BRITISH TROLLEYBUS SYSTEMS

J. JOYCE, J. S. KING AND A. G. NEWMAN

LONDON

IAN ALLAN LTD

First published 1986

ISBN 0 7110 1647 X

Published by Ian Allan Ltd,
Shepperton, Surrey;
and printed by Ian Allan
Printing Ltd at their works
at Coombelands in
Runnymede, England

Back cover, top:
**London: No 1722, an MCW-
bodied Leyland, was part of an
export order destined for South
Africa but diverted to London
during the war. The front exit
(not used in London) and the
tinted window glass (hardly
needed in London) are
apparent.** *Ian Allan Library*

Back cover, bottom:
**Portsmouth: No 24 was the last
of the series of English Electric-
bodied AEC 661Ts of 1935.**
Ian Allan Library

Previous page:
**In a stronghold of the trolleybus: against a background of the Pennines,
two of Huddersfield Corporation's three-axle Sunbeams (No 601, a Roe-
bodied MS2 of 1951, and No 583, a 1949 MS2 with Park Royal body) wait at
the terminus of the lengthy Marsden route.** *R. Brook*

Below:
**In the trolleybus era: two vehicles of the Llanelly & District Traction Co
stand at Llanelli station in the summer of 1951. Utility-bodied Karrier No 47
(later sold to Bradford where it was rebodied) is followed by 1932
Leyland No 7.** *R. W. A. Jones*

Abbreviations used in tables

ADC	Associated Daimler Co
AEC	Associated Equipment Co
A/West	Allen West
BCT	Bradford City Tramways
BRCW	Birmingham Railway Carriage & Wagon Co
B/Roe	Beadle/Roe
BTH	British Thomson Houston
BUT	British United Traction
C/Parkinson	Crompton-Parkinson
C/Smith	Clough Smith
C/West	Crompton West
D/Kerr	Dick Kerr
E/Constr	Electric Construction Co
E/Electric	English Electric
E/Lancs	East Lancashire Coach Works
EMB	Electro Mechanical Brake Co
GEC	General Electric Co
H/Nelson	Hurst Nelson
K/Clough	Karrier/Clough
LGOC	London General Omnibus Co
LPTB	London Passenger Transport Board
MCW	Metropolitan-Cammell-Weymann
MCCW	Metropolitan Cammell Carriage & Wagon Co
N/Counties	Northern Counties
NCB	Northern Coach Builders
P/Royal	Park Royal
R/Kenning	Reeve & Kenning
R/Stevens	Rees-Stevens
RS&J	Ransomes, Sims & Jefferies
S/Clough	Straker-Clough
S/Squire	Straker Squire
T/Stevens	Tilling-Stevens

Contents

Preface

This book originates from a series of articles which appeared in *Buses* from 1966 onward, dealing with those British trolleybus systems which had not at that time been adequately documented. With the addition of further material, including useful contributions from readers of the original articles, it was hoped that ultimately the series could be reprinted in book form, along with details of other systems not covered in the articles, in order to present a concise and convenient record of this mode of transport as it existed in Britain. The present volume is the outcome of that hope.

The first public trolleybus services in Britain started in 1911, and the last ceased in 1972. During that period of some 60 years, almost 50 distinct undertakings came and went. A few, especially in the earlier experimental days, were small and short-lived, while others enjoyed longer lives and each developed an individual character of its own. The trolleybus made its appearance in most of Britain's principal cities and towns, but its role in the overall transport pattern varied; in some cases it provided the major form of local transit, while in others it remained subsidiary to the tramcar or the motorbus. Rising to its greatest popularity during the 1930s, its decline from the 1950s onward reflected changes in both economic and traffic conditions which militated against the costly fixed equipment of the so-called route-bound trolley vehicle. It is perhaps ironical that in the altered environment of the later 1980s trials were beginning with a 'new age' trolley-bus. Our references to the 'last' trolleybuses may therefore require some qualification.

In this book we have prefaced a brief sketch of the rise and decline of the trolleybus, together with a reminder of 'How it Works' (since it is now so many years since we have been able to observe the British trolleybus in normal service operations), before proceeding to the major part of the work: a description of each of the individual undertakings, placed in alphabetical order. We have sought to outline the history of each system together with details of its routes and vehicles and the distinctive features which gave it character. Within the limited space at our disposal it has been impossible to include much more than the basic facts, or to illustrate more than a small selection of the many and varied types of vehicles which once ran beneath the wires. But we hope that, by bringing basic data within the covers of one volume, the book may form a convenient source of reference and that it may stand as a modest tribute to a mode of transport that was formerly a common sight in our cities and towns.

Since our original articles appeared, many books and monographs on individual systems have been published, indicative of a greater appreciation of the subject, and for readers who may wish to seek further information on any particular undertaking we have appended references to each section, in addition to a bibliography of more general works.

Acknowledgements

The principal sources we have used in compiling both the original articles and the additional material for this book we have listed under the respective system and in the general bibliography, and to all these sources we acknowledge our indebtedness. We are no less grateful to the numerous fellow-enthusiasts who have greatly assisted us in our endeavours. In particular we would like to express our thanks to G. H. F. Atkins, J. R. Attridge, D. G Bowen, J. Bray, R. Brook, J. C. Brown, A. R. Burton, R. Chandler, Dr E. R. Clark, B. K. Dyes, H. C. Goldspink, K. E. Griffiths, A. Hinchliffe, J. Hughes, D. G. James, R. E. Jones, S. Lockwood, R. Marshall, J. M. Maybin, A. W. Mills, M. P. M. Nimmo, G. M. O'Connell, A. E. Old, J. H. Price, T. J. Sheppard, J. Smith, E. K. Stretch, C. J. Taylor, D. M. Torbet, A. Tye, J. D. Watson, and P. R. White. Our thanks also go to John Parke, former Editor of *Buses*, and to the present Editor of *Buses*, Stephen Morris, for their help and encouragement and for permission to reproduce material from the published articles. The majority of the photographs we have included are from the Ian Allan Library, including the V. C. Jones Collection, and our thanks go to S. W. Stevens-Stratten for his assistance. For other photographs we are grateful to Roy Brook, C. Carter and R. W. A. Jones.

The Trolleybus and How It Works

The simplest, if not the most technically sophisticated, definition of a trolleybus is 'an electrically-powered bus which collects its current from overhead wires'. The chassis of the trolleybus was generally similar to that of the motorbus, but instead of an internal combustion engine and gearbox it was fitted with an electric motor and resistances, while on the roof of the vehicle were mounted two trolley poles carrying sliding collectors which made contact with twin overhead wires, one positive and the other negative, by means of which current was obtained from a central source.

High-voltage current from this central source (often the municipal generating station) was fed to substations, where it was transformed to 500-600V and rectified from alternating current to direct ·current. Then it went by feeder cables to feed the overhead wires, at intervals of not more than half a mile to minimise voltage drop. The overhead was divided electrically into half-mile sections which could each be cut out if required in case of defect. Of the two overhead wires, the inner wire (nearer the centre of the road) was normally the positive and the outer the negative. The wires were slung at a minimum height of 20ft above the roadway, except where low bridges required a lesser height, and were supported about every 100ft by span wires or brackets. A spacing of 24in between the positive and negative wires was standard, although some earlier installations used a closer spacing. The trolley wires were of copper or copper-cadmium, and were generally of grooved section clamped into 'ears' which were attached to the span wires or brackets. The supporting standards were usually of tubular steel, planted in concrete bases. In many instances existing tramway overhead was converted for use by trolleybuses.

Where two routes diverged, junctions in the overhead incorporated moveable 'frogs' to direct the poles of the trolleybus on to the required route. These frogs were either manually operated from a lever fitted to an adjacent standard, or remotely controlled, in which case the frog was operated by means of an electro-magnet energised by way of a contact on the overhead wire just ahead of the turnout. If the driver wanted to change the setting of the frog, he approached with power on so that

Below:
Electrical circuit of a typical double-deck trolleybus.

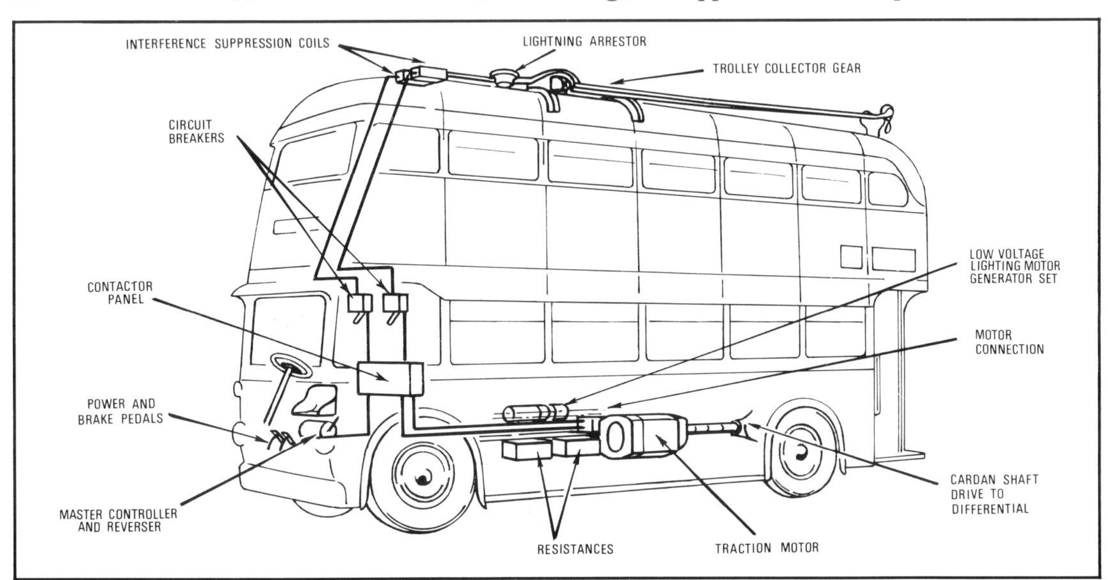

current flowed through the magnet; if no change was needed, the approach was with power off so that no current flowed through the magnet. To avoid having to negotiate a junction in the overhead in the middle of a busy street intersection, the turnout would be situated a little distance in advance of the actual divergence, and the two sets of wires would be run parallel until the two routes diverged.

On the trolleybus itself, the trolley poles were about 20ft long and were pivotally mounted on a roof gantry. The trolley heads were kept in contact with the overhead wires by means of coil springs attached to the bases of the poles. The trolley heads comprised a grooved unit fitted with a carbon insert to make contact with the wire (in some instances, particularly in earlier years, a wheel similar to that used on a tramcar was employed). The carbon inserts needed renewal after about every 1,000 miles running. Suppressors were fitted into the circuit and mounted on the roof to eliminate interference with radio and television.

From the roof, cables took the current via circuit breakers to the contactor panel and control resistances. The two circuit breakers (one in each line) were set to trip in case of an

overload resulting from an electrical fault or from the driver trying to accelerate his vehicle too enthusiastically by giving the motor more current than it could absorb.

The contactor panels, generally situated beside the driver in his cab, contained magnetically-operated switches (contactors) which switched in and out banks of resistances (normally mounted beneath the floor) to control the amount of current reaching the motor, and hence the speed of the vehicle. The contactors were operated by way of the master controller, which was linked to the driver's power pedal; depression of the pedal first brought the contactors into play, and further depression operated relays to cause the contactors to cut out more and more of the resistances until full speed was reached. The typical control equipment, with up to a dozen 'notches', was designed to give an acceleration of about 3-4mph per second up to about 20mph with a lower rate up to full speed, and a balancing speed of 30-35mph.

An alternative to the electro-magnetic contactor was the electro-pneumatic contactor, in which compressed air was employed to operate the contacts. In some earlier trolleybuses, 'direct' control was used, the power pedal being directly linked to a drum-type controller, so that the driver 'notched up' his vehicle by alternately depressing and partially releasing the pedal. In some early trolleybuses, the controller was hand operated, in similar manner to that on a tramcar.

In some of the more modern trolleybuses, automatic acceleration was incorporated. The automatic acceleration unit, brought into action by depression of the power pedal, regulated the speed of progression of the master controller according to both the load on the vehicle and the gradient, thus ensuring a smooth rate of acceleration and obviating jerky starting.

Traction motors were of several types, varying from the earliest which were similar to tramcar motors, to later practice which favoured the compound-wound type or the series-wound, regulated-field motor. Typically rated at around 90-110bhp, the compound motor was a combination of series wound (with the armature and field coils in series) and shunt wound (part of the current could be diverted or 'shunted' from the coils), such an arrangement permitting optimum control over a wide range of speeds as well as electric braking. Early trolley vehicles followed tramcar practice in employing two motors, which could be connected in series for starting and low-speed running, and in parallel for higher speeds. A later variant of this was the tandem motor, with two fields and with two armatures in tandem on the same shaft.

To do its work, the armature shaft of the traction motor was coupled by means of a cardan shaft and universal joint to the differential on the rear axle of the vehicle. A worm reduction gear was incorporated in the differential.

A changeover switch (often housed within the same casing as the controller) enabled the motor to be switched into reverse when required. It also enabled the battery (if fitted) to be switched to feed the traction motor to permit limited manoeuvring in the event of failure of the main

Left:
This view of a 1940 Sunbeam chassis for a double-deck trolleybus shows the contactor panel beside the driver's position, the side-mounted resistances and the traction motor. The two-pedal control of the trolleybus is also apparent. *Ian Allan Library*

Above:
The tower wagon was an essential member of the fleet. This one was serving the Reading Corporation undertaking in the 1940s.
V. C. Jones/Ian Allan Library

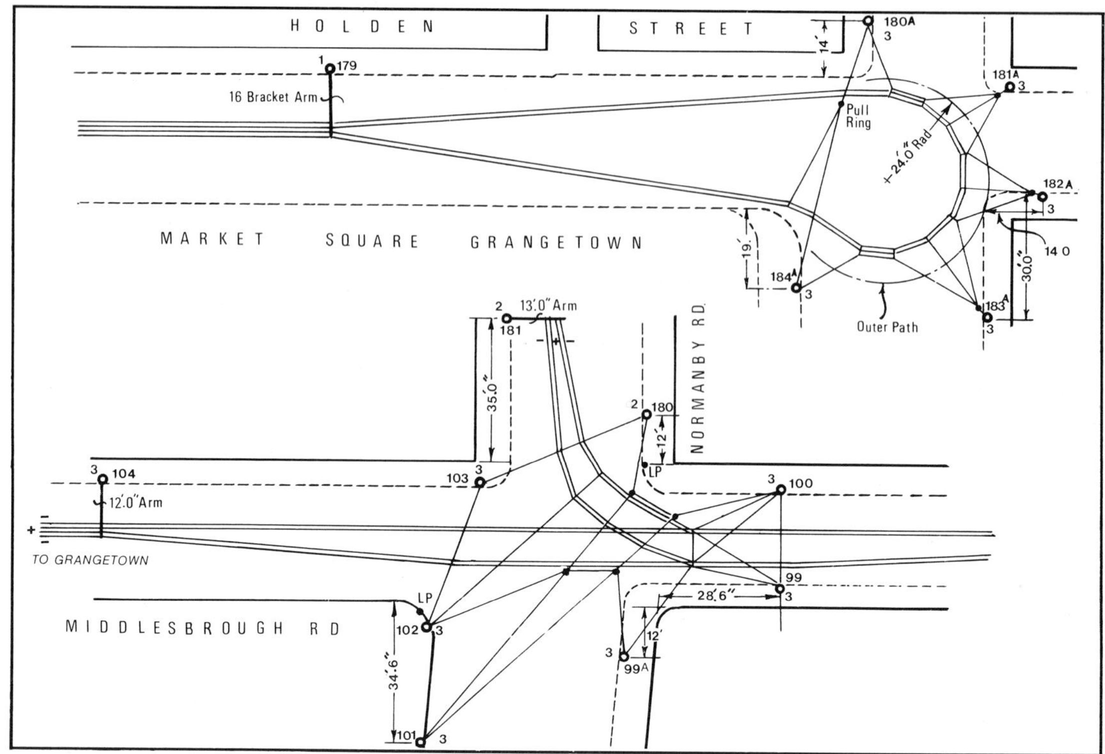

Above:

Examples of overhead wiring layout at a terminal loop and a junction, as installed on the Teesside system in 1919.

power supply. The battery also supplied the lighting; low-voltage lighting was a legal requirement with metal-framed vehicles, whereas older vehicles with wood or composite-built bodywork had their lighting fed direct off the main supply and did not carry batteries. The battery was kept charged by a generator driven off the traction motor or by a separate motor.

While the driver's left pedal operated the controller, the right pedal operated the brakes. There were several types of braking, generally used in combination: regenerative or rheostatic, air or vacuum. In both rheostatic and regenerative braking, the traction motor was switched to act as a generator, the consequent load having a braking effect. In the case of regenerative braking, the current so generated was fed back into the overhead wires, whereas with rheostatic braking it was dissipated in the resistances. Rheostatic braking remained in general use, but the regenerative method tended to fall out of favour, since, although it made for economy in that it fed back the excess current instead of wasting it in heating the resistances, it presented problems with over-voltage surges

which could result in blown-out lamps and damaged equipment. Both methods nevertheless reduced wear and tear on brake drums, but since neither method could bring the vehicle to a halt (the braking effect obviously faded as speed fell) compressed-air or (less commonly) vacuum operated braking was also fitted. For this purpose a compressor or exhauster was installed, driven by a separate motor. There was also of course a hand brake. Electric and power braking systems were coupled; thus initial depression of the pedal brought the rheostatic braking into operation, while further depression activated the air braking.

As with the motorbus, it was usual for chassis and body to be supplied by different makers, with the electrical equipment also being provided by separate specialist manufacturers. Since most trolleybus undertakings served busy urban routes, where high-capacity vehicles were needed, the double-decker was very much in the majority, with the single-decker largely confined to routes hampered by low bridges. Three-axle vehicles were long favoured where maximum capacity was required. Simple two-pedal control with high acceleration and smooth running, combined with silence in operation and absence of exhaust emissions, contributed to the popularity of the modern trolleybus in urban traffic conditions.

The Trolleybus in Britain

'The latest development in connection with electric transport in this country is the introduction of the railless trolley system, which provides an inexpensive and convenient method of transit in districts where, for one reason or another, tramways or railways are impracticable. The first railless trolley lines in England were formally opened in Bradford and Leeds on 20 June of the present year.'

Thus *The Engineer* of 1911 described the advent of the trolleybus in Britain and the role for which it was then cast. This role was evident from its contemporary nomenclature; the railless or trackless tram was intended as a cheap alternative to the tramway. By the end of the first decade of the century the electric tramway boom had almost run its course. Practically all the routes on which its heavy capital expendi-

ture could be justified were already served. Yet there still remained in the growing towns many urban and suburban routes on which a public transport service was desirable, but on which the traffic potential was not sufficient to warrant the cost of installing tracks. The motor omnibus was still viewed with some scepticism, especially by municipal operators wedded to the electric tramcar, and the prospect opened up by the development of the railless electric vehicle seemed to offer the solution. Railless electric traction could bring the well-established advantages of electric transport at modest cost, and could conveniently be installed to supplement an existing tramway undertaking.

At least as early as 1908 several major municipal tramway operators — including Bradford, Manchester, Liverpool, Sheffield and Dundee — were showing an interest in the new mode of local transit, and delegations were sent to the Continent to inspect the various railless installations already in action there. In Britain, the first trolleybus actually to go into operation was demonstrated in London in 1909 by the Railless Electric Traction Co at the Hendon depot of the Metropolitan Electric Tramways. The vehicle did not offer a public service but ran within the confines of the depot in order that interested parties could see tangible evidence of its merits. It is reported to have attained a speed of 15mph and to have safely negotiated foot-deep mud-filled ruts in the roadway, a valuable asset in the eyes of those contemplating adopting this form of transport along poorly-made suburban roads.

The next two years saw something of a 'trolleybus mania' as numerous towns rushed to obtain powers to instal this ideal machine, and while most of these plans fell by the wayside, several schemes did materialise. The first trolleybus systems to begin public service in Britain were inaugurated on the same day in 1911 by Leeds and Bradford. In Bradford the

Left:
The original 'trackless tram' was envisaged as a cheaper substitute for the tramway where conditions did not justify the cost of track construction. A Leeds 'trackless' of 1911 traverses the sparsely-populated Farnley route.

1½-mile route joined two suburban tramways, while in Leeds the 4-mile route connected an outlying suburb with the city centre along sparsely populated roads. Dundee Corporation followed in 1912, again with a short suburban route, and then later in the same year

The trolleybus comes to town: three scenes on the Mexborough & Swinton system in the early 1920s.

Right:
The conductor assumes a proprietorial attitude, one foot on step, as the company's new AEC trolleybus poses for the photographer in the early summer of 1922. *Ian Allan Library*

Below:
Narrow streets suit the flexibility of the trolley vehicle; still new enough to cause heads to turn, the latest AEC trolleybus pulls up behind a steam wagon. *Courtesy R. Brook*

Bottom:
Staff at the Denaby depot stand proudly by their charges, which are already running over the tram tracks and are destined eventually to supersede the tramcars entirely. *Courtesy R. Brook*

Rotherham Corporation started a rural line outside its municipal boundary as a feeder to the town tramways. Other operators followed: Stockport, Keighley and Ramsbottom in 1913, Aberdare and the Rhondda Tramways in 1914, and the Mexborough & Swinton Tramways Co in 1915. With one exception, all these installations were associated with an existing tramway system and served as extensions to it. The exception was Ramsbottom, which had long been considering building a tramway but now boldly decided to go for the 'trackless' system instead.

World War 1 brought problems for all the operators. Not only did wartime conditions hinder further development, but they also caused difficulties in the maintenance of existing equipment and vehicles, as well as in the supply of spares, a problem compounded by the fact that some systems employed Continental-type equipment which was unobtainable during the war. Moreover, not only were roads suffering from the pounding of the heavy trolley vehicles, which in most cases did not traverse the most substantially-made highways, but the vehicles themselves were being badly shaken by the uneven surfaces. Further, much of the existing equipment could still be considered to be of an experimental nature, with consequent 'teething troubles', and there was as yet little standardisation of such features as current collection gear and overhead equipment. Hence services became erratic, and at times ceased altogether. After the war, a virtually new start had to be made. The first postwar system, that of the Teesside Railless Traction Board, was opened in 1919, having been delayed for several years, followed by those of York in 1920 and Halifax in 1921.

By this time the trial period had ended and the much improved trolley vehicle found itself entering upon a whole new phase of its life. Far from being a mere second-best to the tramcar, it was now becoming a serious contender as a substitute for existing tramways. In 1922, trolleybuses replaced a tramway for the first time, when Birmingham converted its Nechells route. This changeover was observed with keen interest by many other operators, whose policies were to be influenced by its success. Tramways throughout the country were still struggling to make up arrears of wartime maintenance, a fight in which they were hindered by the greatly increased costs of new track and equipment. Furthermore, changed conditions were militating against the tramways. Extensions were called for to meet the needs of new housing development beyond the old termini, while at the same time the growing weight of motor traffic was emphasising the obstructive nature of tramcars running on fixed tracks in narrow streets.

By contrast, the trolleybus was not only a more manoeuvrable vehicle, but it possessed the merit of being able to utilise existing overhead, the wires of which could be extended at the fraction of the cost of a tramway. At the same time, it could maintain the valuable traction load for the municipal power station, which in many cases had been established to serve the needs of the town's tramcars. Postwar advances in design had moreover resulted in a vehicle which was not only more efficient and reliable, but was more attractive than either the original trackless cars or the old tramcars, and which could now offer a carrying capacity comparable with the tram. Birmingham's new double-

Into the era of the big trolleybus: the first Sunbeam trolleybus in 1931 (Wolverhampton No 95) was a three-axle 61-seater. *Ian Allan Library*

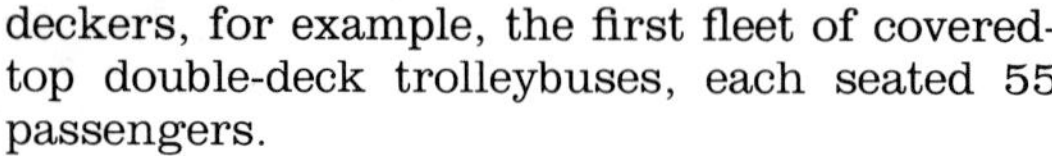

Above left:
Trolleybus interior of the early 1930s: the lower saloon of Derby No 84, a Guy BTX with Brush body, photographed when new in 1931. *Ian Allan Library*

Above:
'The trolley omnibuses in the busy centre of Hastings do not contribute to congestion. They are kept well in to the pavements ... passengers are safely deposited at the kerb before the omnibus moves expeditiously and noiselessly away.' A new AEC of the Hastings Tramways Co loads in this scene from 1940.
Ian Allan Library

Left:
The trolleybus in its ascendancy in the mid-1930s; Portsmouth No 24, an AEC 661T with body by English Electric, proudly sports the city's crest and elaborately-lined livery. *Ian Allan Library*

deckers, for example, the first fleet of covered-top double-deck trolleybuses, each seated 55 passengers.

The 1920s therefore witnessed the trolleybus taking over from many tramways, especially on the more vulnerable systems which did not carry the heaviest loads to justify the high cost of track renewal, or which suffered from poor track layout where any acceleration of service was impracticable and where other traffic was hindered by the slow-moving cars. Ipswich and Wolverhampton both introduced trolleybuses in 1923, Darlington in 1926. In all three cases the tramways were soon virtually entirely super-seded, and in both Ipswich and Darlington for years to come the local services were to be provided solely by trolleybuses. In other towns, too, the process of conversion was under way. Chesterfield, Nottingham and St Helens installed their first trolleybuses in 1927, Doncaster, Maidstone and the Hastings Tram-ways Co in 1928.

A table published in *Tramway & Railway World* early in 1927 showed that 16 municipal operators had opted for the trolleybus, and while most of the systems were still modest in extent, many were in the process of expansion with further routes planned. The largest system in operation was that of Ipswich, with 35 vehicles operating over more than 15 miles of route. Wolverhampton, the Teesside Railless Traction Board, Keighley, Bradford and Dar-lington possessed about 20 vehicles apiece. There was only one company-owned system, that of the Mexborough & Swinton Tramways Co.

A notable convert from 1928 was the Hastings Tramways Co, which soon acquired a fleet of 58 vehicles to become for a time the largest trolley vehicle undertaking in Britain, and indeed in the world. A contemporary description of the system sums up the attractions of the new mode of transport: 'the trolley omnibuses in the busy centre of Hastings do not contribute to conges-tion. They are kept well in to the pavements, but are always ready, by passing slower units, to keep traffic unimpeded. Passengers are safely deposited at the kerb, before the omnibus moves expeditiously and noiselessly away. Practically the only sound that meets the ear is the not unpleasing swish of the trolley wheel'.

The trolley vehicle itself had been undergoing a revolution, in the course of which it was metamorphosed from a trackless tram to an electric bus. Out were the old high frames, the dual motors and hand-operated controllers, the solid tyres and the bodywork built in the substantial upright tradition of the conventional tramcar. Now both body and chassis benefited from designs developed by the motorbus builders. Perceiving the growing market, new makers entered the field with advanced designs. Symbolic of the progress made over the recent past was the first trolleybus to be produced by Guy Motors in 1926. A covered-top double-decker seating 61 passengers, this was the first six-wheel trolleybus with twin rear axles, running on pneumatic tyres. Supplied to Wolverhampton, it was soon followed by others, and similar vehicles were supplied to both Hastings and Maidstone. Other makers in contention by this time included Sunbeam, Garrett, and Ransomes Sims & Jefferies.

The 1930s proved to be the decade of rapid expansion. The need for tramway replacement in nearly all major towns and cities was increasingly urgent. Equipment installed in the tramway boom in the early years of the century was now urgently in need of renewal, while the interwar housing boom was creating new suburbs calling for new routes, and traffic congestion increasing at a greater rate than anyone had envisaged was condemning the inflexible tramcar as unsuited to modern streets. The trolleybus, on the other hand, was

Above:
The typical suburban setting in which the trolleybus found its spiritual home is exemplified by this scene in Kingston-upon-Hull, with No 32, one of the city's 1938 Craven-bodied Crossleys. By the time this photograph was taken in 1961, public transport clearly had its competitors!
V. C. Jones/Ian Allan Library

Below:
Welcome to the trolleybus! The arrival of the first Bournemouth trolleybus at Christchurch on 8 April 1936 is greeted with due ceremony. *Ian Allan Library*

Right:
During World War 2, the trolleybus using electricity generated from home-produced fuel, helped to overcome the shortage of imported oil. Dealing with the wartime crowds in Reading in 1943 is newly-delivered No 132, a Sunbeam W with Park Royal utility body. *Ian Allan Library*

Below:
Wartime bodywork is exemplified by this Bradford AEC 661T, one of a number rebodied by Brush. *Ian Allan Library*

Below right:
Representing the zenith of the conventional double-deck trolleybus, Derby No 216 was the first of a batch of Sunbeam F4As with 60-seat Willowbrook bodies delivered in 1952/3. *Ian Allan Library*

not only tried and accepted as a viable alternative, but the modern vehicles being offered by numerous manufacturers had an obvious allure that was hard to resist. Smart, smooth-running, silent and comfortable, they were a striking contrast to many obsolete tramcars and had already proved their popularity with operators and passengers alike. Big three-axle double-deckers were quite capable of coping with the loads carried on the busiest tram routes where big bogie cars had hitherto retained their dominance for the busiest services. What enlightened town could hold out against the inevitable march of progress? Municipal visits to Wolverhampton or Hastings could clinch the issue.

More operators joined the ranks during the early years of the decade. The small Pontypridd Urban District Council undertaking started running in 1930, as did the extensive system of the South Lancashire Transport Co. Walsall began in 1931, the same year that brought the first trolleybus services in London, followed in 1932 by Derby, Llanelli, and the interurban Notts & Derby network. In 1933, it was the turn of industrial Huddersfield and seaside Bournemouth, both of which were to be numbered among the staunchest supporters, followed in 1934 by Portsmouth, destined to be another major entry.

The London system started on a fairly modest scale but was soon to prove an influential giant. The initial fleet of the London United Tramways Co (LUT) in suburban Surrey and Middlesex numbered 60 vehicles serving routes considered best suited to this form of transport. But after the formation in 1933 of the London Passenger Transport Board (LPTB) which took over not only the LUT but London's other tramways and buses, a drastic changeover was soon under way when the Board embarked on a wholesale replacement of tramways by trolleybuses. Eventually the fleet amounted to some 1,800 vehicles, not only the largest in Britain but in the world. The influence on those wavering on the brink was apparent; if London was doing it, how could anyone else go wrong? Moreover, with the seemingly insatiable London demand,

14

trolleybuses were rolling off the assembly lines in quantity.

New recruits during the later 1930s included some big names: Newcastle in 1935, Reading and South Shields in 1936, Kingston-upon-Hull in 1937, Manchester and Belfast in 1938, Brighton in 1939. Meanwhile, existing systems had been growing. Wolverhampton's fleet of two dozen in 1927 had increased to 120 by 1939 and the route mileage from less than seven to 47, Bradford's fleet from 20 to 135 and route mileage from nine to 35, Nottingham from 10 to 125 and mileage from three to 23. Total route mileage in operation now amounted to more than 650, on which 2,500 trolleybuses were in service carrying over 860 million passengers a year. Of the total number of vehicles, the majority (more than 1,300) were owned by local authorities and only 200 by company operators, but far and away the largest single system, with a fleet almost equalling that of all the local authorities put together, was the London Passenger Transport Board with over a thousand.

After the outbreak of World War 2 in 1939 the rate of expansion was necessarily curbed, but while many proposals had to be deferred and some were never to materialise, the trolleybus nevertheless continued to gain ground. The unfinished London conversion programme was not brought to a halt until the middle of 1940, and an entirely new system was inaugurated in Cardiff in 1942, though this was the only wartime newcomer. In several places, including Newcastle, Manchester and Belfast, the wires were extended so that the electric vehicles could take over from motorbuses and so ease the need for imported fuel oil. The utility-bodied Karrier W became a familiar sight in numerous towns, while the drop in seaside traffic enabled Bournemouth and Hastings to lend surplus vehicles to other more hard-pressed operators.

Conditions in the early postwar world proved vastly different from the palmy days of the 1930s. New vehicles and equipment were not only in short supply, but costs were greatly inflated and were to go on rising at an alarming rate. In the face of stringent material shortages, makers struggled to cope with the more urgent demands for new motorbuses rather than trolleybuses. Only one entirely new system started operation during this period, when in 1949 Glasgow at last took a step towards superseding some of its oldest tramcars. Nevertheless, expansion continued into the 1950s on many of the established systems, including Bradford, Cardiff, Derby, Manchester, Newcastle, Reading and Walsall, while a new generation of vehicles supplanted the prewar veterans which had given yeoman service and brought a new look to their respective fleets.

By the 1950s however, it was obvious that the tide had turned. Operators who had been in the process of replacing their tramcars now completed their conversions with diesel buses rather than trolleybuses. Most ominous of all, London Transport's ambitious prewar scheme was not completed, and the remaining tramcars succumbed to the diesel. Throughout the country there were signs that the passenger boom was ending; numbers were levelling off and would soon start to fall with monotonous regularity. With costs just as steadily rising (but fares barely keeping pace) a reluctance to hazard investment in long-life fixed assets was understandable. The flood of private motor cars taking business from public transport was reflected in road reconstruction schemes to ease traffic flow, but the trolleybus with its elaborate overhead layouts and its alleged tardiness in negotiating junctions and turnouts, was regarded as an obstacle to the smooth working of an improved street pattern. Meanwhile, one of the traditional bulwarks of electric urban transport was removed, when the electricity industry was nationalised and trolleybuses and tramcars were no longer fed from their hometown municipally-owned power stations. Operators already had to run motorbuses on routes which could never be considered worthwhile for trolleybuses, and as the economic squeeze tightened, the complexity of maintaining two different modes of transport became an indulgence that could no longer be afforded.

During the first years of the 1950s some of the more vulnerable brethren began to fall by the wayside. Birmingham, after its early incursion into the trolleybus, had lost enthusiasm and gave up in 1951 even before the city's last trams had made their final journeys. Llanelly & District ceased operation in 1952 after changes in ownership, including ironically a period under the South Wales Electricity Board. West Hartlepool withdrew after differences with neighbouring Hartlepool in 1953, while the widely-strung Notts & Derby system ended in the same year. In 1954 Southend's trolleybuses succumbed under a wider co-ordination scheme with surrounding bus operators. Even if each of these casualties might have been regarded as a special case rather than a trendsetter, there was no gainsaying the impact of London Transport's 1954 announcement that the whole of its vast network was to be scrapped, starting in 1958. The case was forthrightly put: vehicles and equipment were in need of renewal, the trolleybus was less mobile, and integration of services could be better attained if buses only were used. If London's wholehearted conversion programme of the 1930s had encouraged others to embrace the trolleybus, so now its condemnation darkened the horizon. Manufacturers saw their future market effectively halved at a stroke, and other operators were deprived of at least moral support. The surrender of three more long-established strongholds — Darlington in 1957, South Lancashire Transport in 1958 and Hastings in 1959 — seemed to confirm the apparently inevitable outcome.

The end in London came in 1962. But this was only one of the many to cease during this disastrous decade; indeed only four operators were to survive the 1960s. The Grimsby and Cleethorpes system closed in 1960; Mexborough & Swinton (the last of the few company-operated systems) in 1961; Brighton in the same year; Portsmouth, Ipswich and Doncaster in 1963; South Shields and Kingston-upon-Hull in 1964; Rotherham in 1965; Nottingham, Newcastle, Ashton and Manchester in 1966;

Wolverhampton, Maidstone, Glasgow (the last comer) and Derby in 1967; Belfast, Huddersfield, and Reading in 1968, and Bournemouth in 1969.

Those devotees who struggled on during these final years had to face their own special problems. Even if their faith in the merits of the trolley vehicle remained unshaken, not only were new vehicles and equipment unobtainable (except perhaps to special order at made-to-measure prices) but maintenance difficulties increased until the operation of any normal service became a constant tussle with ageing fleets and material. Added pressure came from town-planners impatient to sweep away the wires to implement their new road projects. Some temporary alleviation resulted as closures took place, releasing still serviceable vehicles and fittings which found a ready market in keeping the survivors afloat. Numerous transfers of vehicles took place during these years, in some cases involving rebodying to give a new look and a new (if brief) lease of life. Bradford made good use of this resource, while the gallant little Teesside system almost completely renewed its rolling stock by a combination of rebodying and an intake from Reading, and even opened a new extension as late as 1968.

The final quartet did not endure much longer. Cardiff and Walsall gave up in 1970, Teesside in 1971. This left Bradford, one of the pioneers of 1911, appropriately to be the last, and here the

Below:
The trolleybus being overtaken by the diesel bus — literally and metaphorically — in the 1960s, the disastrous decade for the trolleybus. A Kingston-upon-Hull Corporation AEC Regent passes No 100, a 1948 Roe-bodied Sunbeam.
V. C. Jones/Ian Allan Library

final closure took place in 1972. 'Enthusiasts Mob Last Trolleybus', cried the newspaper headlines. 'The last trolleybus to run in Britain ended its final journey today three-quarters of an hour late after being mobbed by enthusiasts. Crowds cheering and singing Old Lang Syne escorted it into the Thornbury Depot at Bradford. Alderman Herbert Moran, the Lord Mayor, and 52 guests were aboard for the last ride round the city. Among them was Mr Edgar Oughtibridge, 80, a former maintenance superintendent, who was on the first trolleybus 61 years ago.'

So the curtain came down on the trolleybus era in Britain. In many respects the trolleybus had been regarded as no more than a transitional vehicle between the tramcar and the motorbus, filling a gap until electrical equipment installed for the tramways had reached the end of its life and then departing, sometimes after only one generation of vehicles. In its heyday it had enjoyed a measure of popularity with operators and passengers alike, even if in its latter days it shared some of the vilification accorded to its predecessor. Its demise stemmed from economic and traffic conditions rather than from any deficiences in the trolleybus as a vehicle. Perhaps its departure can be best summed up in the words of the Lord Mayor of Bradford on that final day: 'We shall miss the fume-free silent service of our trackless trolleybuses'.

Numbers of Trolleybuses

Operator	1927	1939	1953	Operator	1927	1939	1953
Ashton-under-Lyne	8	7	24	Maidstone	—	15	17
Belfast	—	14	221	Manchester	—	76	193
Birmingham	16	78	—	Mexborough & Swinton	7	36	39
Bournemouth	—	104	105	Newcastle upon Tyne	—	101	204
Bradford	19	135	204	Nottingham	10	125	155
Brighton	—	44	63	Notts & Derby	—	33	—
Cardiff	—	—	65	Pontypridd	—	9	8
Chesterfield	14	—	—	Portsmouth	—	100	115
Cleethorpes	—	13	15	Ramsbottom	7	—	—
Darlington	18	51	37	Reading	—	6	57
Derby	—	86	71	Rotherham	9	55	52
Doncaster	—	44	47	St Helens	4	55	40
Glasgow	—	—	68	Southend	3	20	29
Grimsby	5	17	19	South Lancashire	—	59	70
Hastings	—	58	49	South Shields	—	35	60
Huddersfield	—	140	132	Teesside	21	13	15
Ipswich	35	70	71	Walsall	—	21	33
Keighley	20	—	—	West Hartlepool	7	21	17
Kingston-upon-Hull	—	46	96	Wigan	4	—	—
Leeds	14	—	—	Wolverhampton	26	124	161
Llanelly	—	20	—	York	4	—	—
London	—	1,411	1,811				

British Trolleybus Systems

Aberdare

First in an alphabetical list of British trolleybus systems, Aberdare possessed a number of unusual features. The vehicles used were of a type to be found in only one other town in Britain; the system was part of a co-ordinated electric traction scheme involving both trams and trolleybuses; it was among the first British trackless systems to open, being eighth in line. Aberdare Urban District Council was one of only three in Britain which exercised powers to run trackless cars; and, most remarkable, part of the trolleybus system was replaced by a tramway.

The Aberdare Urban District Council sought powers in 1910 to operate a system of trackless trolleys, and these were granted by an Act of the following year. By February 1913 work had begun on equipping the routes and a trial run was made with one of the cars on 22 September 1913 at Abernant. The system was equipped at the same time as a tram route was constructed, the arrangement being that the trams should provide the backbone, with four trolleybus routes feeding the tramway at different points. The tramway ran between Trecynon Cemetery and Aberaman, while the trolleybus routes ran from Cwmdare to Trecynon Cemetery (½-mile), from Abernant to the centre of Aberdare at Commercial Street (1-mile), and from both Capcoch and Cwmaman to Clarence Street, Aberdare (¾ and 1¼-mile respectively). Three of the four routes were hilly, with an average gradient of 1 in 10.

It was intended to start the tramway and the trackless system on the same date. Although an opening ceremony was held on 9 October 1913, the official Board of Trade returns show this date for the tramway opening for traffic and 15 January 1914 as the date for trackless cars.

The choice of cars was unusual and, in view of subsequent events, unfortunate for the success of the system. An Austrian invention first demonstrated in this country at West Ham in 1912, the Cedes Stoll system, enjoyed considerable success in Austria from 1907 onwards, and

Aberdare: A Cedes-Stoll trolley vehicle negotiates the railway bridge at Aberdare in 1913 on the route to Abernant.

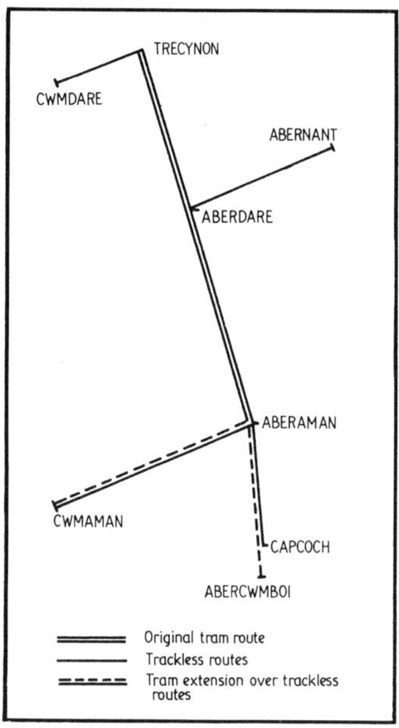

the company was beginning to interest a number of operators elsewhere in 1912 and 1913. Basically the invention differed from others in that current collection was by means of a four-wheeled trolley which ran on top of the overhead wires, while the motors were an integral part of the rear wheels. Most of the routes in Aberdare were equipped with only one pair of wires, and the trolleys were exchanged as vehicles met. Only the Cwmaman route was equipped with a double set of wires.

A depot was built at Gadlys to house up to 12 tramcars and eight trackless cars. The trackless cars were single-deckers with seats for 27 passengers in rear-entrance bodies by Christopher Dodson Ltd. The front-end design included a sloping bonnet (not unlike the Renault motor cars) to house the cable drum of the trolley cable. Provision was made for the cars to have a slipper lowered into the tram track and a boom raised to the overhead so that they could proceed under their own power to the starting point of each route, but it was soon decided to tow them out each morning by tramcar. The war brought increasing problems in keeping the cars on the road, since spares were unobtainable. By 31 March 1919 the two routes from Aberaman had closed and only four trolleybuses were in use.

Now came the unusual and probably unique step of replacing part of the trolleybus system by trams. Tenders were accepted for extension of the tramway beyond Aberaman in 1920 and work began. However, the route was not ready for inspection by the Ministry of Transport officials until December 1922. In January 1923 the Council's tramway committee considered the question of the trackless cars and decided that, in view of the difficulties and the expense of maintenance, the resources of the trackless system should be concentrated on the Abernant route, no further expenditure should be incurred on the purchase of trackless cars, and that only quarterly licences should be taken out in respect of the remaining cars. The active fleet, which had dwindled to three by 1921, was down to two by 1924. The exact date when the system ceased to operate seems to have escaped notice, but the last report seen (in the local newspaper of 8 August 1925) states: 'The Cedes Stoll trolley vehicle has completely broken down. The town clerk of Keighley has offered several single-deck Straker-Clough vehicles for sale. The Aberdare Council will inspect them'. Nothing more was heard of this suggestion.

References
'British Trolleybus Systems: 1 — Aberdare': *Buses Illustrated* October 1966.
'Tramways and Railless Traction at Aberdare': *Tramway & Railway World* 15 January 1914.

Ashton-under-Lyne and Oldham

Through transport services between the various towns of the Manchester area have long been important so it is not surprising that the trolleybus history of Ashton-under-Lyne should have been linked with that of its neighbours. It engaged in an early instance of joint trolleybus

Ashton-under-Lyne

Fleet Nos	Registration Nos	Chassis	Electrical equipment	Body	In service	Withdrawn	Notes
50-57	TD 2362/2497/ 3147/8/3207/8/ 3262/3344	Railless	E/Electric	Short B36C	1925	1937/8	a
48, 52, 55	CTD 547-9	Leyland TB4	Metrovick	E/Electric H36/30R	1937	1956	b
49	CTD 787	Crossley TDD4	Metrovick	Crossley H28/26R	1937	1956	
46, 47, 58	CTF 313/4, CNE 474	Crossley TDD6	Metrovick	Crossley H38/30R	1937/8	1951-5	
50/1/3/4/ 6/7/9/60	ETE 811-8	Crossley TDD4	Metrovick	Crossley H28/26R	1940	1954-60	
61-4	FTE 645-8	Sunbeam W	E/Electric	P/Royal UH30/26R	1944	1963-5	c
65, 66	FTJ 401/0	Sunbeam W	Metrovick	Roe H30/26R	1946	1960	d
77-81	LTC 771-5	Crossley TDD42/2 'Empire'	Metrovick	Crossley H30/28R	1950	1963-5	
82-9	YTE 821-8	BUT 9612T	Metrovick	Bond H32/28R	1956	1966	

Notes:

a Oldham purchased two similar vehicles

b No 52 seating H30/24R

c Nos 61 and 62 rebodied by Roe H33/28R 1958; Nos 63 and 64 rebodied by Bond H33/28R 1955/6

d Sold to Bradford

Preserved vehicles: Nos 80, 87

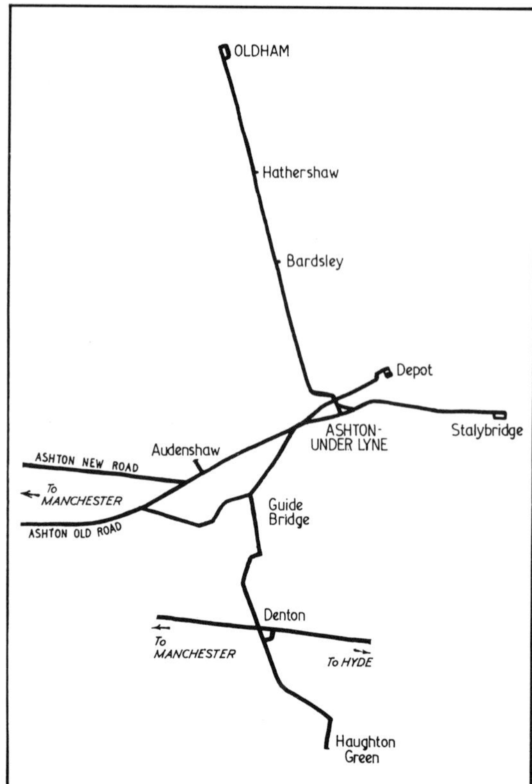

operation, while for almost 30 years its services were closely related to those of Manchester.

The earliest proposals for trolley vehicles in the area seem to have been those of the Oldham & Saddleworth District Railless Electric Traction scheme, for which a Bill was before Parliament in 1911, but nothing of this scheme materialised. In the mid-1920s came Ashton's first trolleybus service, which for a time was operated jointly with neighbouring Oldham. In 1921 through trams started running between the two towns, but only two years later Ashton proposed that, in view of the bad condition of the track, the trams should be replaced by trolley vehicles. Oldham agreed, and in 1924 orders were placed with Railless Ltd for a total of 10 vehicles, eight for Ashton and two for Oldham, all Short-bodied central-entrance single-deckers. The services started on 26 August 1925 between the Market Place in Ashton and Chaucer Street in Oldham, via Waterloo, Bardsley and Hathershaw, a distance of about four miles. The two Oldham vehicles were housed in the former tram depot at Copsterhill Road.

Oldham seems to have been the unlucky partner in the venture. It kept trams going for a time on the section of route as far as its

Top:
Ashton-under-Lyne: No 56 was one of the batch of Short-bodied Railless vehicles supplied to Ashton to inaugurate its trolleybus service in 1925. Oldham purchased two similar vehicles for the joint route.

Above:
Ashton-under-Lyne: The first two-axle trolleybus to be produced by Crossley went to Ashton in 1937, to become No 49.   *Ian Allan Library*

Above right:
Ashton-under-Lyne: No 50 was one of eight Crossleys supplied in 1941.   *Ian Allan Library*

boundary at Hathershaw, and as the two types of vehicle shared the same overhead there were complaints of one being delayed by the other. More complaints came from residents along the way; they objected to the vibrations caused by the solid-tyred trolley vehicles. Within a year Oldham had had enough; it decided to revert to trams on its route to Hathershaw, at the same time cutting the through service since it would not allow Ashton's trolley vehicles to penetrate within its boundaries. Hence on 5 September 1926 the through service was discontinued and Oldham's brief career as a trolleybus operator ended, its two vehicles being left to moulder away in the depot.

Meanwhile Ashton continued to 'go it alone' on the 2½ miles of route from the town centre to Hathershaw, fitting its vehicles with pneumatic tyres and rebuilt bodies. However, the progress of trolleybus design was strikingly displayed when in 1936 the first trolleybus to be produced by Crossley made its trial runs as Ashton No 58, followed shortly after by a four-wheel version which became No 49. Late in 1937 three English Electric-bodied Leylands appeared, while in 1938 the last of the old single-deckers was taken out of service. Now something more ambitious was under way. In 1936 Manchester decided to adopt trolleybuses in place of trams on the Ashton Old Road between Manchester and Ashton via Openshaw, while in the following year it decreed a similar change on the parallel route along Ashton New Road via Droylsden and Audenshaw.

On 1 March 1938 trolleybuses took over from trams on Ashton Old Road, running from Manchester, through Ashton itself to Stalybridge, a distance of nearly nine miles. As well as seeing the end of Ashton's tramcars, this marked the commencement of trolleybus operation by Manchester, which had ordered a fleet of 76 Crossleys and Leylands. Ashton added a further two Crossley six-wheelers. On 31 July trolleybuses took over on Ashton New Road to give the second route between Manchester and Ashton. Later the same year Ashton Council decided that the Hathershaw route should be replaced by motorbuses, in view of the high cost of re-equipment and the inconvenience of the lack of a through service to Oldham; accordingly this trolleybus service ended on 19 February 1939.

More expansion was to come elsewhere; Manchester extended its Guide Bridge route into Ashton from 22 March 1940, while on 1 July a new route was opened through Guide Bridge southwards to Denton, extended on 4 November of the same year to Haughton Green. In order that Ashton could take a more active part in operations, the fleet was augmented early in 1940 by the addition of eight Crossley four-wheelers, while further additions included four Sunbeam Ws in 1944 and another two in 1946. A further five Crossleys came in 1950, and in spite of Manchester's plans to abandon trolleybus operation, Ashton in 1956 added eight Bond-bodied BUTs which were to be the last completely new trolleybuses and which took the place of prewar Leylands and 1940 Crossleys. The four wartime Sunbeams were also rebodied.

On 3 July 1960 the service from Ashton to Haughton Green ran for the last time, and on 10 October 1964 the last runs were made on the route from Manchester to Ashton via Guide Bridge. Both Ashton and Manchester ceased trolleybus operation entirely on 30 December 1966.

References
'British Trolleybus Systems: 2 — Ashton-under-Lyne and Oldham': *Buses Illustrated* December 1966.

Belfast

Although the Belfast system was the only one to exist in Ireland, in its heyday it was among the giants with a fleet totalling around 240 vehicles. The use of trolleybuses in place of tramcars was recommended in 1936 by the general manager, Major R. McCreary: 'Taking all factors into consideration, provided the Electricity Department offers and continues to offer to the transport undertaking — its best customer — the most favourable tariff possible, trolleybuses should be introduced as being the most suitable mode of transport to replace tramcars'. As the first step it was decided to convert one route; Falls Road was selected because it had little connection with other routes, it was of sufficient length (some three miles) to give the newcomers a fair trial, and a depot was situated on it. The vehicles for the experiment, although outwardly similar 68-seat double-deck six-wheelers, were almost a representative cross-section of current manufacturers' products. No fewer than seven different makers had supplied chassis, while bodymakers had been equally co-operative in giving the Corporation the chance of deciding whose wares it would favour.

As a result, 14 vehicles were on hand for the inauguration on 28 March 1938 of operation on the Falls Road route, after two weeks during which motorbuses had been used while Clough Smith completed the overhead work. Before the end of the year the general manager was recommending that the city should go ahead with replacing trams by trolleybuses, and in January 1939 the Corporation agreed, with the changeover to be completed by the end of 1944. Accordingly, during the summer of 1939 contracts were placed for vehicles and overhead equipment. However, the outbreak of war disrupted the plans; 88 chassis ordered from AEC took from 1940 to 1943 to come across, while another 28 were never delivered. Those that did materialise were completed with bodywork by Harkness and took the fleet numbers 15 to 102.

In 1941 it was possible to go ahead with

Below left:

Belfast: The scene in Queens Street at the opening of Belfast's trolleybus service on 28 March 1938, when the Lord Mayor drove the first vehicle, after having driven the last tramcar on the Falls Road route which the new trolleybuses took over.   *Ian Allan Library*

Above:

Belfast: The initial fleet included vehicles of several different makes. Seen in the city centre in 1938 is No T10, a Harkness-bodied Karrier.

Ian Allan Library

Above right:

Belfast: Photographed in service in 1938 was No T14, a Sunbeam with body by Cowieson of Glasgow.

Ian Allan Library

further conversions. Belfast's second trolleybus route, on 13 February, was along Cregagh Road over Albert Bridge, followed shortly after (5 June) by the Castlereagh route over Queens Bridge, both routes extending some distance beyond the former tram termini. On 26 March 1942 trolleybuses reached Stormont, with an impressive new circle around the Parliament Buildings, and two services were put on via Albert Bridge and via Queens Bridge respectively. On 16 November 1942 it was the turn of the Dundonald route, first via Queens Bridge and then (on 8 March 1943) via Albert Bridge.

Belfast

Fleet Nos	Registration Nos	Chassis	Electrical equipment	Body	In service	Withdrawn	Notes
1	EZ 7889	AEC 664T	E/Electric	Harkness H38/30R	1938	1958	
2	EZ 7890	AEC 664T	E/Electric	Harkness H38/30R	1938	1958	
3	EZ 7891	Crossley TDD6	Metrovick	Crossley H38/30R	1938	1958	
4	EZ 7892	Crossley TDD6	Metrovick	Harkness H38/30R	1938	1958	
5, 6	EZ 7893/4	Daimler CTM6	Metrovick	Harkness H38/30R	1938	1958	
7	EZ 7895	Guy BTX	E/Electric	P/Royal H38/30R	1938	1956	
8	EZ 7896	Guy BTX	E/Constr	Harkness H38/30R	1938	1958	
9, 10	EZ 7897/8	Karrier E6A	C/West	Harkness H38/30R	1938	1958	
11, 12	EZ 7899/7900	Leyland TTB4	GEC	Leyland H38/30R	1938	1958	
13, 14	EZ 7901/2	Sunbeam MS2	BTH	Cowieson H38/30R	1938	1958	
15-102	FZ 7800-87	AEC 664T	GEC	Harkness H38/30R	1940-3	1962/3	
103-28	FZ 7888-7913	Guy BTX	GEC	Harkness H38/30R	1947-9	1964-8	
129, 130	GZ 1620/1	Sunbeam W	BTH	P/Royal UH30/26R	1943	1958	
131-42	GZ 2802-13	Sunbeam W	BTH	Harkness H38/30R	1946	1958-60	
143-86	GZ 8507-50	Guy BTX	GEC	Harkness H38/30R	1948/9	1964-8	
187-234	GZ 8551-98	BUT 9641T	GEC	Harkness H38/30R	1948-54	1964-8	
235	DDA 182	Sunbeam MF2	BTH	P/Royal H28/26R	1952	1954	a
236	DDA 986	Sunbeam MF2	BTH	P/Royal H28/26R	1952	1954	a
237-40	DDA 987-90	Sunbeam MF2	BTH	P/Royal H28/26R	1952	1954-6	a
241-5	DDA 991-5	Sunbeam MF2	BTH	Roe H29/25H	1952	1954-6	a
246	2206 OI	Sunbeam F4A	BTH	Harkness H38/30R	1958	1968	

Note:

a Ex-Wolverhampton Nos 282, 286-95 respectively

Preserved vehicles: Nos 98, 112, 168, 183, 246

Obviously the original plan for a complete changeover by 1944 was out of the question, and it was not until after the war that further expansion took place. This included:

6 May 1946: Bloomfield via Albert Bridge.

19 April 1948: Ormeau Road.

24 January 1949: Antrim Road to Glengormley (this terminus was to be unique on the system in having a reversing triangle instead of a turning circle).

30 April 1950: Cliftonville Road and Carr's Glen.

2 October 1950: Shore Road to Greencastle (this proved to be the last tram route to be taken over by trolleybuses; the rest fell to the diesel by 1954).

In 1952 a new branch was opened off Falls Road to Glen Road, followed by a new route along

Holywood Road and a further branch off Shore Road along Whitehall Road.

During these years the fleet had been much augmented to work the expanding network. Several Utility Sunbeams (the first four-wheelers in the fleet) were introduced in 1943 and 1946. Postwar vehicles began to arrive in

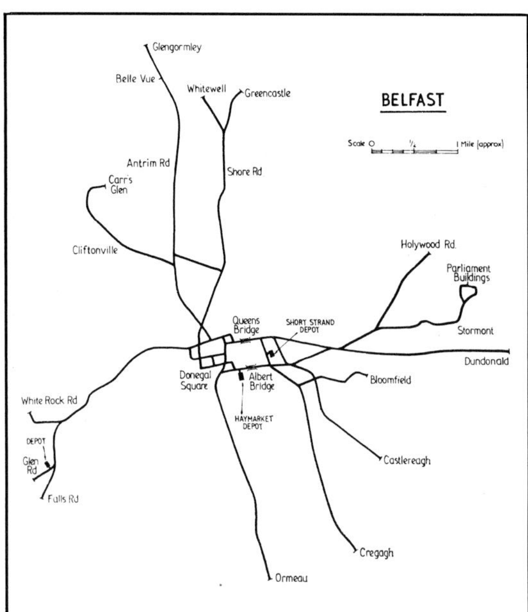

1947, and between then and 1949 Nos 103 to 129 and Nos 143 to 186 were added, all of them six-wheel Guys, followed by BUTs in 1950 and 1953-4. To speed-up the changeover from trams on Shore Road, 11 secondhand Sunbeams were purchased from Wolverhampton in 1952, but these were all withdrawn within the next four years.

New road construction brought the first contraction of the system in 1958 with the closure of the Holywood Road route after the remarkably short life of only six years, and Ormeau Road suffered a similar fate. The year 1958 also witnessed the introduction of what was to prove to be the last addition to the fleet, No 246, a Harkness-bodied Sunbeam generally similar to other members but notable in being a four-wheeler. There were hopes that this might have been the forerunner of others of the same type, but No 246 was destined to remain unique.

A short branch off Falls Road, along Whiterock Road to Springfield Road, was the final new route extension, for in 1959 the transport committee recommended that the whole system should gradually be replaced by motorbuses. The Greencastle route was cut back in 1962, following negotiations with the Ulster Transport Authority into whose sphere of influence it penetrated, although the Whitewell branch continued. In 1963 services over Queens Bridge were terminated, and the rest of the routes in the east of the city were taken off: Castlereagh on 21 January, Stormont and Dundonald on 1 April, Bloomfield and Cregagh on 13 October. Also on 13 October, the Clifton-

Above:
Belfast: The first of the city's order for 114 AEC trolleybuses, including No 18 seen here, went into service in February 1941 on the Cregagh route.
Ian Allan Library

Below:
Belfast: The most spectacular section of the system was the loop around the Parliament Buildings at Stormont, and in this 1942 photograph No 45, one of the Harkness-bodied AEC 664Ts put into service between 1940 and 1943, leaves the precincts for its return journey to the city.   *Ian Allan Library*

ville Road route to Carr's Glen was withdrawn. After 14 June 1965 the Glengormley route was reduced to peak-hours and Saturdays only, and was finally withdrawn from 5 February 1966. The remaining routes (Shore Road, and Falls

Road with its branches to Glen Road and Whitewell Road) continued until the final closure on 12 May 1968.

References
'British Trolleybus Systems: 3 — Belfast': *Buses Illustrated* February 1967.
Belfast Corporation Tramways 1905-1954, J. M. Maybin (Light Rail Transit Association).

Birmingham

The whole trolleybus saga in Birmingham could be regarded as one long experiment. The result was not favourable to the trolleybus and the transport committee decided in the end to standardise on the motorbus. In Birmingham the experiment was confined to what were essentially two routes and a maximum of 90 vehicles.

A Bill was promoted in 1911-12 seeking powers to operate trolleybuses but this was later withdrawn. After the war fresh thought was given to the proposals and in 1921 the Lord Mayor and members of the tramways committee visited Bradford and as a result decided to construct an experimental trolleybus line in Birmingham. At this time Bradford was involved in experiments with double-deck trolleybuses and this encouraged the Birmingham visitors to take the bold step of ordering double-deckers from the start. Powers to operate trolleybuses were obtained during 1921-22. In 1921 orders were placed with Railless for 12 double-deck chassis, with bodies by Charles H. Roe, and delivery commenced about a year later. They were the first fleet of covered-top double-deck trolleybuses in the country. The vehicles had a distinctly tram-like appearance, with a curved outside staircase and seating for 26 passengers on the lower deck and 25 above. Electrical equipment was by Dick Kerr and power was provided by two English Electric 42hp motors linked to a hand-operated tramway-type controller.

Despite the fact that these vehicles made history by replacing tramcars on route 7 from Old Square to Nechells (the first tram-to-trolleybus conversion in Britain), they entered service without ceremony early on 27 November 1922. The vehicles made their way from the Washwood Heath depot using the tramway overhead and a skate return along the tram

Above left:
Birmingham: Demonstrating the manoeuvrability of the trolley vehicle, No 9 shows its paces on the Nechells route in 1922.   *Ian Allan Library*

Left:
Birmingham: The unique EMB trolleybus as Birmingham No 13 in 1924.   *Ian Allan Library*

Above:
Birmingham: An odd one out in the Birmingham fleet, No 67 was later sold to Wolverhampton. A Sunbeam MS2, it had a body by Metropolitan-Cammell-Weymann.   *Ian Allan Library*

Right:
Birmingham: Birmingham's last new trolleybus, MCW-bodied Leyland TB7 No 90 of 1939, leaves the rural-looking terminus at Lode Lane in 1951.
V. C. Jones/Ian Allan Library

Birmingham

Fleet Nos	Registration Nos	Chassis	Electrical equipment	Body	In service	Withdrawn	Notes
1-12	OK 4823-34	Railless	D/Kerr-E/Electric	Roe H25/26ROS	1922	1932	
13	OL 4636	EMB	D/Kerr-E/Electric	E/Electric H28/20R	1924	1926	
14-16	ON 2825-7	AEC604	E/Electric	Short H25/26ROS	1926	1932	
17	ON3261	AEC607	E/Electric	Vickers H26/26ROS	1926	1932	
18	UK 8341	Guy BTX	R/Stevens	Guy H27/26R	1930	1931	a
19	OG 9886	Guy BTX	R/Stevens	Guy H27/26R	1931	1931	b
19	OV 1175	Leyland	GEC	Leyland L24/24R	1931	1931	a b
20	OV 1194	Guy BT	R/Stevens	Guy H24/24R	1931	1931	a
1-11	OV4001-3/13/ 05-7/15/09-11	Leyland TBD2	GEC	Short H27/21R	1932	1940	c
12-16	OJ 1012-6	AEC663T	E/Electric	Brush H33/25R	1932	1940	
17	TJ 939	Leyland	GEC	Massey H34/26R	1933	1933	d
17-66	OC 1117-66	Leyland TTBD2	GEC	MCW H33/25R	1934	1951	
67	OC 6567	Sunbeam MS2	BTH	MCW H31/28R	1934	1934	e
68	TJ 939	Leyland	GEC	Massey H34/26R	1936	1937	f
67-78	COX 67-78	Leyland TB5	GEC	MCW H29/24R	1937	1951	
79-90	FOK 79-90	Leyland TB7	GEC	MCW H30/24R	1940	1951	

Notes:

a Demonstrator

b The first No 19 (OG 9886) never ran in public service and was replaced by new No 19 (OV 1175)

c Originally Nos 1-3, 5-7, 9-11, 13, 15; 13 and 15 renumbered 4 and 8 in 1932 after withdrawal of original Railless Nos 4 and 8

d Later renumbered 68

e Sold to Wolverhampton, where No 222

f Originally No 17

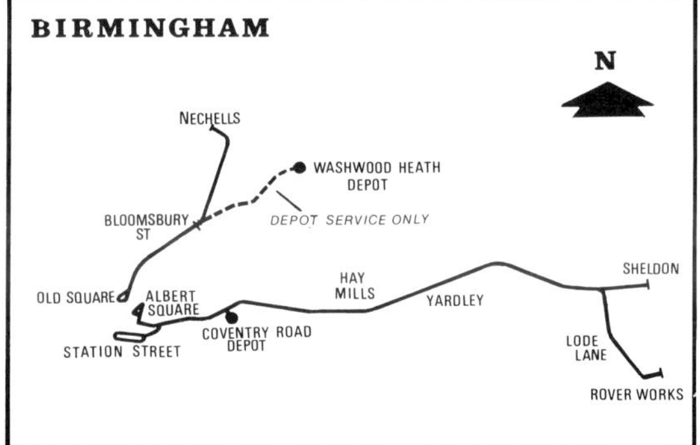

tracks until they reached their own overhead in Bury Street. Although the conversion was by way of an experiment, there was no going back, as lifting of the tram track on the trolleybus route began the same day.

By 1930 consideration was given to ordering replacements for the original Railless vehicles. Three different types of Guy double-decker were delivered in 1930-31, as well as a Leyland. As a result an order was given for 11 Leylands with Short bodies, and these were delivered in 1931, replacing the majority of the Railless vehicles. Fleet numbering commenced at No 1 again with the new Leylands, which were based on the Leyland Titan and had motorbus-type half-cab and bonnet. To complete the replacement of the original vehicles an order was placed with AEC in 1932 for five six-wheel double-deckers.

At about this time a decision was made which had the effect of limiting the spread of trolleybuses in the city. The recently-published Salter Report had recommended that trolleybuses should be liable to licence fees equivalent to the sum that would normally be paid in petrol duties by a bus. With this thought in mind it was agreed to proceed cautiously with the equipping of one further route for trolleybus operation. The tram route to Yardley was chosen and 50 Leyland vehicles were ordered. Services on this route, along Coventry Road from Albert Street and Station Street, began on

7 January 1934. The 50 new MCW-bodied Leylands (Nos 17-66) worked from Coventry Road depot. An extension beyond Yardley to the city boundary at Sheldon was opened on 5 July 1936.

The Corporation was not satisfied that the trolleybus offered sufficient advantage over the bus, and it was decided not to convert any further routes to trolleybus operation. Nevertheless two further batches of vehicles were ordered, again Leylands with MCW bodies, and these were delivered in 1937 and 1939. In 1940 the remaining fleet was concentrated on the Coventry Road services, and the Nechells route was converted to bus operation on 1 October 1940; it was said that flashes from the skate on depot working were an embarrassment during the wartime black-out. So great was the volume of traffic on the surviving route during the war that a special extension was built to serve the Rover Works at Lode Lane, and operation began here on 29 October 1941.

After the war, bus substitution of tram services went ahead in earnest, and the trolleybuses were reckoned as trams in this scheme. Buses took over the Coventry Road services on 1 July 1951 while two further stages of tramway conversion still remained to be carried out. Thus ended a lengthy but limited experiment in the city of Birmingham.

References
'British Trolleybus Systems: 4 — Birmingham': *Buses Illustrated* April 1967.
ABC of Birmingham City Transport: Part 1 Trams and Trolleybuses by W. A. Camwell (Ian Allan Ltd 1950).
The Trolleybuses of Birmingham by F. W. York (British Trolleybus Society 1971).

Bournemouth

'Not only is this town ideally suitable for the operation of trolleybuses, because of its wide thoroughfares and long stretches of straight roads, but there was another factor to be borne in mind by those who were planning to retain the amenities of the borough, and to uphold the name of Bournemouth as a first-class resort: the trolley vehicle did appear to offer something over and above what the motorbus could provide.' Thus stated Bournemouth's Transport Manager, W. D. Reakes in 1951. He pointed to the silence, smooth running and absence of fumes of the trolleybus, as well as its efficiency in tackling the 1 in 8 hill out of the town centre. The decision to adopt trolleybuses, he concluded, was 'a very wise one, and has paid a handsome dividend'.

Above:
Bournemouth: Seen on the first experimental route in 1932, No 70 (an AEC 661T with English Electric body) was later converted to a petrol bus.
S. E. Harrison

Below:
Bournemouth: Far from home! No 132 in Wolverhampton in 1940, one of a dozen Sunbeams on wartime loan to this system. Bournemouth crews who volunteered to transfer their service receive instructions from Wolverhampton's chief inspector.
Ian Allan Library

Above right:
Bournemouth: Bournemouth's first trolleybus was this Weymann-bodied Sunbeam MS2 in 1933.
Ian Allan Library

Proposals for trolley vehicles were in the air as early as 1910, when a service was envisaged in Boscombe, and the tramways manager was instructed to 'keep in touch' with the progress of this type of transport. In 1913 two schemes were the subject of Parliamentary Bills. The Bournemouth District Railless Traction Co proposed a service on Charminster Road, while the Sandbanks Railless Electric Car Co was planning two routes between County Gates, Parkstone and Sandbanks. Neither scheme materialised, but in 1922 Trackless Cars demonstrated their front-wheel drive double-decker (later to become Leeds No 513) at Bournemouth's Southcote Road depot, using a skate in the tram tracks.

Under its Act of 1930 Bournemouth Corporation obtained powers to operate trolleybuses on its tram routes and on 14 other routes, but before going ahead with any general conversion it decided to instal an experimental service over a distance of about one mile along the tramway between the Square and Westbourne. Four vehicles of different types were hired (and later purchased) — two from AEC, one from Sunbeam, and one from Thornycroft (this last was a single-decker, the only one produced by this

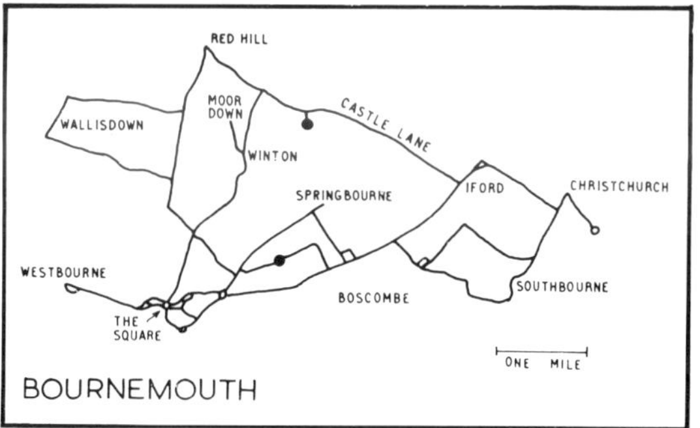

maker). The service began on 13 May 1933.

Such was the success of the experiment that only a few months later (on 7 October 1933) the Council decided that the tramways should be replaced by trolleybuses within three years. Before the end of 1934, orders had been placed for a total of 102 Sunbeams, which were to constitute the largest fleet of one make to be bought by any municipality. The bodies were to Bournemouth's own specification, with rear entrance, dual stairways, and forward exit with manually-operated folding doors. Seating capacity of 56 was low for a six-wheel double-decker, but the use of the front exit was found worthwhile in reducing time at stops while moderate capacity enhanced the high standard of comfort which was a prime objective.

The first permanent service accordingly opened on 22 June 1934, from the Square, via Lansdowne, Holdenhurst Road and Ashley Road to Boscombe, together with a short branch to Queen's Park. The service also incorporated the original line to Westbourne. The new system expanded rapidly in 1935 as follows:

25 March
Iford Bridge.
 7 June
Winton and Moordown.
28 June
Moordown via Lansdowne.
23 August
Charminster and Castle Lane.
21 November
Fisherman's Walk.
23 December
Southbourne.

On 8 April 1936 the route to Christchurch was inaugurated, and on the same day the last

Bournemouth

Fleet Nos	Registration Nos	Chassis	Electrical equipment	Body	In service	Withdrawn	Notes
68	LJ 7701	Sunbeam MS2	BTH	Weymann H32/28R	1933	1952	
69	LJ 7702	AEC 663T	E/Electric	E/Electric H32/28R	1933	1950	a
70	LJ 7703	AEC 661T	E/Electric	E/Electric H26/24R	1933	1950	a
71	LJ 7704	Thornycroft BD	Brush/BTH	Brush B32C	1933	1942	b
72-7	AEL 400-5	Sunbeam MS2	BTH	P/Royal H31/25D	1934	1952-3	
78-83	AEL 406-11	Sunbeam MS2	BTH	E/Electric H31/25D	1934	1952-8	
84-9	ALJ 60-5	Sunbeam MS2	BTH	P/Royal H31/25D	1934	1959-64	c
90-125	ALJ 964-99	Sunbeam MS2	BTH	P/Royal H31/25D	1935	1952-65	d
126-49	BEL 811-34	Sunbeam MS2	BTH	P/Royal H31/25D	1935	1952-65	e
150-73	BRU 1-24	Sunbeam MS2	BTH	P/Royal H31/25D	1935/6	1952-65	f
200-23	KLJ 334-57	BUT 9641T	C/Parkinson-A/West	Weymann H31/25D	1950	1966	g
258-77	WRU 258-77	Sunbeam MF2B	C/Parkinson-A/West	Weymann H35/28D	1958/9	1969	h
278-87	YLJ 278-87	Sunbeam MF2B	C/Parkinson-A/West	Weymann H35/28D	1959	1969	
288-91	HUF 45-8	BUT 9611T	C/Parkinson-A/West	Weymann H30/26R	1959	1965	i
292-4	DNJ 992-4	BUT 9611T	C/Parkinson-A/West	Weymann H30/26R	1959	1965	j
295-303	295-303 LJ	Sunbeam MF2B	C/Parkinson-A/West	Weymann H37/28D	1962	1969	

Notes:

a Converted to petrol bus 1936

b Sold to South Shields as No 236

c Nos 84, 85, 86 and 88 renumbered 205-8 in 1959/60

d Nos 90, 93, 97, 99, 101, 105, 106, 117, 119, 121 renumbered 209-18 1958-60. No 112 renumbered 202 and rebuilt as 69-seat open top 1958

e Nos 129-32, 137, 141, 144, 147 renumbered 219-26 in 1958-60

f Nos 157 and 160 renumbered 200/1 and rebuilt as 69-seat open top 1958. Nos 152/9, 162/3, 167/8, 170 renumbered 227-33 1959/60

g Nos 200-23 renumbered 234-57 1958/9. Nos 234-43 converted to 68-seat 1962/3

h Nos 258/9 and 261-9 originally 62 seats

i Ex-Brighton Corporation Nos 4, 5-8, new 1947

j Ex-Brighton, Hove & District Nos 6391-3, new 1948

Preserved vehicles: Nos 202, 212, 246, 286, 297, 299, 301

trams were withdrawn, thereby completing the changeover. The Christchurch route was notable for its terminal arrangement; in the absence of suitable turning space at Christchurch, a manually-worked turntable was installed in a former stable yard and was brought into use on 19 June 1936. Another unusual feature was the toll bridge at Tuckton. Up to 1942, when the toll was abolished, passengers paid a halfpenny toll in addition to their fare.

Bournemouth had proposed to install trolleybuses to replace tramcars on the two Poole routes which it operated under lease. However, this move was opposed by Hants & Dorset Motor Services, whose buses subsequently took over from the Poole trams on 8 June 1935. Nevertheless, Bournemouth was continuing to expand its network:

11 March 1937
Lawford Road from Moordown to Castle Lane.
5 April 1937
Five Ways-Malvern Road.
8 May 1937
In the town centre, Bath Road and Western Road, to provide an alternative route between Square and Lansdowne.
15 April 1938
Winson, Wallisdown, Columbia Road.
15 April 1939
Ensbury Park.
22 July 1943
Barrack Road, connecting the Iford and Christchurch routes.

During the war the decrease in traffic enabled Bournemouth to assist more hard-pressed undertakings, and no fewer than 30 Bournemouth trolleybuses went on loan to London, Newcastle, South Shields, Wolverhampton,

Above:
Bournemouth: Distinctive in appearance were the dual-doorway Weymann bodies of the 1958/9 Sunbeam MF2Bs.   *Ian Allan Library*

Walsall and Llanelly. The Thornycroft single-decker was sold to South Shields in 1943.

Postwar extensions included Beaufort Road and Cranleigh Road on 16 August 1948, and at Easter 1950 the introduction of wiring to the Pier for the operation of seasonal services as well as a relief to town centre routes. On 15 October 1951 came the last major extension, along Castle Lane to serve new housing at Strouden, thus completing another circle.

In 1953 a new depot and works was opened in Castle Lane, replacing the old Moordown depot, and in 1955 the corporation's generating station ceased to supply power to the trolley-buses, which from then on received their current from the Southern Electricity Board. On 28 August 1955 a section of new routeing was brought into use in Christchurch, where for several months the trolleybuses had had to run wrong-way against the traffic flow in a new one-way street layout.

Postwar fleet renewals took the form of 24 BUTs in 1950 (Nos 200-23), generally similar to the prewar six-wheelers, followed in 1958-59 by 30, 30ft-long, two-axle MF2Bs (Nos 258-87) with Weymann bodies with front exit ahead of the front axle. A further nine (Nos 295-303) were added in 1962 (10 had been ordered but one chassis was destroyed in a fire at the Weymann works), and the last of the batch to be delivered (No 301) earned the sad distinction of being the last trolleybus to be built for operation on an existing British system. In 1959, seven BUTs were purchased from Brighton, to become the only four-wheel double-deckers in the Bournemouth fleet. For the summer season of 1958, three of the prewar Sunbeams were rebuilt as open-toppers for use on a circular service; by removal of the front exit and front

stairway their seating capacity was raised to 69.

On 16 April 1963 Bournemouth Council decided that the trolleybuses should be discontinued within about 10 years. In fact, the process was to take only about six years. As had been discovered elsewhere by this time, there were problems arising from the high cost of new equipment, declining numbers of passengers, and the construction of new road works which would have necessitated costly changes in the overhead layout (though new gyratory layouts in the Square and Lansdowne had been satisfactorily installed in 1947, costs had escalated since then). The changeover was soon under way. On 29 September 1963 services ran for the last time on Lansdowne Road and St Paul's Road. Malvern Road ceased on 4 April 1965, followed on 12 September of the same year by the pioneer Westbourne, Holdenhurst Road and Boscombe route. On 16 April 1966, the Wallisdown route was withdrawn, followed by the withdrawal on 25 September of the services through Moordown, Five Ways and Castle Lane. The remaining routes — along Christchurch Road to Iford, Southbourne and Christchurch — continued until the final closure on 20 April 1969.

References:
Bournemouth Trolleybuses 1933-1969 — Bournemouth Corporation Transport, 1969.
Silent Service; the story of Bournemouth's trolleybuses by D. L. Chalk (Omnibus Society, 1962).
'Corporation Transport in Bournemouth' — *Modern Transport*, 28 April and 5 May 1951.

The Tramways of Bournemouth & Poole by R. C. Anderson (Light Railway Transport League, 1964).

Bradford

The Bradford tramway system reached a maximum of 59 route miles in 1914, by which time the populous areas of the city and its surrounding districts were well served by a fleet of 250 tramcars. There were, however, certain areas whose population was too small to merit the provision of tramway facilities, and a motorbus service was considered and rejected. The Manager, C. J. Spencer, inspected trolley-bus systems in Germany, Austria and Italy in 1909, with the result that an Act was obtained in 1910 for a trolleybus route from Laisterdyke to Dudley Hill, linking two tram routes. The Schiemann system, using twin trolley booms and tramway-type overhead equipment, was adopted.

The route was officially inaugurated on 20 June 1911, simultaneously with the Leeds Corporation route to New Farnley, these being the first regular British trolleybus routes. Public service commenced on 24 June, with the aid of one car, No 240. A second car (No 241) was obtained a few weeks later. Both cars (re-numbered 501/2 in 1913) were rear-entrance single-deckers with Railless chassis, Hurst Nelson bodies and Siemens equipment.

The new installation was sufficiently successful to encourage the Tramways Department to construct a car of its own design at Thornbury works (No 503), and 17 further cars were built between 1913 and 1918 to serve extensions of

Above left:
Bradford: No 572 was a three-axle 56-seater supplied by English Electric in 1929.
Ian Allan Library

Left:
Bradford: Rebodying gave a new lease of life to elderly vehicles. No 605, an AEC 661T of the mid-1930s and originally with an English Electric body, was fitted with this new Brush body in 1944. Note the headlamp masks and white-painted wings in this wartime photograph.   *Ian Allan Library*

Below:
Bradford: In this scene from 1938, new No 679 (one of a series of Weymann-bodied Karrier E4s) pulls in to load for the Clayton route.   *Ian Allan Library*

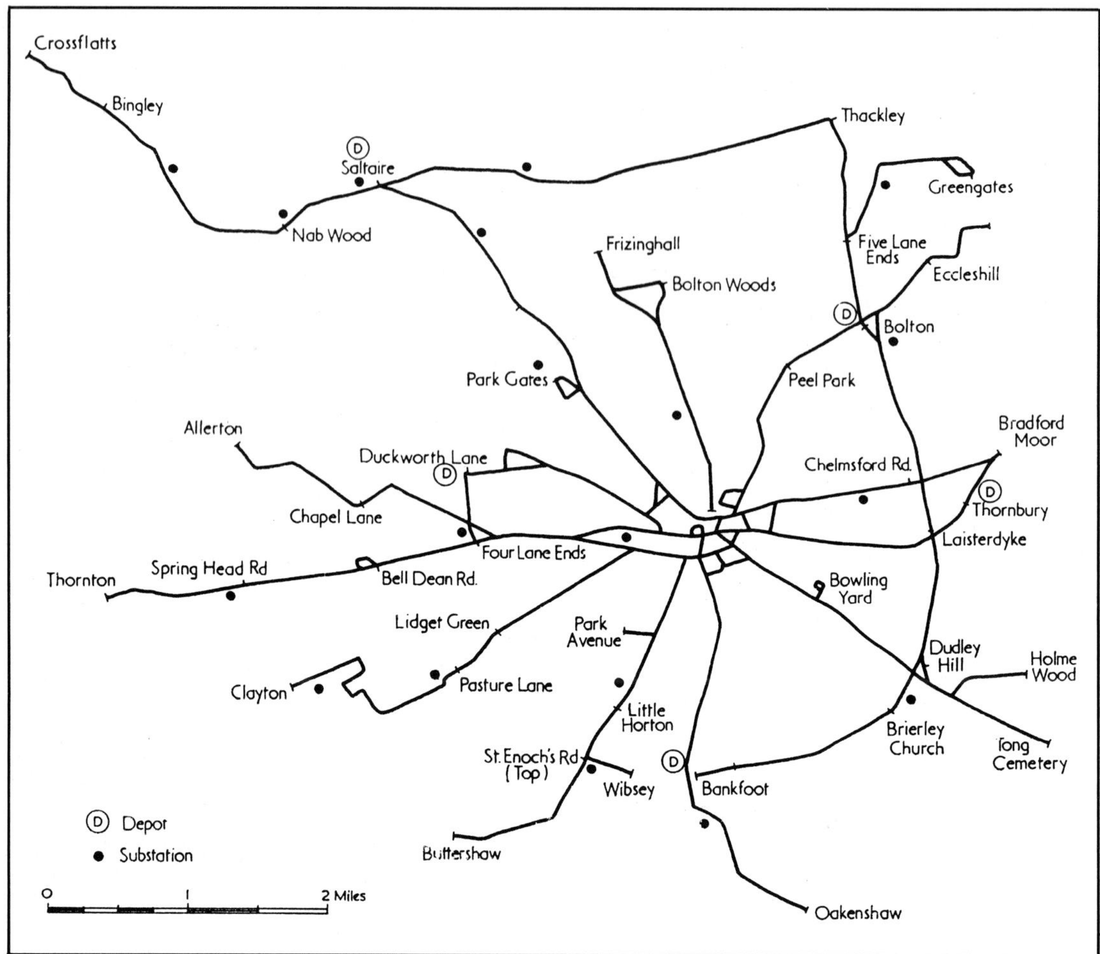

the original route to Bankfoot (17 July 1914) and Bolton (13 October 1914), as well as new routes from Odsal to Oakenshaw (25 June 1914) and from the city to Frizinghall and Bolton Woods (11 March 1915).

The new Manager, R. H. Wilkinson, was impressed with the potentialities of trolleybuses, not only as a feeder to the tramways but also as a possible substitute for them. In 1919 he designed what was virtually a double-deck Bradford tramcar on a four-wheel trolleybus chassis, and this vehicle (No 521) underwent successful trials on 3 November 1920. Although not the first British double-deck trolleybus (open-top versions had run in Keighley, Hove and Brighton) this was the first with a top cover and the first which could be considered as a rival to the tram. Its success prompted tramway conversion in Birmingham and Keighley. No 522, a 59-seat, four-wheel-steering, six-wheel double-decker, followed in 1922, but plans for a large network were not approved.

Wilkinson advocated conversion of the Eccleshill, Idle and Thackley tram routes, while there were also proposals for trolleybuses to Baildon, White Cross, Keighley, Brighouse and Cleckheaton.

Nevertheless, the fleet was continually modernised. AEC one-man cars were introduced in 1923, and pneumatic-tyred Garretts and ADCs in 1926/27. A new route to Clayton — in effect an extension of the Lidget Green tramway along country lanes and winding village streets — was opened on 4 September 1926. The Oakenshaw route was extended from Odsal to the city centre on 24 October 1927, and early in 1928 a through service from Oakenshaw to Clayton was instituted.

The first tram-to-trolleybus conversion took place on 29 November 1929 on the Allerton route, double-deck, six-wheel English Electric vehicles being used. The success of trolleybuses was now assured. No further single-deckers were bought after 1930, and from 1934 the

Above:
Bradford: Another AEC of the 1930s, No 636 was rebodied by Crossley in 1952. *Ian Allan Library*

department standardised on four-wheel double-deckers. Throughout the 1930s the system expanded steadily:

31 March 1930
Saltaire via Thackley.
22 March 1931
Greengates via Idle (an extension beyond the former tram terminus).
1 June 1934
Eccleshill.
21 November 1934
Thornton, and the elimination of trams from the Lidget Green part of the Clayton route.
2 October 1935
Duckworth Lane (extended to the new Royal Infirmary on 20 April 1936).
6 July 1938
Tong Cemetery.
7 May 1939
Saltaire, Bingley and Crossflatts.

A casualty was the Canal Road section, which closed on 30 April 1932 with the withdrawal of services to Bolton Woods and Frizinghall, where traffic had proved inadequate; it was handed over to the West Yorkshire Road Car Co in return for the withdrawal of competition on the Clayton section.

World War 2 hampered progress. The Oakenshaw service was replaced by motorbuses on 1 August 1940, because of the excessive cost of operation, the need for overhead renewals, and unsatisfactory insulation. One new trolleybus entered service during that year: No 692, a Karrier E4 demonstrator which proved to be the last E4 double-decker ever built. Carbon-insert trolley skids were introduced in 1942 and a general conversion began in 1944. In 1942 10 Sunbeam MF2s, part of a batch ordered by

Johannesburg, became the first 8ft-wide vehicles in the fleet. In 1945/46 37 Karrier Ws entered service, and the last of the single-deckers and six-wheelers were withdrawn.

Early postwar developments included the Bradford Moor route, on which trolleybus services started on 4 December 1949, after the last trams had ceased running on 23 July and a temporary motorbus service substituted. New 8ft-wide BUT 96llTs were used. In 1951, authority was given to convert the Thornbury route, which had been wired for depot journeys for many years; this service commenced on 2 March 1952.

The chief problem now was the steeply-rising cost of current, but the new General Manager, C. T. Humpidge, met this challenge by judicious purchases of secondhand vehicles and equipment, and a progressive rebodying schedule

Right:
Bradford: The trolleybuses kept going through snow and ice and wartime blackout; AEC No 663 traverses an exposed section of the Bingley route in February 1940. *Ian Allan Library*

Bradford

Fleet Nos	Registration Nos	Chassis	Electrical equipment	Body	In service	Withdrawn	Notes
240/1	AK 8089/90	Railless	Siemens	H/Nelson B28R	1911	1926	a
503-20	AK 9615-32	BCT	Brown	BCT B28R	1913-18	1927-9	
521	AK 9638	BCT	D/Kerr	BCT H26/25ROS	1920	1927	
522	AK 9963	BCT	Metrovick	BCT H33/24ROS	1922	1927	
523-8	KU 1160-5	AEC 602	D/Kerr	BCT B30F	1923	1931	
529-31	KU 9104-6	ADC 607	Bull	ADC B32F	1926/7	By 1937	
532-9	KU 9101-3, RT 1345, UM 1755, KW 204-6	Garrett	Bull	Roe B36F	1926/7	By 1946	
540-3	KW 200-3	ADC 607	Bull	ADC B32F (540: Strachan)	1926/7	By 1937	
544-60	KW 4590-4606	Leyland	E/Electric	E/Electric B36C	1928/9	By 1947	
561-71	KW 6051-61	E/Electric	E/Electric	E/Electric B36F	1929/30	By 1946	b
572-96	KW 6062-7/ 6654-9/9433/ 9454-64, KY 1360	E/Electric	E/Electric	E/Electric H30/26R	1929-32	1941-6	
597-632	KY 8200-20, AAK 420-34	AEC 661T	E/Electric	E/Electric H30/26R	1934-9	By 1963	c
633	KY 6210	AEC 761T	E/Electric	E/Electric H33/30F	1934	1942	d
634-76	BAK 934, CAK 634-76	AEC 661T	E/Electric	E/Electric H30/26R	1934-9	By 1963	e
677-92	CAK 677-92	Karrier E4	E/Electric	Weymann H30/26R	1938-40	By 1961	e
693-702	DKW 993-9, DKY 2-4	Sunbeam MF2	BTH	Weymann UH30/26R	1942	1968	f
703-14	DKY 703-14	Karrier W	Metrovick	Roe UH30/26R	1945/6	1963	
715-9	DKY 715-9	Karrier W	E/Electric	P/Royal UH30/26R	1945/6	1963	
720-33	DKY 720-33	Karrier W	Metrovick	P/Royal UH30/26R	1945/6	1963	
734-9	DKY 734-9	Karrier W	Metrovick	Roe UH30/26R	1945/6	1963	
740-51	EKU 740-51	BUT 9611T	E/Electric	Roe H33/25R	1949	1968	
752-9	FKU 752-9	BUT 9611T	E/Electric	Weymann H33/26R	1950/1	1968	
760-74	NNU 224-238	BUT 9611T	E/Electric	Weymann H30/26R	1953	1958	g

enabled the fleet to be modernised and additional routes to be opened without heavy capital charges. Public service on the new Wibsey route commenced on 24 April 1954, and on the Buttershaw extension on 8 April 1956. The Clayton route was extended nearly ½-mile from Town End along The Avenue on 15 July 1956.

The extension of the Eccleshill route to Faltis Square, Thorpe Edge, was opened on 9 August 1959. This was the most spectacular section on the system, as vehicles had to contend with a narrow village street, a blind corner and a gradient of 1 in 8. A spur from Tong Street to the Holme Wood housing estate was inaugurated on 6 March 1960, and was the last route extension. The system was now at its zenith, with 47 route miles and 200 vehicles.

The 20 BUTs of 1949-51 were the last new purchases, and thereafter additions to the fleet came secondhand: from Llanelli, Darlington, St Helens, Brighton, Hastings, Notts & Derby, Doncaster, Grimsby, Ashton and Mexborough & Swinton. Many of these were rebodied, as were also a number of older vehicles, the new bodywork incorporating such refinements as forward entrances, platform doors, saloon heaters and trolley retrievers. Noteworthy examples were the nine ex-Darlington 33-seat single-deckers which in 1958 re-entered service with new East Lancashire forward-entrance double-deck bodies with seating for 71. Another former single-decker, from the Mexborough & Swinton system and rebodied by East Lancashire in 1963, became the last trolleybus to enter service in Bradford.

Redevelopment of the city centre led to the abandonment of the routes traversing Forster Square. The Bradford Moor route was closed on 17 November 1962, and the Eccleshill-St Enoch's Road Top through service went over to buses. On 31 October 1963 the Crossflatts trolleybuses were withdrawn, and the last trolleybus to Eccleshill ran on 31 October 1964.

Other closures took place as follows:

28 February 1964
Bolton-Bankfoot service withdrawn. Most of the route continued to be required for depot working until 1967, and only the

Fleet Nos	Registration Nos	Chassis	Electrical equipment	Body	In service	Withdrawn	Notes
580-96	ORB 616-22, HNU 826-30/ 970-4	AEC 661T	E/Electric	Weymann H30/26R	1953-5	1968	g
775-84	CBX 530/1/600/1/ 909-14	Karrier W	BTH (775-8), Metrovick (779-84)	E/Lancs H35/28R	1956	1968	h
785-93	GHN 403/563/4/6/ 9/70/1/4/5	Karrier W	Metrovick	Brush B33C	1958	1972	i
794-801	BDJ 82-9	BUT 9611T	E/Electric	E/Lancs H30/26R	1959	1963/4	j
802/3	HUF 49/50	BUT 9611T	E/Electric	Weymann H30/24R	1959	1963	k
804-15	BDY 796-803/20/ 15	Sunbeam W	BTH	P/Royal H30/26R (814/5: Weymann)	1959-61	1963	l
820/1	FTJ 400/1	Sunbeam W	Metrovick	Roe H30/26R	1960	1961	m
822-5/7	AEE 22-5/7	Karrier W	Metrovick	Roe H31/25R	1960	1961	n
831-5	LHN 781-5	BUT 9611T	E/Electric	E/Lancs H37/29R	1962	1972	o
841-7	FWX 911-4, JWW 375-7	Sunbeam F4	BTH	E/Lancs H37/29F	1962/3	1972	p

Notes:

a Renumbered 501/2 in 1913. No 502 converted to trolley-battery lorry 1916; No 501 converted later

b Nos 573/9/80/4-6/91/2/4/5 sold to Newcastle 1943; Nos 582/90/6 sold to South Shields 1945

c Rebodied by Brush and NCB 1944-9

d Sold to South Shields

e Nos 635-7, 640, 652, 677/8, 682/4/5/8, 691/2 rebodied by Crossley H30/26R 1952; Nos 634/8, 651/4/5/9, 664/6, 674/5 rebodied by East Lancs 1956

f Originally intended for Johannesburg. Rebodied by East Lancs 1956

g Ex-Notts & Derby

h Ex-Llanelly. Rebodied by East Lancs 1956

i Ex-Darlington. Rebodied by East Lancs 1958. Only No 785 (T403) operated as single-decker

j Ex-St Helens

k Ex-Brighton

l Ex-Hastings

m Ex-Ashton-under-Lyne. No 821 never entered service

n Ex-Grimsby

o Ex-Doncaster and Darlington. Rebodied by East Lancs 1962

p Ex-Mexborough & Swinton. Rebodied by East Lancs 1963

Preserved vehicles: Nos 515, 703, 704, 706, 711, 712, 713, 731, 735, 737, 743, 746, 758, 770, 774, 792, 834, 835, 844, 845, 846, 847

Above:
Bradford: No 634, seen when new in 1934, was an AEC 661T with English Electric body. With others in the series, it was rebodied by East Lancashire in 1956. *Ian Allan Library*

Dudley Hill-Bankfoot wiring could be dismantled at this time.
1 April 1967
Tong Cemetery and Holme Wood.
27 February 1971
Allerton.
30 June 1971
Greengates and Saltaire. This ended
    trolleybus operation outside the city.
31 July 1971
Clayton, Wibsey and Buttershaw.

This left only two trolleybus routes operating, not only in Bradford but in Great Britain: from the city to Duckworth Lane, and the cross-city service between Thornton and Thornbury. By the end of 1971 buses had already taken over some duties, and the last public services ran on 24 March 1972. The ceremonial closure took place on 26 March, with nine trolleybuses on tour duties and No 844 as the official last trolleybus to operate in Bradford and Britain.

References
Transport of Delight: the Bradford Trolleybus 1911-1972 by J. S. King (National Trolleybus Association 1972).
'British Trolleybus Systems: No 5 — Bradford', *Buses Illustrated*, June 1967.
Fifty Years of Trolleybuses (Bradford City Transport 1961).
Sixty Years of Bradford Trolleybuses (National Trolleybus Association 1971).

Brighton

Brighton came very near to being one of the pioneer trolleybus towns before World War 1, but in the event it proved to be one of the last to adopt the trolley vehicle. As early as 1909, Brighton Town Council was trying to find a way to instal a trackless trolley system without going to the lengths of promoting a Bill in Parliament. In the following year it must have been brought up with a jolt to find that two rival concerns were preparing to promote separate private Bills for trackless trolley systems in the next Parliamentary session.

These were far-reaching schemes. The Brighton District Tramways Bill (backed by the British Electric Traction Co) included a tramway from Worthing to Brighton and sought powers to construct a trackless trolley route from Brighton's Preston Circus northwest to the borough boundary within three years. The Brighton, Hove & District Railless Traction Co's Bill (promoted by the Brighton, Hove & Preston United Omnibus Co) was for trackless trolleys from Worthing (Marine Parade) through Brighton to Rottingdean (White Horse Inn). To have any chance of succeeding, each Bill needed the support of the local road authorities. This was not forthcoming, and by May 1911 the first battle was over. The Tramways Bill was limited to the section between Lancing and Portslade, while the rival's Bill was amended to cover only a short section from Ovingdean to Rottingdean.

In October 1911 it was stated that important negotiations were in hand between Brighton and Hove Councils for a scheme of trackless trolleys from east to west, and that plans had been formulated for the two councils to proceed simultaneously with Bills for a joint system. However, this project was rejected by Hove Council. After this, each council went ahead with its own scheme: Brighton for a Bill for a route through Hove from Kemp Town to Shoreham with several branches, and Hove with a Bill for a route to run from Hove to Shoreham. After much discussion, both Bills received the Royal Assent on 7 August 1912.

In 1913 the Board of Trade gave Brighton Corporation permission for 690yd of London Road, Brighton, between Trafalgar Road and Rosehill Terrace to be equipped for trials with a double-deck trackless car. The Railless Electric Traction Co offered to provide a car, which had been on trial in Leeds and was the first of its type built. It had two 20hp motors and seats for 38 passengers. It arrived in Brighton on 23 December 1913 and a number of trials were made over a period of several weeks.

Hove Council, meanwhile, favoured the Cedes Stoll system, and for the purpose of trials, overhead was erected from Hove railway station, down Goldstone Villas and George Street to Church Road. Trials in Hove began on 18 September 1914. The vehicle was smartly painted in blue and cream and embellished with the borough arms. The body was built by Christopher Dodson with seats for 33 (18 on upper deck and 15 inside) and two 20hp motors provided traction power.

Brighton: The transition: at the Old Steine in 1939 just before the last of the tramcars had succumbed to the trolleybuses, No 3 is flanked by tram No 49 and AEC Regent III No 71. *Ian Allan Library*

Brighton

Brighton Corporation

Fleet Nos	Registration Nos	Chassis	Electrical equipment	Body	In service	Withdrawn	Notes
1-44	FUF 1-44	AEC661T	C/Parkinson-A/West	Weymann H30/24R	1939	1959-61	
45-50	HUF 45-50	BUT9611T	C/Parkinson-A/West (45-48) E/Electric (49, 50)	Weymann H30/24R	1947	1959	a
51, 52	LCD 51/2	BUT9611T	C/Parkinson-A/West	Weymann H30/24R	1953	1959	b

Brighton, Hove & District

Fleet Nos	Registration Nos	Chassis	Electrical equipment	Body	In service	Withdrawn	Notes
6340-7	CPM 61/2, 53, 375, 101/2, 521, 997	AEC661T	C/Parkinson-A/West	Weymann H30/24R	1945/6	1959	c
6391-3	DNJ 992-4	BUT9611T	C/Parkinson-A/West	Weymann H30/26R	1948	1959	d

Notes:

a Nos 45-48 sold to Bournemouth, Nos 49, 50 to Bradford

b New in 1947, registered in 1951. Sold to Maidstone in 1959

c In stock 1939

d Sold to Bournemouth in 1959

Preserved vehicle: No 6340

When the trials ended in November 1914 Brighton Council renewed its pressure for the matter to go to arbitration. Neither side was willing to give way, and with the war now in progress it was agreed to leave the matter in abeyance for six months from December 1914. This was effectively the end of it. Although there were several flickers of a renewal of interest — in 1925, 1929 and 1935 — it was not until the 1938 Act for the pooling of transport in the town that the way was clear for trolleybuses to arrive in Brighton.

Under the 1938 Act, which created a joint working area from 1 April 1939 between Brighton Corporation and the Brighton, Hove & District Omnibus Co, the tramways were to be replaced by trolleybuses within three to five years. The Corporation was to be responsible for the fixed equipment, and the company was to have the right to operate 20% of total trolleybus mileage. A fleet of 44 Weymann-bodied AEC 661Ts (Nos 1-44) was ordered by Brighton Corporation and the first were put into service on 1 May 1939 on the Lewes Road route. This was followed on 1 June by the Preston Drove circular and an extension along Ditchling Road, and on 17 July by the route to Brighton station and Seven Dials. The final conversion on 1 September saw trolleybuses on the Elm Grove and Race Hill route, as well as from Queens Park Road to Old Steine. For its share, the company bought eight trolleybuses, but these were not put into service until 1946.

On 3 March 1946, to meet new housing

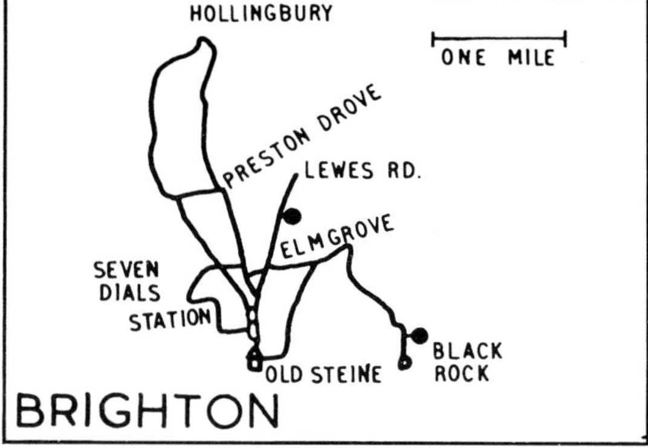

development the Race Hill route was extended along Manor Hill and Whitehawk Road to reach the seafront at Black Rock. This passed Brighton, Hove & District's Whitehawk Road garage which housed the company's trolleybuses, and these were now brought into use for the first time. On 28 November 1948 the Ditchling Road route was extended to Larkfield Way, and then to Carden Hill on 23 March 1949, again to serve housing development. On 12 August 1951 a two-mile extension was opened along Surrenden Road and Carden Avenue through the Hollingbury Estate to connect the Preston Drove and Carden Hill routes and enable an 'outer circle' service to be worked. Meanwhile the corporation's fleet was increased by a further eight vehicles and the company's by another three.

Two of the extensions envisaged under the

1938 Act did not materialise: in Balfour Road, and from Carden Avenue to Ladies Mile Road. Powers for further extensions were also obtained in 1947 for a route from Seven Dials, along Dyke Road to Queens Road and West Street and then along the seafront by Kings Road to Old Steine, and for a branch from Lewes Road to Coombe Road and Baden. In 1952 powers were obtained for an extension from Carden Avenue to Crowhurst Road. Again, none of these proposals reached fruition.

By the 1950s changing conditions prompted a reconsideration of the joint working arrangements between the corporation and the company, and eventually a new agreement (also including Southdown) became effective from 1 January 1961. In 1954 there was a proposal that the corporation's trolleybuses should be replaced by buses so that its fleet could be more flexible within the co-ordination scheme. This was narrowly rejected at the time, but in 1956 the Town Council agreed that the trolleybuses should be withdrawn.

On 24 March 1959 trolleybuses made their last journeys on the routes to Seven Dials, Lewes Road, Elm Grove, Queens Park Road and Black Rock. This change brought the end of trolleybus operation by Brighton, Hove & District, which had remained the only Tilling group company to run this form of transport. The remaining routes continued until 30 June 1961, when the honour fell to the original No 1 to make the official last journey.

References
British Bus & Tram Systems: No 35 — 'Brighton Corporation and the Brighton Hove & District Omnibus Company' by V. H. Darling; *Buses Illustrated*, February, March, April 1963.
'British Trolleybus Systems; No 6 Brighton and Hove'; *Buses Illustrated*, October 1967.
'Transport in Brighton'; *Modern Transport*, 22 April 1950.

Below:
Brighton: Standard units in the Brighton fleet were the Weymann-bodied AEC 661Ts which lasted the lifetime of the system. *Ian Allan Library*

Cardiff

Cardiff was late on the scene with trolleybuses (later than any English undertaking and followed only by Glasgow) but its system developed a strongly individual character, not least in the design of the vehicles which reflected the flat-fare 'pay-as-you-enter' method of working used over a lengthy period. The idea of trackless vehicles seems to have been considered at least as early as 1911, but it was 1939 when it was agreed that the city's tramcars should be replaced by trolleybuses. As a first step orders were placed with Leyland for 10 six-wheel chassis which were to be provided with Northern Counties bodies, but wartime conditions brought delays, and since Leyland were not in a position to supply, the chassis were eventually obtained from AEC. It was not until 1942 that the complete vehicles were on hand as Nos 201-10 in the Corporation fleet. Like the tramcars, they were of special low height design (just under 15ft) to negotiate low bridges, and in view of the danger of flooding in certain places the chassis were designed to navigate through 6-8in of flood water in safety.

Operation started on 1 March 1942 when five vehicles began a service between the city centre at Wood Street and the Docks at Clarence Road. Delivery of the remaining five vehicles enabled the route to be extended northwards along Cathedral Road to Llandaff Fields on the following 8 November. Of particular interest was the 'pay-as-you-enter' system introduced with the trolleybuses, employing a coin box and a flat fare of one penny; no tickets were issued and no change was given. So successful was the system that it was extended to the trams by 1944 as well as to many bus routes.

No more route extensions took place during the war, but the transport department's chief engineer prepared a design for a postwar trolleybus in co-operation with East Lancashire Coachbuilders and orders for 20 vehicles were placed. Features of the new design exploited the 'pay-as-you-enter' method and included a forward exit with sliding door, served by a front stairway, and a seat for the conductor on the near side of the rear entrance. As things turned out, the new vehicles were not to make their debut until 1948.

Meanwhile attention was being given to another route which presented its own problems. A low bridge on the Bute Street route prevented the use of double-deck trolleybuses between the city centre and the docks. Trams were replaced by buses in 1946, but when it was desired to replace these in turn by trolleybuses

Above:

Cardiff: Cardiff's first trolleybus in 1941 was fitted for pay-as-you-enter operation. The boards in the lower saloon windows exhort passengers to 'Have Your Penny Ready Please'. *Ian Allan Library*

Below:

Cardiff: Still in wartime livery, No 205 takes on its load in the shadow of the Castle in 1945. *Ian Allan Library*

Cardiff

Fleet Nos	Registration Nos	Chassis	Electrical equipment	Body	In service	Withdrawn	Notes
201-10	CKG 191-200	AEC6641T	E/Electric	N/Counties H38/32R	1941-3	1962-5	
211-30	DBO 471-80, DUH 716-25	BUT9641T	GEC	E/Lancs H38/29D	1948	1966-70	
231-7	TG 379/81/83/85/ 87/89/91	E/Electric	E/Electric	E/Electric B32C	1947	1949-50	a
238-42	EBO 891-5	BUT9641T	GEC	E/Lancs B38D	1949	1964	
243	KBO 961	BUT9641T	GEC	E/Lancs B40R	1955	1964	
245-64	EBO 902-21	BUT9641T	GEC	E/Lancs H38/29D	1949	1965	b
265-74	FBO 85-94	BUT9641T	GEC	E/Lancs H38/29D	1950	1965-8	b
275-87	KBO 948-60	BUT9641T	GEC	E/Lancs H40/32R	1955	1968-70	

Notes:

a Ex-Pontypridd 1-7, new 1930

b Nos 245 and 251-74 had East Lancs body frames completed
by Bruce Coachworks

Preserved vehicles: Nos 203, 243, 262

it was necessary to employ single-deckers. With new vehicles still unobtainable, eyes turned to the secondhand market and fell on seven 1930 single-deckers which had become redundant at nearby Pontypridd. With these veteran English Electric six-wheelers, trolleybus operation along Bute Street commenced on 17 August 1947; this was to be the only Cardiff trolleybus route to be worked by single-deckers.

The years 1948 to 1950 saw considerable expansion, with the fleet greatly augmented and taking over from the last of the trams. Trolleybuses started running to Victoria Park on 6 June 1948, Roath Park on 4 December 1949, Gabalfa on 20 February 1950, and along Newport Road to Pengam on 15 October 1950. A total of 50 new double-deckers arrived, all of the

Below:
Cardiff: No 203 seen in the short-lived 'streamlined' livery. *V. C. Jones/Ian Allan Library*

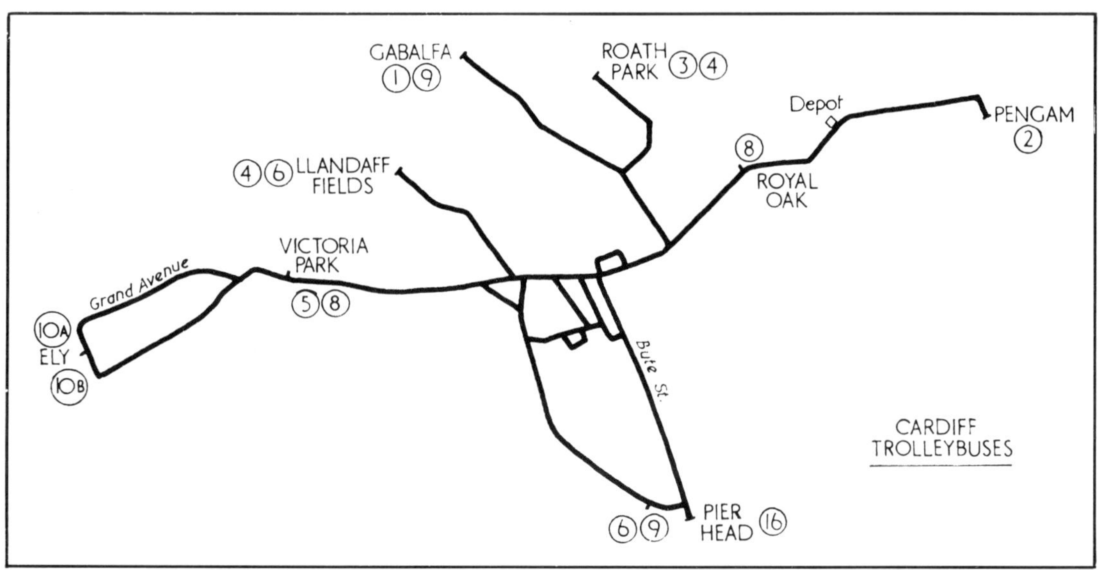

Above:

Cardiff: Postwar vehicles were designed for pay-as-you-enter operation with forward exit, visible here on No 229, a BUT 9641T with East Lancashire body, dating from 1948.   *V. C. Jones/Ian Allan Library*

Right:

Cardiff: One route — to the Pier Head via Bute Street — was restricted to single-deckers, of which No 239 was one of five delivered in 1949. A BUT 9641T, it had a 38-seat East Lancashire body.
V. C. Jones/Ian Allan Library

front-exit design conceived during the war; they were on BUT chassis with East Lancashire bodies, though some had bodywork completed by the local firm of Bruce on East Lancashire frames. Also added were five single-deckers of basically similar pattern to replace the ex-Pontypridd vehicles in 1949.

With rising costs the flat fare (now raised to 1½d) was no longer an economic proposition, and in November 1950 the 'pay-as-you-enter' system was given up and the front exits were later taken out of use. In view of the change, the last additions to the fleet were of more orthodox design with single entrance and staircase; BUTs with East Lancashire bodywork, they entered service in 1955, the year of the last major route extension.

Opened on 8 May 1955, this continued from the Victoria Park terminus to Ely, making a large loop along Green Farm Road and Grand Avenue. Another single-decker was also added in this year; No 243 was generally similar to its predecessors but had no front exit. It was to be the last single-deck trolleybus to be built for operation on a British system.

In 1961 it was decided that replacement by diesel buses should be carried out over a period of eight to 10 years. On 24 November 1962 the last trolleybuses operated to Pengam when the route was cut back to the Royal Oak. The Bute Street route ceased on 11 January 1964. On 22 July 1965 peak-hour services 5A and 5B between Wood Street and Victoria Park or Beda Road via Neville Street ran for the last time, followed on 24 July by service 5 between Windsor Lane and Victoria Park. After 16 December 1965 services 6 and 9 were cut back from Docks to Central Bus Station, while their northern sections to Llandaff Fields (6) and Gabalfa (9) ceased after 16 April 1966. Service 4 between Roath Park and Llandaff Fields ran for the last time on 17 September 1966. In the city centre during 1965, one-way alterations brought wiring for the first time along Kingsway and Cathays Park Road, passing the Civic Buildings. This proved to have a short life, for the final trolleybuses ceased on 11 January 1970.

References
'British Trolleybus Systems: 7 — Cardiff': *Buses Illustrated* January 1968.
The Cardiff Trolleybus by D. G. Bowen and J. Callow (National Trolleybus Association 1969).
City of Cardiff: 68 Years of Electric Transport (National Trolleybus Association and City of Cardiff Transport 1970).
'Cardiff's Pay-as-you-Enter Trolleybuses': *Transport World* 12 March 1942.
'Progress of Cardiff's Tramway Conversion Scheme': *Transport World* 12 August 1948.

Chesterfield

Although the trolleybus system in Chesterfield ran for the comparatively short span of 11 years, the history begins before World War 1 when the town could have been numbered among the pioneers of British trolleybus operation. The Chesterfield Corporation Railless Traction Act of 1913 provided for five routes representing projections from the existing tram route. However, it was not until the mid-1920s that it was decided to replace the trams between Brampton and Whittington Moor, and in 1926 the first order was placed for 14 Straker-Clough trolleybuses, with single-deck bodies by Reeve & Kenning of nearby Pilsley. The first vehicle was delivered on 21 April 1927 and made a run the following day to Brampton for trials.

The first section from Market Place (West Bars) to Brampton was opened to traffic on the evening of 23 May 1927 with a minimum of

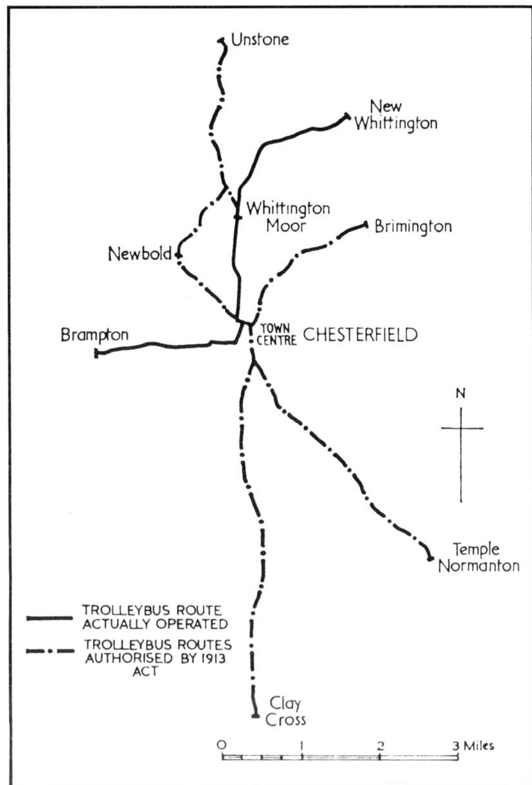

ceremony. In the interim period motorbuses covered the northern section of the former tram route until the new trolleybuses were able to take over the whole route from Brampton to Whittington Moor (3¾ miles) on 27 September 1927, when a formal opening ceremony took place. A month later it was decided to apply for an extension of the route beyond Whittington Moor to New Whittington. This was opened for traffic on 29 July 1929 and added just over two miles to the existing route mileage. No further extensions were built.

The only two double-deckers in the fleet (Nos 16 and 17) were delivered at the end of 1931; they were Ransomes with lowheight Ransomes bodies. In 1936 three Karrier Clough E4s were purchased from York, and these became Nos 18-20 in their new home. This was to be the limit of expansion of the system, for in 1937 the decision was made to abandon the trolleybuses in favour of motorbuses. Among the reasons for the decision were the need for extensive overhead renewal, the high cost of

Left:
Chesterfield: The only two double-deckers in the fleet (Nos 16 and 17) were Ransomes productions of 1931. *Ian Allan Library*

Fleet Nos	Chassis	Electrical equipment	Body	In service	Note
1-12, 14, 15	S/Clough	BTH	R/Kenning B32C	1927	
16, 17	Ransomes D2	BTH	Ransomes L24/24R	1931	
18-20	Karrier E4	BTH	Roe B32R	1936	a

Note:

a Ex-York Nos 30-32

electricity, low railway bridges preventing route extensions, and the Corporation's connections with the network of company bus services. Accordingly, on 24 March 1938 two single-deckers filled with councillors made the last journey.

References

'British Trolleybus Systems: 8 — Chesterfield': *Buses* April 1968.

'Chesterfield's New Transport System': *Tramway & Railway World* 13 October 1927.

Darlington

After World War 1 Darlington's tramways were in a rundown condition, and in 1924 Birmingham's Manager Alfred Baker was invited to advise on future policy. Replacement by trolleybuses was recommended, and following the Darlington Corporation (Transport etc) Act 1925, a contract was placed with Clough Smith for the supply of 20 single-deck trolleybuses and the conversion of the overhead line. The vehicles were Strakers with central-entrance Roe bodies and BTH equipment, and the first (No 1) arrived in December 1925. The first route, to Haughton, opened on 17 January 1926, and the last tram (to Harrowgate Hill) ran on 10 April. The new routes covered all the tram routes except for 250ft of track at Cockerton, where the service now extended to Faverdale.

A circular service to Cockerton (Travellers' Rest), via North Road, Willow Road and Woodland Road, was opened on 25 March 1928. Other routes were opened to Neasham Road (6 April 1928), Park Lane (23 February 1930) and Coniscliffe Road (27 March 1932), while the Haughton route was extended to the Gatehouse on 5 November 1933.

Below:
Darlington: This animated scene from the 1930s includes No 19 (one of the original 1925/6 Strakers) and No 33 (an AEC 662T of 1934). *Ian Allan Library*

The most interesting feature of the system was that the department relied entirely on trolleybuses. The chief reason for this was that the transport and electricity departments were under the same manager. Moreover Darlington electricity department consumed Durham coal: charity begins at home! The fleet expanded continually to keep pace with developments. The original 20 Strakers were joined in 1926 by four all-English Electric vehicles, two Ransomes in 1928, and six further English Electrics in 1929-30. They were followed by AEC 662Ts, and four Ransomes from Rotherham, as well as by eight Leyland TB5s in 1937.

The Manager, Mr I. R. P. Lunn, was remarkably conservative in his specifications for bodies, insisting that new vehicles should closely resemble existing ones, and as a result the vehicles ordered in 1937 were scarcely distinguishable from the 1930 products. He was, however, aware of the limitations of single-deckers, and in 1936 recommended the purchase of eight lowbridge double-deckers for the busy Harrowgate Hill-Eastbourne route, but no action was taken.

After the retirement of Lunn in 1937, the transport department was separated from the electricity department, and the first vehicles bought under the new regime (Leyland TBS Nos 56-63) were noteworthy in that their Brush bodies were of an attractive modern semi-streamlined type in a new light blue livery. The outbreak of war interrupted the normal process of renewal, but wartime deliveries included two Karriers (Nos 1 and 2) in 1942, the last of the E4 type ever built, as well as austerity-bodied Karrier Ws in 1943 (the first of the type to be built), enabling the veteran Strakers to be withdrawn. A short route extension was opened to Lingfield Lane (Eastbourne) at the end of 1942.

In 1947 the decision was made to replace the trolley vehicles by motorbuses in stages, in view of the need for costly re-requipment as well as increasing road congestion. Nevertheless the McMullen Road extension to serve Patons & Baldwins factory opened on 16 March 1949. Also in 1949, six BUT double-deckers, ordered in anticipation of the lowering of the road under certain bridges, arrived and were put into service, though not on the routes intended as the bridges had not yet been dealt with; in 1952 these vehicles were sold to Doncaster.

The first stage of the conversion programme

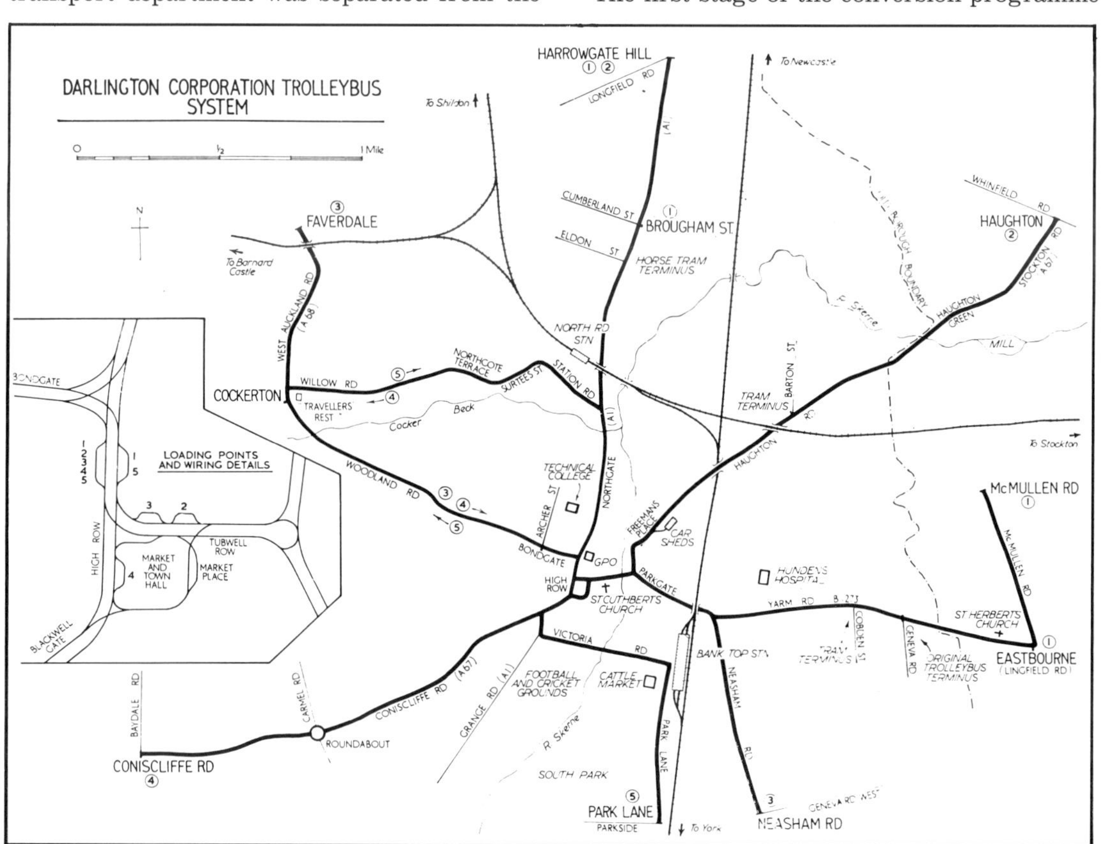

Darlington

Fleet Nos	Registration Nos	Chassis	Electrical equipment	Body	In service	Withdrawn	Notes
1-20	HN 4370-89	S/Squire	BTH	Roe B31C	1925/6	1939-44	
21-4	HN 4770-3	E/Electric	E/Electric	E/Electric B31C	1926	1939/44	
25/6	HN 6204/3	RS&J	RS&J	RS&J B22C	1928	1949	
27-32	HN 6879-84	E/Electric	E/Electric	E/Electric B32C	1930	1949/50	
33-40	HN 9657/8, AHN 185-90	AEC 662T	E/Electric	E/Electric B32C	1934	1950/1	
41-3	BHN 188-90	AEC 662T	E/Electric	Brush B32C	1935	1951	
44-7	ET3217/4820/ 4818/9	RS&J	RS&J	RS&J B32C	1937	1937	a
48-55	DHN 231-8	Leyland TB5	Metrovick	Brush B32C	1937	1951/2	
56-63	FHN 231-8	Leyland TB5	Metrovick	Brush B32C	1939	1953	
64-7	FHN 974-7	Leyland TB5	Metrovick	E/Lancs B32C	1940	1953	
1/11	GHN 321/2	Karrier E4S	E/Electric	E/Lancs B32C	1942	1953/4	b
17, 19, 24, 44-7, 8	GHN 401-8	Karrier W	E/Electric	Brush B33C	1943	1954	c
2-9, 13	GHN 561-8	Karrier W	E/Electric	Brush B33C	1944	1954-7	d
10, 12, 14, 16, 18, 20, 21, 22	GHN 569-76	Karrier W	Metrovick	Brush B33C	1944	1954-7	e
68-73	LHN 780-5	BUT9611T	E/Electric	E/Lancs H30/26R	1949	1952	f

Notes:

a Ex-Rotherham

b No 11 sold to Bradford

c In 1953-4 No 44 renumbered 15; 45 later 23; 46 later 48, then 1; 47 later 11. Sold to Bradford

d Nos 2-7 and 13 sold to Bradford

e Sold to Bradford

f Sold to Doncaster; resold to Bradford 1959

Right:
Darlington: Newly arrived in its wartime livery, Karrier W No 45 of 1943 had a Brush utility body.
Ian Allan Library

was effected on 30 November 1951 when the Harrowgate Hill-Haughton service was withdrawn. Eastbourne (Lingfield Lane) ceased on 16 June 1952, but trolleybuses continued to run for duplication and works traffic between Brougham Street and McMullen Road until June 1956. Park Lane and Willow Road closed on 7 December 1953. Coniscliffe Road trolleybuses then ran to and from a new turning circle at Travellers Rest until buses took over on 30 November 1954. The Suez crisis prolonged the life of the remaining route (Faverdale-Neasham Road) but early in 1957 the press announced that 'the last trolleybus of the summer will pass like the last rose, with a touch of sentimental regret'. Accordingly on 31 July the remaining eight vehicles (all Karrier Ws) made their final journeys; they later went to Bradford, where they were rehabilitated for further service.

References
British Trolleybus Systems: 9 — Darlington':
Buses July 1968.

Derby

Powers to operate trolley vehicles in Derby were applied for as early as 1913, but nothing materialised at this time. In 1929 a committee was appointed to consider the future of the tramways, with the result that in 1930 a Bill provided for running trolleybuses, and the Council approved a recommendation that trolleybuses should replace the town's 78 tramcars. At the beginning of 1932 permission was given for the operation of trolleybuses on the Nottingham Road route, and the service started on 9 January with the Mayor driving the first vehicle for a short distance. The 2½-mile route was worked by six Brush-bodied three-axle Guy BTX double-deckers, Nos 79-84.

Two more routes commenced in 1932: Alvaston Road on 24 July, and Osmaston Road to the borough boundary at Allenton on 13 November. More Guy six-wheelers (Nos 85-98) were obtained, this time with Dodson bodies, but meanwhile the committee had decided to buy three vehicles of different types to find out which would best meet future requirements: they were respectively a Karrier and a Sunbeam (both with Dodson bodies) and a Ransomes. Also acquired was a lone Thornycroft. Later purchases revealed that Guys remained in favour.

Trolleybuses took over the Burton Road and Uttoxeter Road tram routes on 13 August 1933, while at the end of the year they also took over Ashbourne Road as far as Kingsway. The last regular tram service ceased in March 1934 (though a few cars were still about until the end of June) and trolleybuses were put on to Normanton Road to complete the changeover on 18 March. With the addition of further Guy BTX six-wheelers, the fleet had now grown to a total of 56.

Other extensions followed beyond the former tramways: Kedleston Road on 28 April 1935, and from Cavendish to Browning Circle on 30 June of the same year. In 1936, Osmaston Park Road and Chaddesden Park Road followed on 29 November. On 17 October 1937 the Duffield Road route was inaugurated as far as Broadway, while on 6 November 1938 the Osmaston Road route was extended to Shelton Lock. The addition of more Guys, plus the first four-wheelers (five Daimler CTM4s in 1938), brought the prewar fleet total to 86 vehicles.

A wartime extension was inaugurated on 30 August 1943 along Sinfin Lane to replace motorbuses, though this required only a short length of new wiring, while the first postwar extension was the Duffield Road route to Kingscroft, introduced on 14 September 1947. Only three years later brought the first contraction, when on 3 June 1950 the Chaddesden Park Road service was withdrawn, although the wires were kept up for the use of specials until November 1962. The Ashbourne Road route was extended into the Mackworth Estate to Prince Charles Avenue on 8 June 1952 and to Morden Green on 26 July 1953. April 1958 saw the last extension, along Ascot Drive, though this was used for specials and depot workings only. This brought the system to its maximum extent of just on 28 route miles.

Half a dozen single-deck Guys from Hastings helped out during the war, while utility-bodied

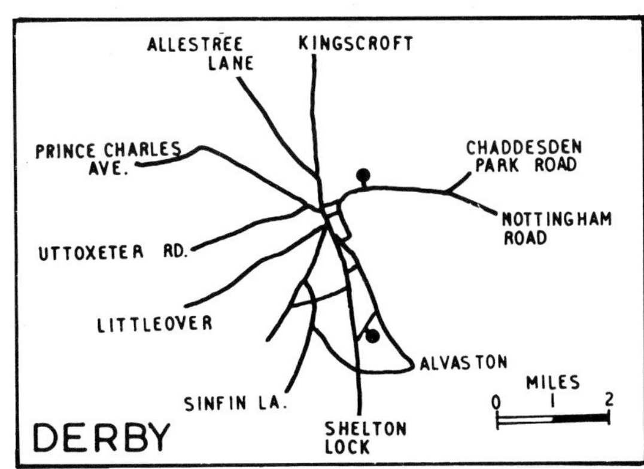

Above:

Derby: A member of the original fleet of 1932, No 82 was a Guy BTX with Brush body. *Ian Allan Library*

Below:

Derby: Also dating from 1932 was the only Ransomes in the fleet, No 101. *Ian Allan Library*

Sunbeam Ws made their appearance in 1945, the last of these destined to survive until as late as 1965. Postwar re-equipment took the form of further Sunbeams, with bodies by Brush and Willowbrook. The final new vehicles (Nos 236-243) comprised a batch of Sunbeam F4As with Roe bodies in 1959/60.

With the 1960s came abandonment in earnest, though the position right to the end was complicated by the fact that even after nominal withdrawal of normal services, the wires often remained in position and trolleybuses still worked some special services, or even put in an appearance to replace 'replacing' diesel buses. The main closures included:

30 January 1960 — Browning Circle.
10 November 1962 — Nottingham Road and the last of the services on the branch to

Left:
Derby: Six-wheelers of the early 1930s included, (*above*), No 100, a Sunbeam with Dodson body, and (*below*), No 114, a Brush-bodied Thornycroft. *Ian Allan Library*

Right:
Derby: Standing over the pits while receiving the attentions of the high-pressure lubrication machine in 1937 is No 132, a Brush-bodied Guy BTX of 1933 vintage. *Ian Allan Library*

Below right:
Derby: Outside the Midland station in 1965 No 221, a 1952 Sunbeam F4A, is followed by a utility-bodied Sunbeam W. *V. C. Jones/Ian Allan Library*

Derby

Fleet Nos	Registration Nos	Chassis	Electrical equipment	Body	In service	Withdrawn	Notes
79-84	RC 401-6	Guy BTX	BTH	Brush H29/27R	1932	1948	
85-92	RC 544-51	Guy BTX	BTH	Dodson H29/27R	1932	1948/9	
93-8	RC 793-8	Guy BTX	BTH	Dodson H29/27R	1932	1948/9	
99	RC 799	Karrier E6	BTH	Dodson H29/27R	1932	1951	
100	RC 800	Sunbeam MS2	BTH	Dodson H29/27R	1932	1951	
101	RC 801	RS&J	RS&J	RS&J H29/27R	1932	1951	
102-13	RC 1102-13	Guy BTX	BTH	Weymann H30/26R	1933	1946-50	
114	RC 1414	Thornycroft	BTH	Brush H30/26R	1933	1951	
115-48	RC 1615-48	Guy BTX	BTH	Brush H30/26R	1933/4	1949-53	
149-58	RC 4349-58	Guy BTX	BTH	Brush H30/26R	1935/6	1949-53	
159-64	RC 6659-64	Daimler CTM4	Metrovick	Brush H30/26R	1938	1959/60	
165-70	DY 5113/5/?/37/ 40/5584	Guy BTX	R/Stevens	RS&J B32C	1942	1946	a
171-85	RC 8751-5/ 8876-85	Sunbeam W	BTH	P/Royal UH30/26R	1945/6	1965	
186-215	ARC 486-515	Sunbeam F4	BTH	Brush H30/26R	1948/9	1967	
216-35	DRC 216-35	Sunbeam F4	BTH	Willowbrook H32/28R	1952/3	1967	
236-43	SCH 236-43	Sunbeam F4A	BTH	Roe H37/28R	1959/60	1967	

Notes:

a Ex-Hastings Nos 11, 13, ?, 35, 38 and 57

Preserved vehicles: Nos 172, 175, 215, 224, 237

Chaddesden Park Road.

3 October 1964 — Burton Road and Kingscroft.

1 January 1966 — Wyndham Street and Sinfin Lane.

26 November 1966 — Uttoxeter Road and Normanton.

11 February 1967 — Kedleston Road.

The last day of operation was 9 September 1967.

References

'British Trolleybus Systems: No 10 — Derby'; *Buses* May 1969.

'British Bus & Tram Systems: Derby Corporation' by E. G. Hunt & P. J. Taplin; *Buses Illustrated* No 17, 1954

'Derby's Trolleybus Services' by J. G. T. Simpson; *Trolleybus Magazine* January 1973.

Doncaster

In an era of intense private bus competition, Doncaster Corporation obtained powers to run its own motorbuses in 1922 and began its first service in that year. In 1925 the first double-deckers took over from tramcars on the Avenue Road route, with the new service extended to Wheatley Hills, for the purpose of determining whether motorbuses or trolleybuses would be the best replacement for a tramway system which the manager described as 'hopelessly inadequate'. The buses to Wheatley Hills did not impress the Corporation as the ideal mode of transport. The trolleybus was seen as having the higher acceleration needed to maintain a fast schedule on short routes with many stops, while it also had the merit of consuming electricity which could be supplied from the municipal power station. Hence in 1926 the Corporation obtained powers to operate trolleybuses over its existing tramways (except the Brodsworth route) as well as on the bus route to Wheatley Hills.

A batch of six-wheel double-deck trolley vehicles was accordingly ordered in 1927, comprising both Garretts and Karrier-Cloughs (the latter being the first of the E6 type to be produced), all fitted with 60-seat Roe bodies. In the spring of 1928 driver training was being carried out on the Race Course route, along part of which trolleybus wiring had already been strung, a skate in the tram track being used on other parts. The Bentley route was the first to be ready for operation, and trolleybuses took over on 22 August 1928, continuing beyond the former tram terminus to traverse a large loop around Bentley village.

The success of the new service soon stimulated further conversions. The next changeover took place on the Hexthorpe route on 1 July 1929, and this was closely followed on 31 July by the Beckett Road route which was extended beyond the erstwhile tram terminus to Wentworth Road. Conversion of the Hyde Park route followed on 16 January 1930, again with a continuation beyond the tramway, this time along Carr House Lane to the Great North Road at the Race Course where it met the Race Course tramway to complete a circle back into town by way of Bennetthorpe. Tramcars were displaced from the Race Course service two months later, on 20 March 1930, the tramway in Grandstand Road being abandoned and the trolleybuses operating a circular service.

On 4 March 1931 trolleybuses took over from buses on the Avenue Road and Wheatley Hills route, on which buses had displaced tramcars in 1925, and were extended along Thorne Road to a terminus at the Wheatley Hotel. The Warmsworth route was replaced on 26 July 1931, but the trolley vehicles went only as far as Austen Avenue, Balby, about a mile short of the Warmsworth tram terminus, and this last section was covered by a motorbus service. Motorbuses took over the last tramway, to Brodsworth, in 1935.

The trolleybus complement meanwhile had been strengthened by another 20 Karrier E6s (Nos 11-30), and these were joined by further E6s up to 1939, by which time the fleet numbers had reached 68. An unusual and almost unique member was No 31, one of the only two

Top:

Doncaster: Dating from the start of the system in 1928 is this Karrier E6 with Roe body.
V. C. Jones/Ian Allan Library

Above:

Doncaster: Another Roe-bodied Karrier of later vintage, No 45 of the 1937 batch stands at the terminus of the Racecourse route in 1938. Not far from this point, new overhead was erected in 1985 for trials with a 'new age' trolleybus. *Ian Allan Library*

trolleybuses built by the Bristol Tramways & Carriage Co. Dating from 1929 when it was displayed at the Commercial Motor Show, it spent some time as a demonstrator before coming to Doncaster. With bodywork by Beadle on Roe framework, it was generally similar in appearance to its Karrier companions. The first four-wheelers to be obtained came during the war in the shape of three utility-bodied Karrier

Doncaster

Fleet Nos	Registration Nos	Chassis	Electrical equipment	Body	In service	Withdrawn	Notes
1-4	DT 821-4	Garrett	BTH	Roe H32/28R	1928	1943-5	
5-10	DT2002/3, 2165-8, 2633	K/Clough E6	BTH	Roe H32/28R	1928	1943-5	
11-16	DT 1745-50	K/Clough E6	BTH	Roe H32/28R	1929	1943-5	
17-23	DT 1099, 1118, 1143/6, 1198, 1206, 2935	K/Clough E6	BTH	Roe H32/28R	1930	1943-5	
24-30	DT3153-9	K/Clough E6	BTH	Roe H32/28R	1931	1943-5	
31	DT 2620	Bristol	BTH	B/Roe H32/28R	1931	1945	
32	DT 4718	Karrier E6	BTH	Roe H32/28R	1933	1945	
33-36	DT 5772-5	Karrier E6	Metrovick	Roe H32/28R	1935	1952-7	
37-42	DT 6539-44	Karrier E6	Metrovick	Roe H32/28R	1936	1952-7	
43-48	ADT 181-6	Karrier E6	Metrovick	Roe H32/28R	1937	1952-7	
49-68	BDT 114-29/31-4	Karrier E6	Metrovick	Roe H32/28R	1939	1952-7	
69-71	CDT 312-4	Karrier W	Metrovick	P/Royal UH30/26R	1943	1961-3	a
72-74	CDT 624-6	Karrier W	Metrovick	Brush UH30/26R	1945	1961-3	a
75-77	CDT 636-8	Karrier W	Metrovick	P/Royal UH30/26R	1945	1961-3	a
*							
378-83	LHN 780-5	BUT 9611T	E/Electric	E/Lancs H30/26R	1952	1959	b
384-92	BHJ 827-9, 898-903	Sunbeam W	BTH	Roe H34/28R	1954	1961-3	c
393-8	EWT 478-80, 513-5	Sunbeam W	Metrovick	Roe H34/28R	1955	1961-3	d
351/2	FNY 983/4	Sunbeam W	E/Electric	Roe H34/28R	1957	1961-3	e
353/4	FWX 898, 902	Sunbeam W	Metrovick	Roe H34/28R	1958	1961-3	f

Notes:

a Rebodied by Roe H36/26R 1954-8

b Ex-Darlington Nos 68-73. Sold to Bradford 1959

c Ex-Southend Nos 130-8. Rebodied 1956-9

d Ex-Mexborough & Swinton Nos 1-6 rebodied

e Ex-Pontypridd Nos 10 and 11 rebodied

f Ex-Mexborough & Swinton Nos 14 and 18 rebodied

* (Nos 32-77 renumbered as 332-377 in 1948)

Preserved vehicle: No 375

Ws in austerity grey in 1943, followed by six more in 1945 in brown.

Two short extensions were made to the system during the war. To serve new housing, in April 1941 the Beckett Road route was extended by about half a mile. Then in July 1942, the Balby route was extended a few hundred yards from its original terminus at Austen Avenue to a turning circle at Barrel Lane. In both cases, terminal working was improved in that the old triangular reversers were eliminated.

By the early 1950s the advancing years of the six-wheel Karriers stimulated thoughts of motorbus replacement, but after the arrival of T. Bamford as General Manager in 1953 it was decided that the trolleybuses should be retained. Six BUTs had been purchased from Darlington to replace an equal number of six-wheelers. Then in 1954 began the somewhat unusual modernisation programme. Eight of the utility-bodied Karriers were sent for rebodying with new Roe 62-seat bodies, and these were backed up by the purchase of secondhand vehicles which were similarly rebodied, so that by 1957 the last of the prewar six-wheelers could be withdrawn. The purchases included nine Karriers from Southend, which entered service with original utility bodies before their transformation was completed in 1959, eight Sunbeam Ws from Mexborough & Swinton where they had carried single-deck bodies, and two utility-bodied Karriers from Pontypridd. By the end of the 1950s, therefore, Doncaster possessed a completely revitalised trolleybus fleet.

Extensive road works in the North Bridge area which would have necessitated considerable alterations in the overhead for what was virtually an isolated route, sealed the fate of the Bentley route, which was taken over by buses on 12 February 1956. Nevertheless, two short extensions were later made elsewhere. On

Above:
Doncaster: Waiting to take up their new duties in 1955 are six Sunbeams, originally single-deckers on the Mexborough & Swinton system but purchased by Doncaster and given new Roe 62-seat double-deck bodies. *Ian Allan Library*

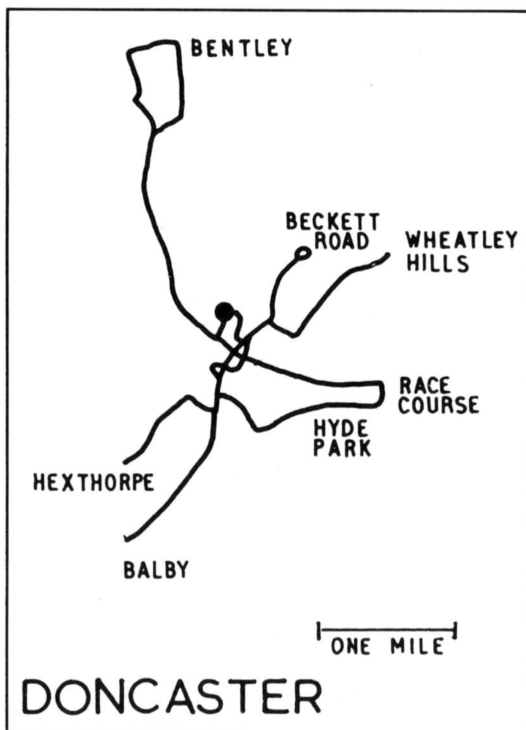

17 February 1958 the Beckett Road route was extended by about half a mile to a new terminus at Parkway, followed on 14 October 1958 by about a quarter of a mile on the Wheatley Hills route to Sandal Park Avenue. A branch of about a mile off the Balby route to Broomhouse Lane was also proposed but this did not materialise.

The usual problems confronting trolleybus operators by this time were pressing no less heavily on Doncaster. The difficulty of obtaining spares to keep vehicles running, the high cost of new equipment, and the prospect of changes in street layouts necessitating costly reconstruction of overhead resulted in the decision to abandon the trolleybuses.

The changeover was generally a gradual process, with buses being inserted into the schedule in place of trolleybuses as they became available. The Hyde Park route was converted to bus operation after 10 December 1961, although trolleybuses continued to run one way round the circle (the 'Race Course' service) until 13 October 1963. The Hexthorpe route was closed on 17 March 1962, and the last trolleybuses ran to Balby on 8 September, and to Wheatley Hills on 30 December. The final withdrawal came on 14 December 1963, when No 375 (the only trolleybus left in service by this time) made the last runs on Beckett Road. In an unusual aftermath, 20 of the Roe trolleybus bodies were transferred to motorbus chassis as they became redundant, thus allowing them to enjoy their allotted span of life.

This was not to be the last that Doncaster was to see of the trolleybus. In 1985, not far from the old Race Course terminus, standards and overhead were erected for the demonstration runs of the 'new age' trolleybus developed by GEC Transportation Projects.

References
'British Bus & Tram Systems: No 20 — Doncaster Corporation Transport by Leslie Flint and Michael Fowler, *Buses Illustrated*, March, April, May 1960.
'Quiet Flows the Don' by Charles S. Dunbar, *Passenger Transport*, January 1964.
Doncaster's Electric Transport 1902-1963 by Peter Tuffrey (author, 1983).

Dundee

In 1908 a deputation from Dundee visited trolley vehicle systems in Germany and reported that the trackless system was 'undoubtedly practical' and that 'the Clepington Road (from Forfar Road to Strathmartine Road) should without delay be equipped with this form of traction'. An extension to Lochee via Loons Road should also be undertaken as soon as possible. Further ideas envisaged a ring route via Ninewells and the Esplanade, but it was not until 1911 that the City Council decided to introduce the trackless system on Clepington Road to act as a feeder to the Maryfield and Downfield tramways. On 3 September 1912 the 1¼-mile route was examined by the Board of Trade Inspector, Lt-Col von Donop (the first

such system he had been called upon to inspect) and two days later the system opened to the public, when 1,200 passengers were carried during the day.

The two cars, numbered 67 and 68 in the tramcar series, were obtained from Railless Electric Traction and had Milnes Voss 28-seat open-platform rear-entrance bodies. They were powered by two Siemens motors. The *Dundee Courier* described the cars as 'most comfortable and commodious'. Turning circles were provided at each end of the route, and the trolley vehicles used the tramway overhead in conjunction with a skate in the track to reach the depot at Maryfield.

Operation began with great optimism, but by

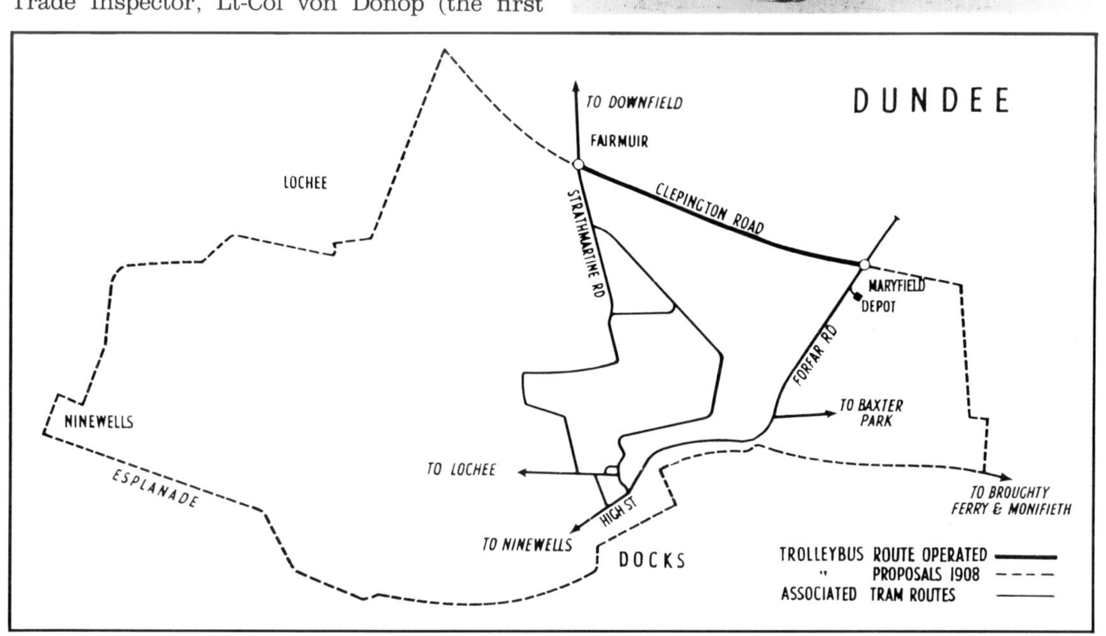

early 1913 there were difficulties about the roads. The dust in dry weather was appalling and few people chose the bumpy ride. In 1914 local residents were complaining of the 'intolerable nuisance' caused by the dust, and the tramways committee decided to abandon the trackless cars and share with the works committee the cost of remaking the road. The service ran for the last time on 13 May 1914, thus gaining the distinction of being the first trolleybus abandonment in the British Isles. The cars remained in Maryfield depot until 1919, when Halifax decided to purchase them.

References
'British Trolleybus Systems: 11 — Dundee', *Buses*, February 1969.
'Railless Trolley Traction in Dundee', *Tramway & Railway World*, 20 October 1912.
Tramways of the Tay Valley by Alan W. Brotchie, Dundee Museum & Art Gallery, 1965.

Glasgow

With more than a thousand tramcars, Glasgow might have looked like a rich field for the trolleybus. Indeed, as early as 1921 some thoughts had turned in the direction of trackless trolleys, at least as feeders to the tramways. But the tramcars were well entrenched, and it was not until 1949 that the trolleybus made its debut in Glasgow's streets. This was by several years the last British system to be inaugurated and the only one after World War 2. It grew to a respectable size (with almost 200 vehicles it became one of the largest) and it could boast an array of interesting and innovative vehicles. But perhaps it had come too late; it never seemed to be wholeheartedly

received, and in less than 20 years the entire system had disappeared.

Powers to run trolleybuses on tram routes were obtained in 1933 but were not then exercised. Opponents of any major changeover emphasised the likely effects on employment both at the Corporation's Coplawhill works (where the Corporation built its own tramcars but was not permitted to build trolleybuses) and among permanent-way staff, as well as the worsening of congestion at junctions and in narrow streets if both forms of transport were used together. However, after six years of war had taken their toll on the tramways, in 1945 plans were announced for an experimental trolleybus installation in place of tramcars between Provanmill and Polmadie, for which purpose 20 vehicles would be required. Before they were introduced, however, it was agreed to extend the proposed system to Rutherglen and to Kings Park and Blackhill, and accordingly an additional 44 vehicles were ordered in 1947.

The first service started on 3 April 1949 as number 102 between Polmadie and Riddrie, after an interim period of several weeks during which the former tram service had been worked by motorbuses, some of which continued until the end of the month before enough trolleybuses were available to take over completely. The route was extended to Hampden Park on 3 July 1949, although again it was several weeks before full trolleybus operation was possible. In 1950 the new Hampden depot was opened to provide better accommodation for the trolleybuses than their first home in Larkfield bus garage. The new depot was laid out with open-air parking and with gradients to permit gravity manoeuvring to reduce the need for elaborate overhead installations within the depot precincts.

Glasgow

Fleet Nos	Registration Nos	Chassis	Electrical equipment	Body	In service	Withdrawn	Notes
TB1-32	FYS 701-32	BUT 9641T	E/Electric	MCCW H40/30R	1949	1960-6	
TB33/4	FYS 733/4	BUT 9641T	C/Parkinson	MCCW H40/30R	1949	1960-6	
TD1-30	FYS 735-64	Daimler CTME	Metrovick	MCCW H40/30R	1950/1	1958-64	
TB35	FYS 765	BUT RETB1	Metrovick	Weymann B26D	1951	1964	a
TBS2-11	FYS 766-75	BUT RETB1	E/Electric	E/Lancs B27D	1953	1964	b
TG1-5	FYS 776-80	Sunbeam F4A	E/Electric	Alexander H34/28R	1953	1965/6	
TG6-20	FYS 781-95	Sunbeam F4A	E/Electric	Weymann H34/28R	1953	1965/6	
TB35-64	FYS 796-825	BUT 9613T	GEC	Crossley H36/34R	1957-9	1965-7	c
TB65-114	FYS 826-75	BUT 9613T	Metrovick	Crossley H37/34R	1957-9	1965-7	
TB115-24	FYS 977-86	BUT 9613T	Metrovick	Crossley H37/34R	1957-9	1965-7	
TBS12-21	FYS 987-96	BUT RETB1	Metrovick	Burlingham B50F	1958	1961-7	

Notes:

a Renumbered TBS1 in 1953

b Rebuilt to B36C in 1959-61

c H37/34R in 1960/1

Preserved vehicles: Nos TB78 and TBS13

Next to come was the first part of the Rutherglen route, as far as Shawfield, to which service 101 started on 6 November 1949. It was more than two years before the next route was brought into operation. This was on Cathcart Road and Clarkston Road to Muirend, to which service 104 started on 31 August 1952. Almost a year after this, on 5 July 1953, the wires were extended along Clarkston Road to Clarkston (service 105), while at the same date they were also continued northward through the city, via George Square, to Queens Cross. Further extension to Milngavie was envisaged, but this was postponed.

As part of the tram replacement programme, the Corporation in 1975 decided to buy 135 more trolleybuses, as well as 150 buses. The trolleybus part of the package was influenced by the desirability of maintaining a load for the Corporation's Pinkston power station, which had long supplied the tramways and had just been extensively modernised. Later, in 1955, it was agreed to purchase another 75 trolley-buses.

The relative role seen for the trolleybus in the transport system at this period was outlined by the General Manager, Mr E. R. L. Fitzpayne, when he wrote in 1952: 'It is probably true to say that an efficient tramcar service, augmented to some extent by trolleybuses and motorbuses, is still best suited to the city proper, but where new areas such as housing schemes and industrial estates are being developed, the lower capital outlay involved in the operation of trolleybuses would favour the adoption of this type of vehicle'. As it turned out, this situation did not come to pass; not only did the trams go, but the trolleybuses were not projected into the newer developing areas.

Nevertheless the system continued to expand. On 19 February 1956 the Shawfield route was extended beyond the city boundary to its originally proposed destination at Rutherglen. On 7 July 1957, the 107 service was introduced along Victoria Road to give an alternative route between the city and Muirend. On 15 June 1958 the lengthy 106 service was introduced to

Left:
Glasgow: No TB35, a 1951 BUT RETB1 with Weymann dual-doorway body, was an experiment in large-capacity standee single-deck operation. In 1953 it was renumbered TBS1. *Ian Allan Library*

Right:
Glasgow: No TB36 was one of the fleet of Crossley-bodied BUT 9613Ts delivered between 1957 and 1959.
Ian Allan Library

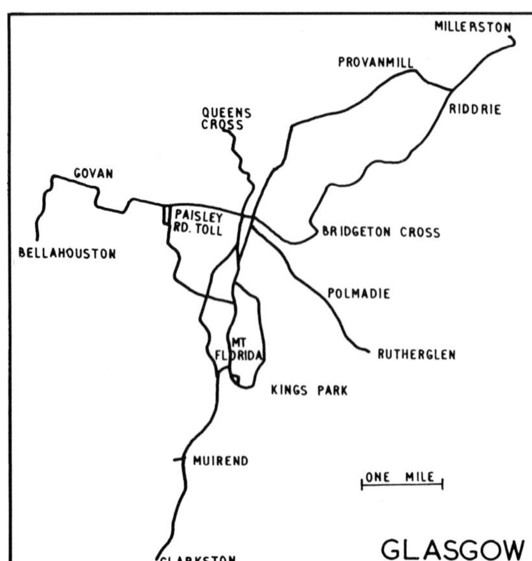

Below:
Glasgow: Notable trolleybuses introduced by Glasgow were the 10 two-axle 35ft-long BUT RETB1s with 50-seat Burlingham bodies. This one was exhibited at the Commercial Motor Show in 1958.
Ian Allan Library

Millerston along Cumbernauld Road, and south of the Clyde westward to the dock area and Ballahouston, with peak-hour workings along Govan Road to Linthouse and Shieldhall. Finally, on 15 November 1958 came the 108, the last new trolleybus route, and the last tram-to-trolleybus conversion in Britain; an out-of-town suburban route, it ran between Mount Florida and Paisley Road Toll, with peak-hour extension to Linthouse and Shieldhall.

In that same year of 1958 it was agreed that the city's remaining tramcars should be replaced by motorbuses and that the trolleybus fleet should be limited to a maximum of 200 vehicles. Replacement of the trams by trolleybuses, it was claimed, would have cost £2 million more than replacement by buses. Moreover, the Corporation's Pinkston power station was to be sold to the South of Scotland Electricity Board, from which power for transport would henceforth be purchased. The removal of the tramway load was undoubtedly the deciding factor in the move, but in its turn this put the trolleybuses in a less favourable situation.

The system already had its own built-in problems. Far from being an intensive compact network, it was really a collection of straggling individual routes. This was inherent in its growth, since a cardinal objective had been the segregation of trolleybus from tram; with the aim of avoiding congestion, trams had as far as practicable been removed from the streets as the trolleybuses were introduced, involving a considerable amount of re-routeing of the remaining tram services. Since the tramcars used bow collectors instead of trolley poles, the

trolleybuses could not share their wires. Moreover, trolleybus overhead had to be kept far enough away from tram wires to clear the bows, while at junctions long dead sections were necessary where tram bows crossed trolleybus wires. Ministry of Transport regulations enjoined that no trolleybus should overtake a tramcar. Although the trolleybuses could offer a higher scheduled speed (an average of nearly 11mph against the trams' 9½mph) they were generally confined to the older tram-served areas and were not extended into the newer developing districts.

By the mid-1960s their fate was sealed. Some services had already been cut: the 103 had been withdrawn in 1959 and the 104 in 1962. The first route closure came on 14 November 1964 when the last services ran on the peak-hours-only Linthouse and Shieldhall section. In the following year the general manager recommended the withdrawal of all the remaining trolleybuses, and this was approved early in 1966. An influencing factor was the rising cost of operation, partly due to higher electricity charges. The closure took place fairly rapidly, with the respective last days of operation as follows:

30 April 1966 Services 101 and 102: Rutherglen-Riddrie.
1 October 1966 Service 106: Millerston-Bellahouston.
4 March 1967 Services 107 (Victoria Road) and 108 (Mount Florida-Paisley Road Toll).

The final day of operation was 27 May 1967 when the 105 service made its last runs on the

Clarkston-Queens Cross route. So the last trolleybus ran a bare five years after the last tram and only 18 years after the first trolleybus.

The fleet was worthy of a longer and happier career, even if its varied character must have been reflected in enhanced operating costs. The design for Glasgow's first trolleybuses envisaged a distinctive six-wheel double-decker with separate entrance and exit, but since the production of a non-standard type would have delayed delivery, the first vehicles materialised as replicas of similar designs already being delivered to Newcastle and London. All with Metropolitan-Cammell bodies, Nos TB1-34 were on BUT chassis and Nos TD1-30 on Daimler chassis.

Single-deckers made their debut in 1951 with TB35 (later renumbered TBS1), the first experimental standee-type (or 'transit' type as it was described). 'One of the most interesting public service vehicles of recent time', as *Modern Transport* termed it, TB35 was of rear-entrance front-exit layout, with a large platform fitted with a cash desk for the conductor. Seats were provided for only 26, but there was space for another 40 standing. It was followed in 1953 by a further 10 (TBS2-11) with the exit repositioned behind the front axle. They did not prove popular with passengers or crews, and all were rebuilt in 1959-61 as conventional single-deckers, with the rear doorway closed up and the seating increased to 36.

Arrivals in 1953 also were two-axle Sunbeam double-deckers TG1-20, of which 15 had Weymann bodies while the other five had bodies by Walter Alexander, the only trolleybus bodies ever built by this maker. No TG1 for a time was fitted with a unique experimental double-headed single trolley, but this did not prove successful. In 1957/8 came Nos TB35-124, the first two-axle 30ft-long members of the fleet. BUTs with Crossley bodies, they were the last Crossley-bodied trolleybuses to be built.

The year also saw another experiment in large-capacity single-deckers with the advent of BUTs Nos TBS12-21. Notable for their length, at 35ft they were longer than the then permitted maximum for two-axle vehicles, and special approval had to be obtained from the Ministry of Transport for their use on the new 108 route between Mount Florida and Paisley Road Toll, on which they were to spend their brief working lives. Their front-entrance Burlingham bodies provided 50 seats, with room for another eight passengers standing. Originally it had been proposed that 20 vehicles of this type should be introduced, but in the event only 10 were ordered and another 10 double-deckers were added instead. After closure, No TBS13 was

given a place in Glasgow's Museum of Transport as a reminder of a short-lived era in the city's transport history and a glimpse of what might have been.

References
Glasgow's Trolleybuses by Brian T. Deans (Scottish Tramway Museum Society, 1977).
'Transport in Glasgow'; *Modern Transport*, 27 June and 4 July 1953.

Grimsby-Cleethorpes

'Grimsby Corporation has decided to start a trackless trolley service between Riby Square and Weelsby Road with five single-deck omnibuses purchased from Richard Garrett of Leiston at a cost of £1,475 each', reported the *Electric Railway & Tramway Journal* at the beginning of 1926. The 'omnibuses' (Nos 1-5) duly arrived, and the service started on 3 October 1926 with free rides on the first day. The new vehicles replaced trams between Riby Square and Welholme Road via Freeman Street, and then continued along Hainton Avenue to Weelsby Road. Traffic soon demanded another two Garretts and these (Nos 6 and 7) were put into use early in 1927. All were of the central-entrance type and ran on pneumatic tyres, and skates were fitted for operation along the tram tracks to and from the depot in Victoria Street.

The success of the venture encouraged an application in 1926 for quite a network of routes: along Weelsby Road from the existing terminus to Laceby Road, Sutcliffe Avenue and the borough boundary; along Bargate and Deansgate to the Bull Ring to replace more of the trams; and in a loop around Cleethorpes

Below:
Grimsby/Cleethorpes: Grimsby No 12, an AEC 663T with Roe body, dated from 1936.
V. C. Jones/Ian Allan Library

Grimsby-Cleethorpes (amalgamated from 1 January 1957)
Grimsby

Fleet Nos	Registration Nos	Chassis	Electrical equipment	Body	In service	Withdrawn	Notes
1-5	EE 6461-5	Garrett S	Bull	Roe B22CD	1926	1939-44	a
6, 7	EE 7097/8	Garrett S	Bull	Roe B22CD	1927	1944/5	
8-12	JV 5001-5	AEC 663T	E/Electric	Roe H34/24CD	1936	1955-7	
14-18	JV 5007-10/6	AEC 663T	E/Electric	Roe H34/24CD	1936	1955-7	
1-3	JV 8701-3	Karrier W	E/Electric	P/Royal UH30/26R	1944	1958	
19-24	AEE 22-7	Karrier W	Metrovick	Roe H31/25R	1946/7	1959/60	b

Cleethorpes

Fleet Nos	Registration Nos	Chassis	Electrical equipment	Body	In service	Withdrawn	Notes
50-9	FW 8986-95	AEC 661T	E/Electric	P/Royal H30/26R	1937	1954-60	c, d
60-2	AFU 153-5	AEC 661T	E/Electric	P/Royal H30/26R	1938	1954-60	c, d
59-62	GFU 692-5	BUT 9611 T	Metrovick	NCB H28/26R	1950	1960	e
63, 64	HEE 541/2	Crossley 'Empire'	Metrovick	Roe H29/25R	1951	1960	e

Notes:

a No 3 renumbered 5 in 1944, scrapped 1945

b Nos 19-22 and 24 sold to Bradford as Nos 822-5/7

c Nos 59 and 60-2 sold to Nottingham 1940 as Nos 437-40; scrapped 1953

d After amalgamation, Nos 54/5/8 renumbered 154/5/8; withdrawn 1957-9

e Sold to Walsall

Preserved vehicle: No 154

Road, Victor Street, Wellington Street, South Durban Street and Eleanor Street. However, in 1927 the Corporation put on its first motorbus service, and none of these proposed trackless schemes reached fruition.

Attention then turned to the main tram route between Grimsby and Cleethorpes, operated jointly by Grimsby Corporation and the Great Grimsby Street Tramways Co. Up to 1925 the route had been run solely by the company, but then Grimsby had taken over the tracks within its own boundaries, while leaving the rest of the 'main line' into next-door Cleethorpes still worked by the company. The two operators maintained a joint through service between the two towns. By 1932 the company was looking at the possibility of replacing its tramway in Cleethorpes by trolleybuses, and Grimsby agreed that if this were done, it would convert its part of the route, in order to continue the through service. However, it was not until 1935 that the company was reported to be seeking powers to operate trolleybuses, while at this time Grimsby was determined to go ahead with trolleybuses and to purchase 10 vehicles.

In 1936 Cleethorpes took over from the company within its area and set up its own transport department. Meanwhile Grimsby's new AEC 663Ts had arrived, and on 22 November 1936 they inaugurated the service between

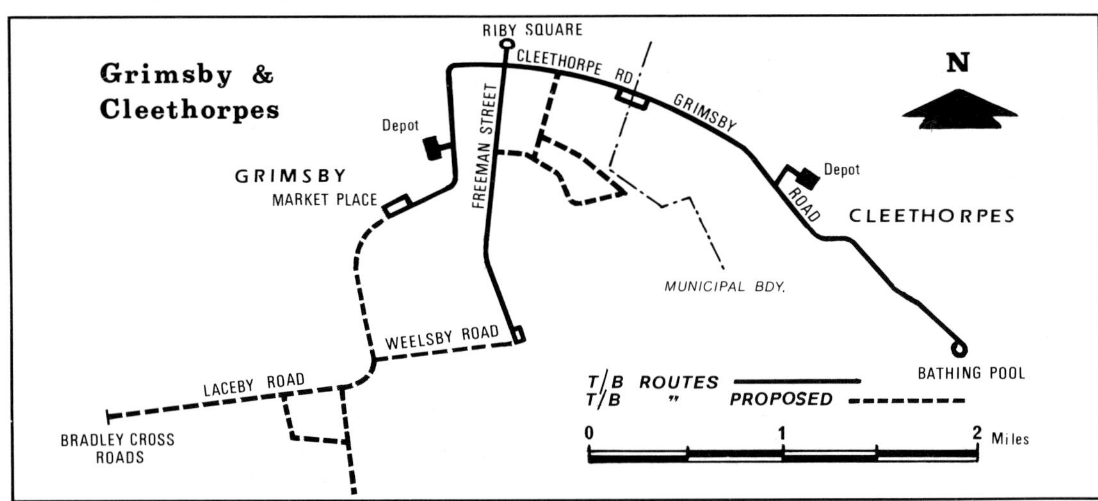

Old Market and the Grimsby-Cleethorpes boundary at Park Street. Trams continued to run between Riby Square and Park Street and on to Cleethorpes, while Cleethorpes installed its own trolleybuses. Consequently the last trams ran on 17 July 1937, followed the next day by the inauguration of the Cleethorpes installation and the introduction of a joint trolleybus service between the two towns. The wires were extended at the Cleethorpes end from the old Kingsway tram terminus to a new turning circle at the Bathing Pool, while Cleethorpes also installed a turning loop on its side of the boundary at Park Street. For its part of the working Cleethorpes had obtained a batch of 10 AEC 661Ts with Park Royal bodies.

In Grimsby, trolleybuses had not taken over the section of tramway between the Market Place and Weelsby Road (People's Park) on which buses had been substituted in 1928, but as late as 1949 there were proposals to extend the wires along Bargate and Laceby Road (as envisaged in 1926) and to Bradley Cross Roads. However, nothing of this materialised. Meanwhile the Grimsby fleet had been augmented in 1944 and 1947 by the addition of nine Karrier Ws, while Cleethorpes obtained four BUTs in 1950 and two Crossleys in 1951. In 1955 Grimsby's pioneer Freeman Street and Weelsby Road route was replaced experimentally by buses for a three-month period and from 1 October the replacement motorbus service was made permanent.

Amalgamation of the Grimsby and Cleethorpes undertakings, after discussions on a merger had been on and off for many years, at last became a reality in 1957, and on 1 January of that year the new 'Grimsby-Cleethorpes Transport' was established under the control of a joint committee. It was agreed that the abandonment of the trolleybuses should not take place without the approval of both authorities. In the new combined fleet the three surviving Cleethorpes trolleybuses Nos 54, 55 and 58 were renumbered 154, 155 and 158. The Cleethorpes depot at Pelham Road was closed on 2 March 1957, leaving operations to be maintained from the Grimsby depot. From September 1958 trolleybuses did not run on Sundays, while in October 1959 a report was prepared for the abandonment of the system and in November the committee sought the approval of the councils of both towns for the changeover. This was forthcoming, and accordingly the trolleybuses were discontinued entirely from 4 June 1960.

References
History of Trolleybuses in Grimsby and Cleethorpes by P. R. White and A. Tye (unpublished paper).
'Great Grimsby Street Tramways' by J. H. Price; *Tramway Review* Nos 119-123, 1984/5.
'Cleethorpes Trolleybus System'; *Transport World*, 9 September 1937.

Below:
Grimsby/Cleethorpes: Cleethorpes No 61 was one of four BUT 9611Ts with bodies by Northern Coachbuilders introduced in 1950 and sold to Walsall in 1960. It is seen here at the Grimsby terminus.
Ian Allan Library

Below right:
Grimsby/Cleethorpes: The last new trolleybus added to the Cleethorpes Corporation fleet was No 64, one of two Roe-bodied Crossley 'Empire' vehicles delivered in 1951. They were later sold to Walsall.
Ian Allan Library

Halifax

'Are we to have electric cars without lines of rails?' asked the *Halifax Courier* in 1903. By this time most of the surrounding areas of Halifax were served by electric tramcars, and consideration was given to the needs of some of the smaller outlying villages and hamlets. The Corporation, however, was beginning to realise that sparsely populated routes were not suitable for tramway operation, and in that year the tramways committee resolved to invite estimates from various firms for the construction of 'an electric car to run on paving or macadam road without rails, being equipped with two trolleys, positive and negative'. However, no constructive action was taken, and although interest revived from time to time the arrival of the motorbus helped push 'trackless' into the background for some years. Meanwhile, the adjacent towns of Bradford, Keighley and Leeds became enthusiastic trackless operators, and finally, on hearing that Dundee's vehicles were for sale, Halifax decided that the time was opportune for an experiment. The Dundee vehicles were duly inspected in December 1917, and purchased a month later, but wartime conditions ruled out any proposals for route construction.

When hostilities ceased, it was decided that a trial should be made on the existing motorbus route from Pellon via Mount Tabor to Wainstalls, and tenders for overhead equipment were invited and received in 1919. The ex-Dundee tracklesses received the fleet numbers 103 and 104 (CP 2021/2) and were renovated at Skircoat Road works. The route was opened without publicity on 20 July 1921, after receiving a Ministry of Transport inspection a month previously. The route was scenic and pleasant in character, and the road along which the tracklesses ran was really a country lane. Within two months of the opening, the manager complained of the damage to the vehicles caused by the bad road surface, and road works were put in hand.

It would seem that by 1923 the ex-Dundee cars were becoming the worse for wear, the rough road surfaces no doubt being to blame. A resolution was therefore made to purchase a further trackless car, and the tender of Tilling-Stevens Motors for a chassis with two 25hp Bull motors was accepted. The forward-entrance body was built by the tramways department, and the car received the fleet number 2 (CP 3457), entering service at the beginning of June 1924.

The ex-Dundee cars may have been renumbered 1 and 2 (in theory at least) some time previously as tramcars bearing the numbers 103 and 104 entered service in 1925 and 1921 respectively. Trackless No 1 was probably ex-No 103, and presumably No 2 (ex-104) was withdrawn when the Tilling-Stevens car arrived, though it was not disposed of.

The municipal motorbuses were now beginning to offer some degree of comfort and reliability, and the retention of the tiny isolated trolleybus route became increasingly difficult to justify. The turning point came when Ben Hall, Manager since 1922, left in 1926; his successor was Walter Young, Manager at Dundee since 1921, and a firm advocate of tramcars but no admirer of trolleybuses. He lost no time in recommending the abolition of the tracklesses, and the service therefore ceased on 24 October 1926. In 1936 the electricity committee urged the transport committee to consider using trolleybuses when abandoning tram routes, but

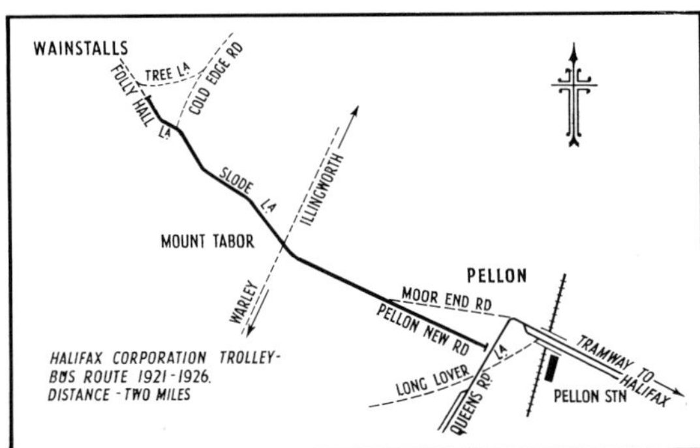

Right:
Halifax: The Tilling-Stevens car with Corporation-built body, photographed at Pellon. *C. Carter*

the Manager, G. F. Craven, stated that power costs on Halifax's gradients would be too great.

Reference
'British Trolleybus Systems: 12 — Halifax', *Buses*, September 1969.

The Hartlepools

Tramways in the twin towns of Hartlepool and West Hartlepool were owned by two British Electric Traction subsidiaries, the Hartlepool Electric Tramways Co and the General Electric Tramways Co, until in 1921 West Hartlepool Corporation bought the lines in its area, together with the fleet of 21 cars, though the section of route within Hartlepool remained the property of the GET, which leased it to West Hartlepool. In 1922 the Corporation debated the future of the tramways and decided to introduce trolleybuses on the Foggy Furze route. Accordingly, trams on this route ceased running in October 1923, being replaced by a temporary bus service while new poles and overhead were erected, and four Short-bodied Railless vehicles

were bought. Ministry of Transport approval was received on 27 February 1924 and the service commenced the next day.

By October it was felt the experiment had been successful, and plans to instal trolleybuses on the Park and Seaton Carew routes were therefore considered. In January 1925 it was decided to convert the Park route, and the trolleybus service commenced on 4 February 1926. Two more single-deckers were obtained, together with a double-decker (No 7) which was unique in many respects. The driver's cab, stairs and upper deck were open, and the trolleys were mounted on a column at the front of the upper deck. Ministry sanction for its use was withheld on account of insufficient ground clearance, and when larger front wheels were fitted in 1927 and the vehicle entered service, passengers complained of the dust which swirled into the saloon via the open rear

Below:
The Hartlepools: In its pristine state outside the Roe works in 1938 is West Hartlepool Corporation Daimler CTM4 No 1. *Ian Allan Library*

platform. No 7 lay disused in the depot from 1928 and was broken up in 1936.

In 1924 the two corporations and the GET had begun to consider the future of the inter-town route, the company's tenure of the tramway in Hartlepool being due to expire in 1925, but no decision was reached. West Hartlepool wanted trolleybuses, but Hartlepool wanted motor buses and went ahead to obtain powers. In 1925 it was agreed that Hartlepool should buy out the GET and obtain powers for joint operation with West Hartlepool of the through trolleybus service, which would be worked by West Hartlepool. Hartlepool took over the tramway, continuing the lease to West Hartlepool, and in 1926 obtained its trolleybus powers. Orders were placed for 12 Straker-Clough single-deckers and overhead installation went ahead.

The vehicles began to arrive at the beginning of 1927; they were jointly owned and were intended for use on the joint route only. The Ministry inspector approved the route in February 1927; the tramcar service ceased on 22 February and the trolleybuses took up their duties the next day. A joint committee of the two corporations had been set up to administer the route. Meanwhile, work on converting the Seaton Carew route had been going ahead; trial runs were made on 26 March, and the last tramcars (the last in the Hartlepools) ran without ceremony on the day after. The new service commenced in full on 28 March.

By the mid-1930s the need for modernisation (including double-deck vehicles) was apparent, and C. A. Hopkins, the Sunderland Transport Manager, was engaged as consultant. On his advice it was decided in 1937 to develop and extend the trolleybus system, and further powers were obtained in 1938. West Hartlepool ordered six Daimler double-deckers, and the two corporations agreed to buy eight similar double-deckers to replace single-deckers on the joint route. The first double-deckers entered service in May 1938 on the Park and Foggy

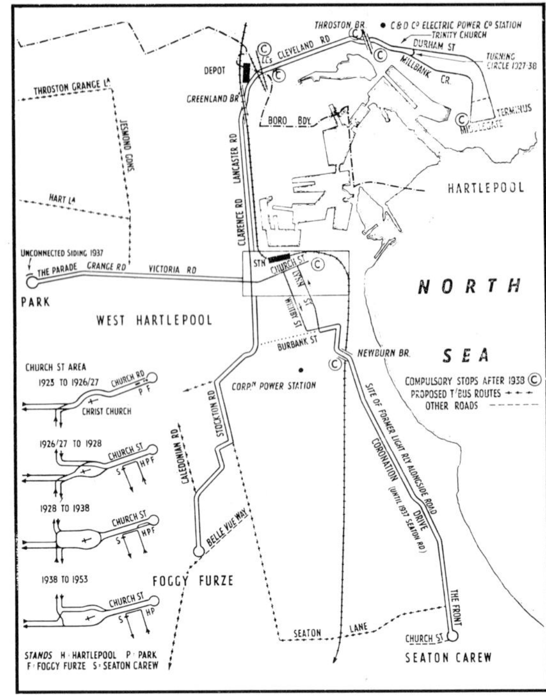

Furze routes, and those on the joint route by the end of the year. One proposed extension was from Foggy Furze to Seaton Carew but this did not materialise. Surprisingly it was decided to operate the Foggy Furze route for the time being with motor buses, and this started on 15 October 1938; the poles and bracket arms were removed and never replaced.

In the summer of 1946 West Hartlepool Corporation decided that the trolleybus system should gradually be replaced by motorbuses, which already outnumbered the electric vehicles by two to one. The decision was due to the fact that the feeder cables from the Burn Road power station were over 30 years old and increasingly subject to failure; ideally a new central substation was required, but this was

West Hartlepool

Fleet Nos	Registration Nos	Chassis	Electrical equipment	Body	In service	Withdrawn	Notes
1-4	EF 2121-4	Railless	E/Electric	Short B36F	1924	1930	
5, 6	EF 3025/6	Railless	E/Electric	Short B36C	1926	1937/8	
7	EF 3027	Railless	E/Electric	Short OT22/26ROS	1927	1928	
8-19	EF 3358-69	Straker-Clough LL	BTH	Vickers B32C	1927	1937-40	a
20-31	EF 3370-81	Garrett O	Bull	Roe B32C	1927	1937/8	
1-6	EF 6701-6	Daimler CTM4	Metro-Vick	Roe H29/25R	1938	1953	
32-39	EF 6892-99	Daimler CTM4	Metro-Vick	Roe H29/25R	1938	1953	a
7-9	EF 7037-9	Leyland TB7	Metro-Vick	Roe B32C	1939	1950	

Note:

a Jointly owned with Hartlepool Corporation

ruled out on grounds of cost. No action was taken at first, and it was not until 18 November 1949 that trolleybuses finished on the Seaton Carew route, and the Park route was converted on 7 March 1953.

West Hartlepool had declined to extend the agreement with Hartlepool, taking the view (perhaps unfairly) that the smaller authority had reaped benefits for years without responsibility. Both corporations successfully applied for consents to operate motorbuses on each other's part of the route, and for licences. Hartlepool could not, however, begin actual operation, owing to the prohibition on the use of motorbuses in Cleveland Road contained in its 1925 Act, and also because there had not yet been time to acquire vehicles. Thus when motorbuses began to operate on 3 April 1953 the service was provided exclusively by West Hartlepool Corporation; the last trolleybuses had run on the previous evening, without ceremony, and the era of electric traction in the Hartlepools had come to an end.

References
'British Trolleybus Systems: No 13 — The Hartlepools', *Buses*, February 1970.

'Trolley Omnibuses at West Hartlepool', *Tramway & Railway World*, 17 April 1924.

Hastings

From 1905/06 the Hastings Tramways Co had been working some 60 tramcars on its routes in Hastings and Bexhill. Under the 1905 Act the local councils had an option to purchase the system in 1925, but as the option was not taken up, the company gave consideration to the replacement of the open-top tramcars by the railless system and called in Alfred Baker from Birmingham. Factors favouring the installation of trolleybuses included the fact that the company already owned its own power station, while the routes included hills as steep as 1 in 9. Following Baker's recommendations (but not without some opposition from Hastings Corporation) the Hastings Tramways Co (Trolley

Below:
Hastings: Among the original fleet of the Hastings system from 1928 were eight Guy BTX with open-top Dodson bodies, including No 3 seen here when new. Later, one was preserved as a museum specimen.
Ian Allan Library

Above:

Hastings: A contrast between then-new 1940-vintage Weymann-bodied AEC 661T No 1 and 1928-vintage single-deck Guy No 28 in this scene at Silverhill in the summer of 1940. *Ian Allan Library*

Vehicles) Act 1927 gave powers for the operation of trolleybuses over existing tram routes and on certain limited extensions. The Act also contained some special clauses: the trolleybuses were to be fitted with pneumatic tyres and were to be operating by 31 March 1930, and the tram rails were to be removed within six weeks of the substitution. Options for the purchase of the undertaking would arise from both Hastings and Bexhill Corporations on 30 June 1945 and at five-yearly intervals thereafter.

The first trolleybuses went into service on 1 April 1928, taking over the tram route between Hollington and the Memorial via Silverhill and Bohemia and also continuing eastwards from the Memorial to the Fish Market along a road where trams had not run. The route from Silverhill to the Esplanade and along the sea front to the Memorial was next, on 21 May 1928, followed on 30 July by Alexandra

Park and a further part of the sea-front 'main line' between Park Cross Roads and West Marina. On 18 September the long run through Bexhill to Cooden was completed. Trolleybuses got through to Ore and St Helens on 24 January 1929, followed on 4 March by a connecting route from the Fish Market along the narrow High Street (which the trams had never penetrated). The 'top of the town' line between St Helens and Silverhill via Baldslow was completed on 15 May, making a circular route nearly nine miles round. With over 21 miles of route, the company could by this time claim to be the largest trolleybus undertaking in the world.

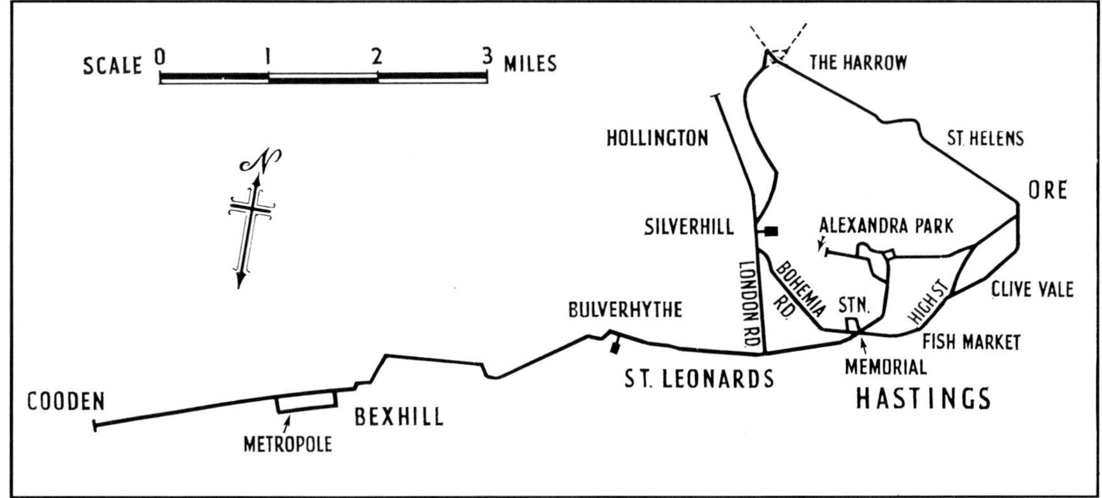

Powers for an additional mile or so were obtained in 1930. These included a 'short cut' along Elphinstone Road in the Mount Pleasant area (opened on 10 August 1930), a loop (opened on 18 January 1931) to Hastings railway station, and another short cut in Bexhill from Devonshire Road to Cooden Road (1 July 1931). The only later extension was made in 1947 at the Hollington terminus in order that the triangular reverser at Glen Road could be replaced by a turning circle. The 1930 Act had authorised a section of route at the eastern end of Hughenden Road which was never equipped for trolleybuses. The main depot was at Beaufort Road, Silverhill; a small depot off Bexhill Road, Bulverhythe, was closed in 1941. The company's power station at Ore was closed in April 1936 and thereafter municipal power was used.

To operate its network the company introduced a fleet of 58 vehicles, all Guy BTX six-wheelers but of two contrasting types. Perhaps the best known were the eight open-toppers (Nos 1-8) with 57-seat Dodson bodies; they were intended particularly for summer duties and were kept clear of the severest gradients. All the other members of the fleet (Nos 9-58) were central-entrance single-deckers with 37-seat bodies by Ransomes Sims & Jefferies. Equipment included air and electric brakes and the Rees-Stevens control system which incorporated regenerative braking. Delivery was completed during 1929.

Replacement of the original vehicles began in

Hastings

Fleet Nos	Registration Nos	Chassis	Electrical equipment	Body	In service	Withdrawn	Notes
1-8	DY 4953/4/65-70	Guy BTX	Rees-Stevens	Dodson O30/27ROS	1928/30	1940	a
9-38	DY 5111-40	Guy BTX	Rees-Stevens	RS&J B32C	1928/30	1941-55	b
39-48	DY 5452-61	Guy BTX	Rees-Stevens	RS&J B32C	1928/30	1941-55	b
49-58	DY 5576-85	Guy BTX	Rees-Stevens	RS&J B32C	1928/30	1941-55	b
1-10	BDY 776-85	AEC 661T	E/Electric	Weymann H28/26R	1940	1959	
11-20	BDY 786-95	AEC 661T	E/Electric	P/Royal H28/26R	1940	1959	
21-30	BDY 796-805	Sunbeam W	BTH	P/Royal H30/26R	1946	1959	c
31-45	BDY 806-20	Sunbeam W	BTH	Weymann H30/26R	1948	1959	c, d

Notes:

a No 3 restored 1953, as No 3A. Later fitted with diesel engine

b Nos 9, 18, 19, 24, 40 and 51 sold to Nottingham 1941; Nos 11, 13, ??, 35, 38 and 57 sold to Derby 1942; Nos 16, 29, 47, 48, 52 and 53 sold to Mexborough & Swinton 1943

c Nos 21-30, 40 and 45 sold to Bradford 1959

d Nos 31, 33, 36-9, 41 and 44 sold to Walsall 1959; Nos 32, 34, 35, 42 and 43 sold to Maidstone 1959

Preserved vehicle: No 3A

1940 when 20 four-wheel double-deck AECs arrived (Nos 1-20). However, during the war years traffic in the coastal resorts declined, and the company was able to send some of its surplus vehicles to help more hard-pressed operators; six each of the single-deckers went to Nottingham, Derby and the Mexborough & Swinton system. Most of the rest were disposed of, but it was still possible to glimpse one on the home system as late as the 1950s. By this time the modernisation had been completed with the delivery of Sunbeam Ws Nos 21-30 in 1946 and Nos 31-45 in 1946-47. The only later 'addition' to the fleet was restored open-topper No 3; after languishing at Bulverhythe depot since 1938, in 1952 it was rescued and restored as nearly as possible to its original state. Embellished with lights and flags, it made its appearance on seafront service in the Coronation summer of 1953 and in subsequent summers until the closure, after which it was fitted with a diesel engine to provide its power.

Although the company became a wholly-owned subsidiary of Maidstone & District Motor Services in 1935, after which the livery was changed from brown to green, the undertaking retained a distinctive identity, helped by the legend 'Hastings Tramways' boldly emblazoned on the vehicles. However, this situation ended in 1957 when the Hastings company ceased to have a separate existence and was merged with Maidstone & District, whose name thereafter took its place. The trolleybus route numbers were also prefixed with the letter 'T'. At the same time it was reported that diesel buses were to replace the trolleybuses, with the object of route integration in the area. Consequently, public services ceased on 31 May 1959, though a ceremonial last journey was made the following day. Most of the trolleybuses were sold for further services in Bradford, Maidstone and Walsall.

References
'British Trolleybus Systems: No 14 — Hastings', *Buses*, August 1970.
'Trolley Omnibus System of Hastings and Bexhill', *Tramway & Railway World*, 15 May 1930.

Right:
Hastings: One of the 1946 Park Royal-bodied Sunbeams, No 24 was among the vehicles sold to Bradford in 1959.   *Ian Allan Library*

Below:
Hastings: Retired from active service, a Hastings Guy single-decker finds a new role as office and waiting room.   *V. C. Jones/Ian Allan Library*

Huddersfield

The introduction of railless cars in nearby Bradford and Leeds aroused interest in Huddersfield, and as early as March 1912 experiments were under discussion. However, although powers for trolleybus operation were sought later in the same year, second thoughts prevailed. In 1931/2 various trolleybus proposals were again under consideration and following proposals for a route to Lowerhouses (dropped after residents complained) Parliamentary powers were obtained for the conversion of the Almondbury tramway to trolleybus operation as an experiment. The tram service was withdrawn in stages, and a temporary motorbus service operated as overhead was erected and the carriageway in Somerset Road reconstructed.

Six vehicles of different types were ordered, to decide which would best suit Huddersfield's needs. No 1 had a Ransomes chassis with Brush body and Ransomes electrical equipment; Nos 2 and 3 were Karriers with Park Royal bodies and BTH equipment; No 4 had a Sunbeam chassis, Park Royal body and BTH equipment; No 5 was a Karrier with body and equipment by English Electric, while English Electric also supplied the body and equipment for No 6, which had an AEC chassis. Thereafter, Karrier chassis, Park Royal bodies and Metrovick equipment were generally favoured for bulk orders. Karrier was a local firm, and the association continued long after the local premises had closed. It is noteworthy that all Huddersfield vehicles were six-wheelers, initially a wise choice as they were thus able to provide accommodation equal to that of the tramcars they displaced.

The Almondbury service was ceremonially opened on 4 December 1933 and received the route number 65. Meanwhile, the Corporation was so confident of success that it had resolved to convert the Lindley and Outlane routes, and later the Waterloo route as the three routes formed part of a cross-town service. The new services opened on 11 November 1934 as 71 (Waterloo-Lindley), 72 (Moldgreen-Marsh) and 73 (Waterloo-Outlane). The Outlane terminus was the highest one reached by trolleybuses in Britain (909ft above sea level) during its lifetime (Wainstalls in Halifax was slightly higher at 1,027ft, but this route had been abandoned by the time Outlane opened as a trolleybus route).

During 1935 the decision was taken to replace all the tramcars, and the subsequent order for 85 Karrier E6s (Nos 41-125) placed in September 1936 was the largest single order for trolleybuses ever placed at that time. The next conversions were the Newsome route on 2 May 1937 and Crosland Hill on 3 October 1937, the latter being extended cross-town to Birkby on 7 November. Further conversions came as follows:

10 April 1938 — Marsden.
19 June 1938 — Sheepridge, Bradley and Woodhouse.
1 January 1939 — Longwood.
12 January 1939 — Lockwood.
28 May 1939 — West Vale.
30 June 1940 — Brighouse; this was the last tramway.

By this time the trolleybus fleet had reached a total of 140 vehicles.

Although all the Huddersfield routes had some scenic interest, the Marsden route outshone them all as it climbed along the Colne Valley. At Spurn Point it left the borough (the first route to do so) and entered the Colne Valley Urban District; the terminus was beyond the former tram terminus. On the long and spectacular West Vale route, the outer terminus lay so far beyond the borough boundary that it had until recently adjoined Halifax's tramway to Stainland. The Longwood route abounded in narrow roads and sharp curves, while at the outer terminus a turntable had to be built out on to the hillside to provide a means of turning. Originally trolleybuses ran onto the turntable and were pushed round by hand, but with the difficulty of replacing the poles on the wires in the wartime blackout, plus the employment of

Below:
Huddersfield: A member of the first fleet in 1933, newly-delivered Karrier E4 No 2 poses with its proud crew. *Ian Allan Library*

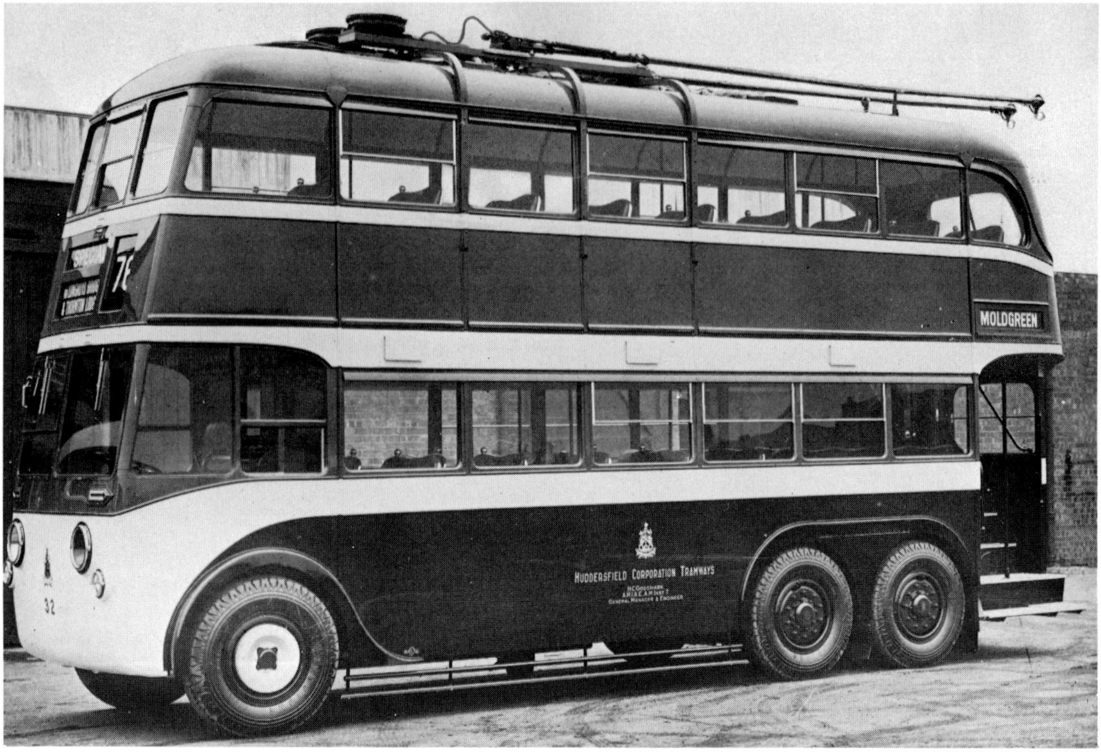

women conductors who could not be expected to assist in the pushing, the turntable was made immovable and vehicles reversed on to it. In view of the many long steep gradients on the system, the Ministry of Transport required coasting brakes to be fitted in order to prevent vehicles becoming out of control in case of dewirement or power failure; their use was compulsory on sections of the Newsome, Woodhouse, West Vale and Crosland Moor routes, and on a 150yd section of the Longwood Road route from 1939 to 1949. These brakes were fitted to all vehicles numbered over 30 (later 430).

The advent of peace in 1945 enabled many improvements to be carried out, and new vehicles were ordered to replace the original trolleybuses. Standardisation was maintained, with Karrier chassis, Park Royal bodies and traction lighting being insisted upon. Some of the older vehicles were also rebodied; the first Roe bodies entered the fleet in this way, and quickly supplanted Park Royal in the department's favour. In 1954 an unexpected break in tradition occurred with the entry into service of a dozen BUTs with English Electric equipment and East Lancashire bodies. A second batch arrived two years later, while East Lancashire was asked to rebody some of the early postwar Karriers. The last new additions, Sunbeams

Above:
Huddersfield: The arrival of Karrier E6 No 32 in 1936 heralded a fleet of similar Park Royal-bodied vehicles. *Ian Allan Library*

Below:
Huddersfield: Brush-bodied Karrier E6 No 115 of 1938 tackles some of the town's hills on the West Vale route. *Ian Allan Library*

Below right:
Huddersfield: No 600 was among the 1951 delivery of Sunbeam MS2s with Roe bodies. *Ian Allan Library*

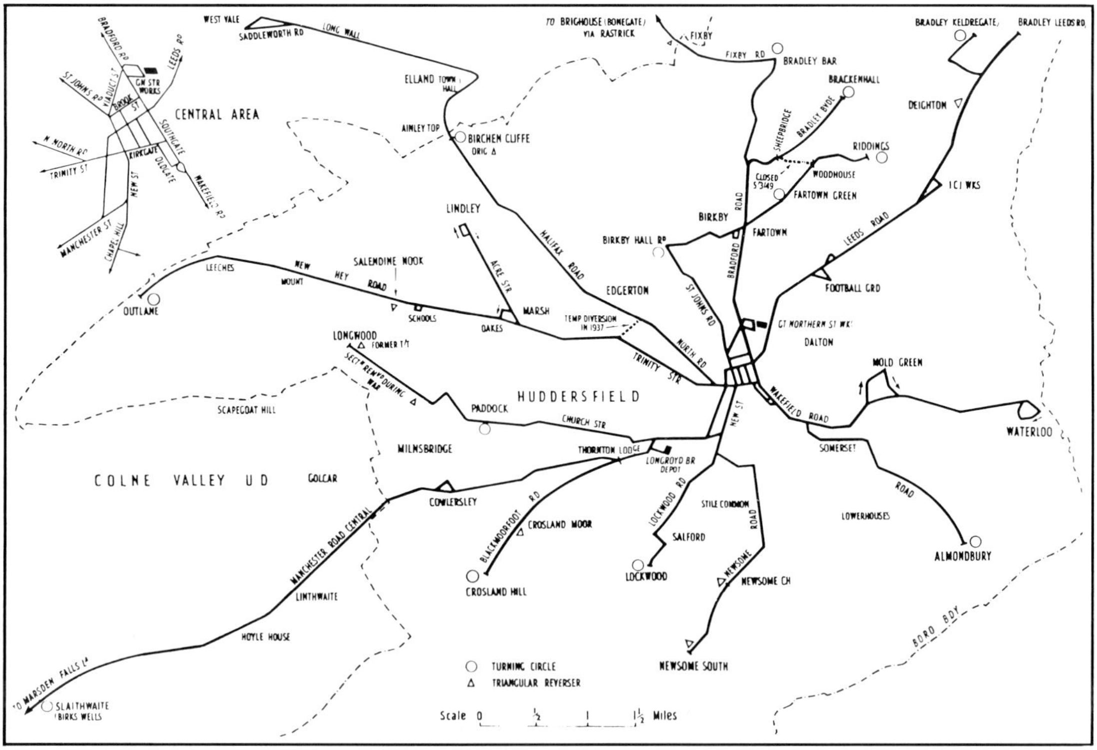

Nos 601-40 in 1959, were the last three-axle trolleybuses built for a British system.

In November 1947 the Marsden, Crosland Hill and Longwood services were diverted along a newly constructed section of route via Outcote Bank, along which wiring had been up since 1942, but the roadway had to be reconstructed before it was suitable for trolleybuses. This change necessitated alterations to several through services. The Sheepridge-Woodhouse circular service ceased operation on 5 March 1949, and next day the Sheepridge section was extended to Brackenhall and the Woodhouse section to Riddings. The last trolleybus to Brighouse ran on 9 July 1955, when the route was cut back to the borough boundary at Fixby; the Brighouse route was barely profitable and suffered from an unsatisfactory terminus.

The last route extension was opened on 2 April 1956 from the Bradley route to a new estate at Keldregate. Proposals were made for extensions to Dalton (Black Horse Hotel) and Balmoral Avenue, but the high cost of power and the undesirability of paying rates for overhead installations to the county council were used as reasons for closing the routes which passed outside the borough boundary. The West Vale route closed on 8 November 1961 and Marsden on 30 January 1963.

The next casualty was the through service from Birkby to Crosland Hill, which ceased on 5 February 1964; this involved also the 'football specials' to Fartown. On 14 July 1965, the through service from Almondbury to Fixby was closed; this caused the withdrawal of the last of the Park Royal-bodied vehicles which had been so typical of Huddersfield. In 1966, routes closed simultaneously on 13 July were the Brackenhall to Lockwood, and Riddings to Newsome through services. The Longwood to Bradley (Keldregate and Leeds Road) services

Huddersfield

Fleet Nos	Registration Nos	Chassis	Electrical equipment	Body	In service	Withdrawn	Notes
1	VH 5723	Ransomes D6	Metrovick	Brush H32/28R	1933	1946	
2, 3	VH 5724/5	Karrier E6	BTH	P/Royal H30/30R	1933	1947	
4	VH 5726	Sunbeam MS2	BTH	P/Royal H30/30R	1933	By end 1943	
5	VH 5727	Karrier E6	E/Electric	E/Electric H32/28R	1933	1947	
6	VH 5728	AEC 663T	E/Electric	E/Electric H32/28R	1933	By end 1946	
7-18	VH 6750-61	Karrier E6	Metrovick	Brush H34/30R	1934	1948/9	
19-30	VH 6762-73	Karrier E6	Metrovick	P/Royal H34/30R	1934	1948/9	
31	VH 8722	Karrier E6	Metrovick	Weymann H34/30R	1935	1949	
32	VH 8530	Karrier E6	Metrovick	P/Royal H34/30R	1936	1949	
33-40	VH 9933-40	Karrier E6	Metrovick	P/Royal H34/30R	1937	1949	
41-61	AVH 441-61	Karrier E6	Metrovick	P/Royal H34/30R	1937	1949/53	
62-98	AVH 462-98	Karrier E6	Metrovick	P/Royal H34/30R	1938	1950-62	a
99-105	AVH 499-505	Karrier E6	Metrovick	P/Royal H34/30R	1939	1945-62	a
106-15	AVH 506-15	Karrier E6	Metrovick	Brush H34/30R	1938	1942-62	a
116-25	AVH 516-25	Karrier E6	E/Electric	Weymann H34/30R	1940	1955-63	a
126-40	BVH 126-40	Karrier E6	Metrovick	P/Royal H34/30R	1940	1955-63	a
*							
541-8	CVH 741-8	Karrier MS2	Metrovick	P/Royal H40/30R	1947	1964-7	a
549-68	DVH 49-68	Karrier MS2	Metrovick	P/Royal H40/30R	1948	1963-5	a
569-92	ECX 169-92	Karrier MS2	Metrovick	P/Royal H40/30R	1949	1964-7	a
593	FCX 293	Sunbeam MS2	Metrovick	Roe H40/30R	1950	1965	
594-9	FCX 294-9	Sunbeam MS2	Metrovick	Roe H40/30R	1951	1965/6	
600-3	FCX 800-3	Sunbeam MS2	Metrovick	Roe H40/30R	1951	1966	
604-6	FCX 804-6	Sunbeam MS2	Metrovick	Roe H40/30R	1952	1966	
607-18	GVH 807-18	BUT 9641T	E/Electric	E/Lancs H40/32R	1954	1966-7	
619-30	KVH 219-29/930	BUT 9641T	E/Electric	E/Lancs H40/32R	1956	1967/8	
631-40	PVH 931-40	Sunbeam S7A	Metrovick	E/Lancs H40/32R	1959	1967/8	

* In 1942 fleet renumbered 401-540

Note:

a 69 vehicles were rebodied by Roe and East Lancs 1950-63.
   Roe: 475, 484, 491-4, 496-9, 501-3, 508/9, 517-9, 523-5,
   527-9, 532, 535/6, 540, 550, 567-9, 571/2, 574-81 and 589;
   E/Lancs: 543/5/6/8, 551-66, 570/3 and 582-5

Preserved vehicles: Nos 470, 541, 619 and 631

---

closed on 12 July 1967. On the last day of operation — 13 July 1968 — only a skeleton service of trolleybuses was provided on the remaining routes from Waterloo to Lindley and Outlane, but on the final procession from Waterloo to Outlane a convoy of five BUTs and Sunbeams appeared.

References
'British Trolleybus Systems: No 15 — Huddersfield'; *Buses* January 1971.
The Trolleybuses of Huddersfield by Roy Brook (Manchester Transport Museum Society, 1976).

Ipswich

In the summer of 1922 Ipswich tramways department, anxious about the state of the roads and the tram tracks in the town centre, agreed to hire three Railless single-deck trolleybuses for experiments. By May 1923 the adaptation of the tramway overhead had been completed on the ¾-mile route from Cornhill to the main railway station, but delivery of the cars was delayed and it was not until 2 September 1923 that operation began. The vehicles (Nos 1-3) were solid-tyred with tramway-type controllers, and their Short bodies had an open smoking compartment at the rear and were of front-entrance construction designed for one-man operation. A flat fare of 1d was charged. The experiment was a success; the hired vehicles were purchased, and in 1924 an order was placed with Ransomes Sims & Jefferies for an experimental trolleybus.

The next route chosen for trolleybus operation was Wherstead Road to Bourne Bridge. It was decided to continue the experimental stage further by arranging for vehicles of different manufacturers to be placed in service, and the three makers chosen were Tilling-Stevens, Garrett and Ransomes. As a result, the first bulk orders for 25 each were placed with Garrett and Ransomes. Trolleybuses took over from trams on the Bourne Bridge route on 17 July 1925.

Further routes to begin operation under the Ipswich Corporation Act 1925 were:

27 May 1926
Felixstowe Road.
9 June 1926
Lattice Barn, with a spur to Derby Road station.
27 July 1926
Whitton and Branford Road.
22 December 1926
Foxhall Road.
29 March 1927
London Road (Ranelagh Road).
18 March 1928
Nacton Road-Hatfield Road-Derby Road station, providing the first of the loops which became a feature of the routes.

More Ransomes single-deckers entered service in 1928 and 1930, but the final single-deck trolleybus to join the fleet was a wholly Garrett-built vehicle (No 45) which arrived in 1931. The first double-deckers appeared in 1933; they were thoroughbred Ransomes (Nos 46-9) and were followed by a further 10 in 1934 and eight in 1935. One-man operation had not proved entirely successful and had ceased by about 1932.

Further extensions included:

28 July 1931
Nacton Road to Gainsborough Estate at Clapgate Lane.
25 April 1934
From Lattice Barn to Rushmere Heath.
6 December 1936
Rushmere Road, and a new terminal arrangement at Electric House.
13 December 1936
Foxhall Road from the Isolation Hospital to Bixley Road.
30 January 1938
Landseer Road-Holbrook Road.
31 October 1938
London Road-Hadleigh Road loop.
23 April 1939
Priory Heath loop via Lindbergh Road and Nacton Road.
26 February 1940
Landseer Road extension to town centre.

A new depot and workshop were opened at Priory Heath in 1937.

In 1939 Ransomes published a pamphlet in which it was claimed that the Ipswich fleet consisted entirely of Ransomes' trolleybuses. However, this was never true. Although in 1939 the fleet included 61 of this make, the advertisement appears to have overlooked the

Below:
Ipswich: No 3, one of the system's original Railless vehicles of 1923. The open rear platform was a distinctive feature.

Below right:
Ipswich: A long-lived Ransomes single-decker, No 41 dated from 1929 and was still handling a good load when photographed at Ipswich station in 1949.
V. C. Jones/Ian Allan Library

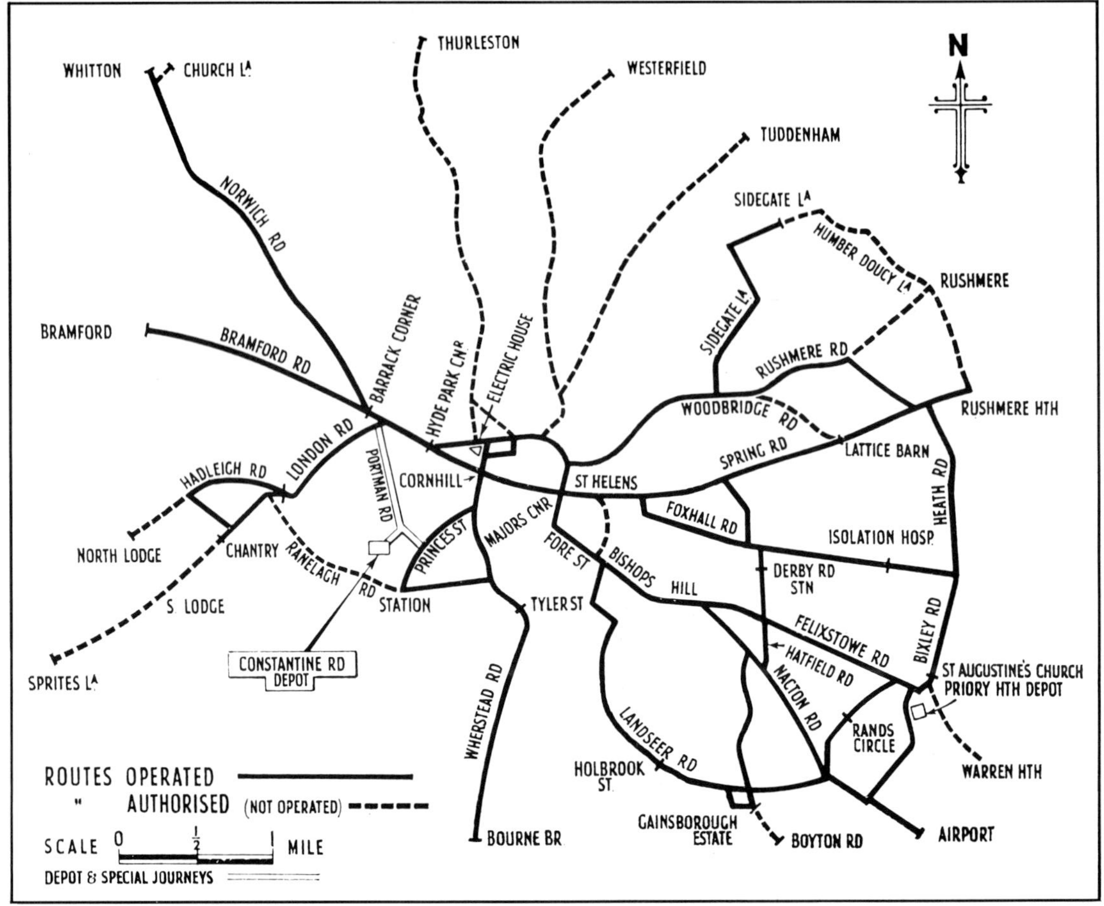

10 Garretts (built 1926) which still continued in service. By the time these vehicles became due for withdrawal, a number of wartime Karriers had arrived, thus removing all possibility of the exclusive claim. One further Ransomes' trolleybus (No 86) was delivered in 1940. It was the 66th of this make to be purchased by Ipswich and the last to be delivered to a United Kingdom operator, although Ransomes continued to supply trolleybuses to Trinidad, Singapore and Norway.

The first postwar extension came on 17 December 1945 to Clapgate Lane, followed by Sidegate Lane on 10 April 1947 and the extension from Nacton Road to the airport on 17 August 1947. This was to be the final extension, apart from the town-centre wires along the new Lloyds Avenue brought into use on 10 July 1949. Further routes proposed under the 1946 Act would have left few roads out of the town without a trolleybus service, but these did not materialise.

Proposals in the 1946 Act included new routes from the town centre to Thurleston Lodge on the Henley Road, Westerfield (Church Lane), and Westerfield House on the Tuddenham Road; extensions from the London Road terminus to Sprites Lane, from the Whitton terminus along Church Lane, from the Sidegate Lane terminus to Rushmere St Andrew; and links between London Road and the main railway station via Ranelagh Road, and between Crown Street and High Street via Fonnereau Road as part of the Henley Road route.

Proposals under the 1948 Act would have served to round out the network. As well as a short extension to the borough boundary on Felixstowe Road, various new links were proposed. Proceeding clockwise from the Constantine Road depot, these would have been: between Constantine Road and London Road via Portmans Walk and West End Road; between London Road and Norwich Road via Chevalier Street and Yarmouth Road; between Bramford Road and Norwich Road via Shafts Road, Bramford Lane and a new road; between Norwich Road and Henley Road via Dales Road; between Whitton Church Lane and Henley Road

Fleet Nos	Registration Nos	Chassis	Electrical equipment	Body	In service	Withdrawn	Note
1-3	DX 3970/98, 4006	Railless	E/Electric	Short B30F	1923	1933-5	
4	DX 3648	RS&J	RS&J/EE	RS&J	1924	1933-5	
5	DX 5217	Tilling Stevens		RS&J B30F	1925	1933-5	
6	DX 5409	RS&J	RS&J/EE	RS&J B31D	1925	1926	
21-35	DX 5626/3-5/8/9, 5627/30-3/4, 5833/5/7	Garrett O	Bull/Garrett	Garrett B31D	1926	1937-51	
6-20	DX 5622/08-16/17-21	RS&J	RS&J/EE	RS&J B31D	1926	1937-54	
36	DX 6014	RS&J	RS&J/EE	RS&J B31D	1928	1937-54	
37-41	DX 7620/33/51/68/83	RS&J	RS&J/EE	RS&J B31D	1928/9	1937-54	
42-44	DX 8869-71	RS&J	RS&J/EE	RS&J B31D	1930	1937-54	
45	DX 9610	Garrett O	Bull/Garrett	Garrett B31C	1931	1937-54	
46-9	PV 817-20	RS&J	RS&J/EE	RS&J H24/24R	1933	1945-58	
50-9	PV 1253-6, 1350-3/4/5	RS&J	RS&J/EE	RS&J H24/24R	1934	1945-58	
60-7	PV 2727-34	RS&J	RS&J/EE	RS&J H24/24R	1935/6	1945-58	
68-85	PV 4061-6, 4540-5, 4788-93	RS&J	RS&J/EE	Massey H24/24R	1937/8	1945-58	
86	PV 6426	RS&J	RSJ/EE	Massey H24/24R	1940	1960/1	
87-90	PV 6875-8	Karrier W	E/Electric	Weymann UH30/26R	1944	1960/1	
91-102	PV 6891-6/6950-5	Karrier W	Metrovick	P/Royal UH30/26R	1945	1960/1	
103-8	PV 8268-73	Karrier W	Metrovick	P/Royal H30/26R	1948/9	1961-3	
109-14	PV 8866-71	Karrier F4	Metrovick	P/Royal H30/26R	1948-9	1961-3	
115-26	ADX 185-96	Sunbeam F4	Metrovick	P/Royal H30/26R	1950	1961-3	a

Note:

a Nos 119-26 sold to Walsall

Preserved vehicles: Nos 8, 16, 41, 44, 56, 58 and 126

via a new road; between Norwich Road and the same new road, via Ashcroft Road and another new road; between Westerfield Road and Rushmere Road via Valley Road and Colchester Road; and between Woodbridge Road and St Johns Road via Cauldwell Hall Road. A minor diversion was also planned near Myrtle Road on the Landseer Road route. The Bill leading to this Act had also included proposals for a service to Belstead Road, where a new housing development was subsequently served by motor buses.

In 1948 the electricity undertaking was nationalised, and one of the mainstays of the trolleybus system was thereby broken away. In 1949 a one-way traffic scheme in the town centre brought about some rerouteing and no doubt raised further questions regarding the long-term future of the system.

The 24-year unrivalled supremacy of the trolleybus ended in 1950 when the Corporation's first motorbuses were introduced, but it was not until 6 September 1953 that the motorbus won its first route from the trolley-buses when the last single-deck Ransomes were withdrawn from Bramford Road. Withdrawal dates of other routes are difficult to establish accurately, since in some cases there was temporary reinstatement or a limited service during certain hours, but the following are from official records:

23 May 1954
Bourne Bridge.
29 July 1956
London Road and St John's Road.
1 June 1958
Foxhall Road.
31 May 1959
Heath Road and Bixley Road.
1 October 1960
Sidegate Lane and Colchester Road.
29 April 1962
Rushmere Heath and Norwich Road.

The final withdrawal of the remaining four routes (Priory Heath, Airport and Gainsborough Estate via Clapgate Lane and via

Above:
Ipswich: The last new trolleybuses to be acquired were 12 Park Royal-bodied Sunbeams in 1950. This is No 15 when new. The characteristic burnished side panels are apparent. Eight of this batch were later sold for further service in Walsall. *Ian Allan Library*

Landseer Road) took place on 23 August 1963.

The very comprehensive nature of the route layout which was necessary in an all-trolleybus system was both an asset and a liability. It resulted in capital being sunk into lightly loaded suburban sections where a reasonable return could not be expected.

References
'British Trolleybus Systems: No 16 — Ipswich', *Buses*, July 1972.
Public Transport in Ipswich by R. Markham (Ipswich Information Office, 1970).

Keighley

Keighley possessed two distinct trolleybus systems in succession. The first, using the unsatisfactory Cedes-Stoll method, was started in 1913 and worked three separate routes in extension of the tramways. This installation was practically defunct by the time the second and more conventional system was started in 1924 to take over from the trams and to give Keighley the distinction of being the first town in Britain to replace its tramways entirely by trolleybuses. Yet these were all withdrawn as early as 1932.

The trolley vehicle first came to Keighley's notice in 1910, when Bradford and Leeds applied for powers to experiment with this type of vehicle. The Council voted to send a deputation to inspect Continental systems (later cancelled in favour of a visit to Bradford and Leeds when those systems opened in 1911) and to obtain powers for trackless routes from Utley tram terminus to Sutton, from Stockbridge tram terminus to Nab Wood, from the town centre to Oakworth, and from Ingrow tram terminus via Cross Roads to Oxenhope. It was not until 1911 that a Bill was promoted following a proposal by Railless Electric Traction to seek powers for tracklesses in Keighley, a proposal which the Corporation rejected.

The Trackless Bill aroused a storm of opposition from local authorities concerned about the effects of the vehicles on their roads and from the Midland and Great Northern railway companies fearing the effects of competition. The Stockbridge to Nab Wood route was struck out (Bradford was to extend its own tramways to Nab Wood) but the other routes remained in the Bill, which became law in August 1912.

During 1912 the Corporation debated the comparative merits of the various types of trackless. The tramways manager recommended that a trial be made with the Cedes system on the Cross Roads route. The Council therefore accepted the offer of the Cedes agents, Trackless Trolley Ltd, to erect 1 mile 1,400yd of overhead line from Ingrow to Hebden Road end and to supply one car on three months' free trial. If the trial proved unsuccessful, the overhead would be adapted for use by the under-running trolleys at no extra cost.

The official inspection of the Cross Roads route, the first Cedes route in the country, took place on 24 April 1913 and a public service commenced on 3 May 1913. The car, a 24-seat single-decker, had been built in Austria and had operated in Vienna before being brought to England for demonstration at West Ham. The Corporation later purchased the car and numbered it 'O'. An order was placed with Trackless Trolley for the two cars (Nos 1 and 2) for the Cross Roads route at a price of £710 each. In October the Corporation declared itself satisfied with the new system and accepted a Cedes tender for the installation of 6 miles 7 furlongs of overhead line on the Oakworth and Eastburn routes and for a further four cars. Another two cars were ordered later.

The overhead line on these two routes was ready long before the new vehicles arrived. The two routes were inspected on 15 December 1914 and service to Oakworth commenced immediately, but the Eastburn service was deferred until the final batch of cars was delivered. This service came into operation in January 1915, but the full service was not working until the end of February.

The extension from Cross Roads to Oxenhope was made during 1916, using equipment from the demonstration line installed at Hove, and a trial run took place on 29 June. The official inspection was made on 2 July, but following objections from the County Council, the Corporation agreed not to use the extension until the war was over. The Cedes company was wound up in 1916 and the Corporation had to seek new sources of supply for motors and equipment. At the sale of Cedes plant and effects, Keighley bought the Cedes double-deck car which had been used at Hove.

Lack of spares and new equipment rendered the service chaotic. By April 1920 only one trackless remained in service, on the Cross Roads route. The Eastburn section was reopened at Whitsun 1920, and the Oakworth service resumed as far as Slaymaker Lane in July, after nearly two years, but the car failed again a few days later. Things improved in 1921, when from 25 March four cars operated a regular service to Cross Roads and along the Sutton route as far as Crosshills, and the extension to Oxenhope was opened at last. Attempts to improve the vehicles included conversion to front-wheel drive instead of the original Cedes hub motors. However, the Oxenhope extension closed again on 24 October 1921, and the last runs on the Oakworth route were made on 2 December of the same year.

In 1923 the Council agreed to replace the tramcars by modern trackless vehicles, and a

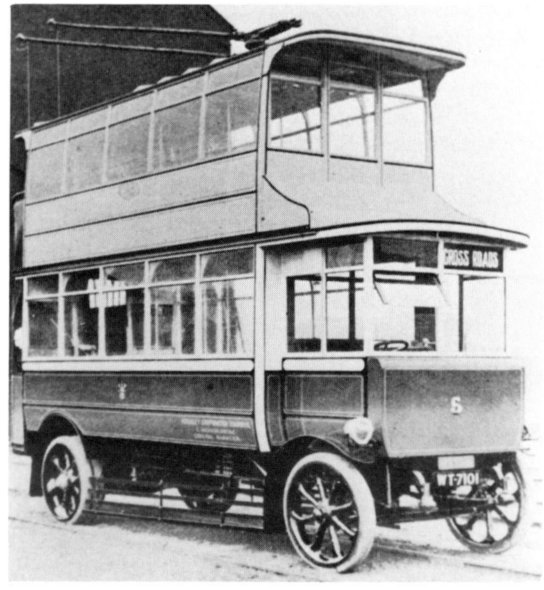

Below:
Keighley: No 5, a Brush-bodied Straker of 1924, was one of the undertaking's second generation of trolley vehicles. *V. C. Jones/Ian Allan Library*

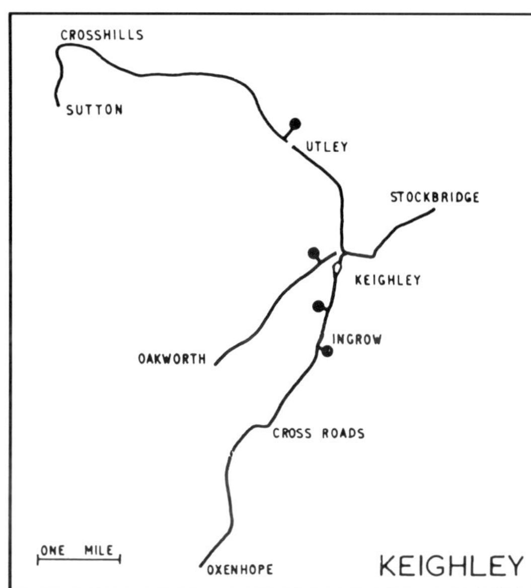

Keighley

Fleet Nos	Registration Nos	Chassis	Electrical equipment	Body	In service	Withdrawn	Notes
0		Cedes Stoll	Cedes	Austrian-built B24F	1913	1924	a
1, 2		Trackless	Johnson-Phillips	Dodson B28R	1914		a
3		Cedes Stoll	Johnson-Phillips	Dodson B29R	1914		a
4	WR 8165	Cedes Stoll	Johnson-Phillips	Dodson B29R	1914		a b
5-7		Cedes Stoll	Johnson-Phillips	Dodson B29R	1914/15		a
8	WY 243	Cedes Stoll	Johnson-Phillips	Dodson B29R	1915	1924	a
9		Cedes Stoll	Johnson-Phillips	Dodson H17/16ROS	1917	1924	a
1-4	WT 6336/5/58/57	Straker Squire	BTH	(Note c)	1924	1925/6	c
5-10	WT 7101-6	Straker Squire	BTH	Brush H26/24ROS	1924	1932	
11-14	WT 7107-10	Straker Squire	BTH	Brush B32F	1924	1932	
15-18	WU 2585-8	Straker Squire	BTH	Brush H26/24ROS	1925	1932	

Notes:

a Nos 0-9 renumbered 50-59 in 1920/1

b Given new Straker chassis in 1923

c Originally Cedes vehicles of the first 1-6 series. Seating capacity: No 1: 33, No 2: 29, Nos 3 and 4: 27

Preserved vehicles: No 5 (1924 Straker).

Bill to operate trolley vehicles on the Utley, Ingrow and Stockbridge routes received the Royal Assent on July 1924. It was also intended to modernise the Sutton and Cross Roads trackless routes for use by conventional vehicles; however, the Sutton service ran for the last time on 23 May 1924.

The Utley tramcars were replaced by trackless on 20 August 1924, using new Nos 1-4 which comprised bodies taken from the Cedes cars mounted on new Straker chassis. The Stockbridge service started on 21 November 1924, and the Ingrow service on 14 December 1924. As well as Nos 1-4, the new trackless fleet put into operation during this year comprised more Strakers; Nos 5-10 were two-motor double-deckers, while Nos 11-14 were single-deckers, all with Brush-built bodies. Four more double-deckers (Nos 15-18) were added in 1925.

The Cross Roads route continued to operate on the Cedes system, and Straker No 2 was fitted with Cedes trolley attachments to enable it to work on the route. After various vicissitudes, and after the practicability of conversion had been considered to enable a through service to be run, operation finally ceased on 3 May 1926. Thus the first Cedes-Stoll route in the country was also the last.

During the 1920s, motorbus competition and the growing need for through routes and co-ordinated services into neighbouring areas culminated in 1931/2 in plans for a new company, to be jointly owned by Keighley Corporation and the West Yorkshire Road Car Co. Under the scheme it was anticipated that the trackless would be withdrawn. In August 1932 the Council resolved to abandon the tracklesses at the end of the month and to operate a replacing bus service until the start of the new joint company. And so, on the evening of 31 August 1932, a crowd of several hundred persons gathered to witness the closure of the trackless system. The official last car was double-decker No 17. On 2 September, the new joint company was registered as Keighley-West Yorkshire Services, and the last Corporation buses ran on 30 September 1932.

The Corporation could hardly have foreseen that its later tracklesses would be so quickly rendered obsolete by the rapid technical advances of the later 1920s. The cars, though hardly eight years old when scrapped, could not withstand comparison with the new vehicles continually placed in service by their competitors as the latter strengthened their hold on the Corporation's routes.

References
Keighley Corporation Transport by J. S. King (Advertiser Press 1964).

Kingston-upon-Hull

The first trolleybus plan by Kingston-upon-Hull proved abortive. After examination of the Doncaster and Rotherham systems in 1929, Hull's tramways committee considered that the Paragon Square-Preston Road motorbus service was such as to support trolleybus operation and it proposed to obtain the necessary powers. However, the Bill (which also covered other projects) was rejected by a town's meeting, whereupon the committee, which had already ordered the vehicles in confident expectation of approval, had the 12 Guy six-wheelers fitted with petrol engines and put into service on the route as motorbuses.

By 1934, with the co-ordination agreement with East Yorkshire Motor Services, consideration was given to the possibility of replacing the city's tramways, and in 1936 the Kingston-upon-Hull Corporation Act gave the necessary powers. However, the first route to be inaugurated was not a tramway but a motorbus route: the Chanterlands Avenue trolleybuses were officially inaugurated on 23 July and public

Kingston-upon-Hull

Fleet Nos	Registration Nos	Chassis	Electrical equipment	Body	In service	Withdrawn	Notes
1-26	CRH 925-50	Leyland TB4	Metrovick	Weymann H28/26R	1937	1952-4	
27-46	ERH 27-46	Crossley TDD4	Metrovick	Craven H28/26R	1938	1954-62	a
47-66	FRH 547-66	Leyland TB7	Metrovick	East Lancs H28/26R	1939	1957-61	a
67-78	GRH 287-98	Sunbeam W	Metrovick	Brush H30/26R	1945	1962	a
79-84	GRH 355-60	Sunbeam W	Metrovick	Roe H30/26R	1945	1962	a
85-90	HRH 85-90	Sunbeam F4	Metrovick	Roe H31/29R	1947	1962-4	
91-100	HRH 91-100	Sunbeam F4	Metrovick	Roe H31/29R	1948	1962-4	
101	NRH 101	Sunbeam MF2B	Metrovick	Roe H30/24D	1953	1964	
102-16	RKH 102-16	Sunbeam MF2B	Metrovick	Roe H30/24D	1954/5	1964	

Notes:

a Nos 27-84 reseated H31/29R 1947/8

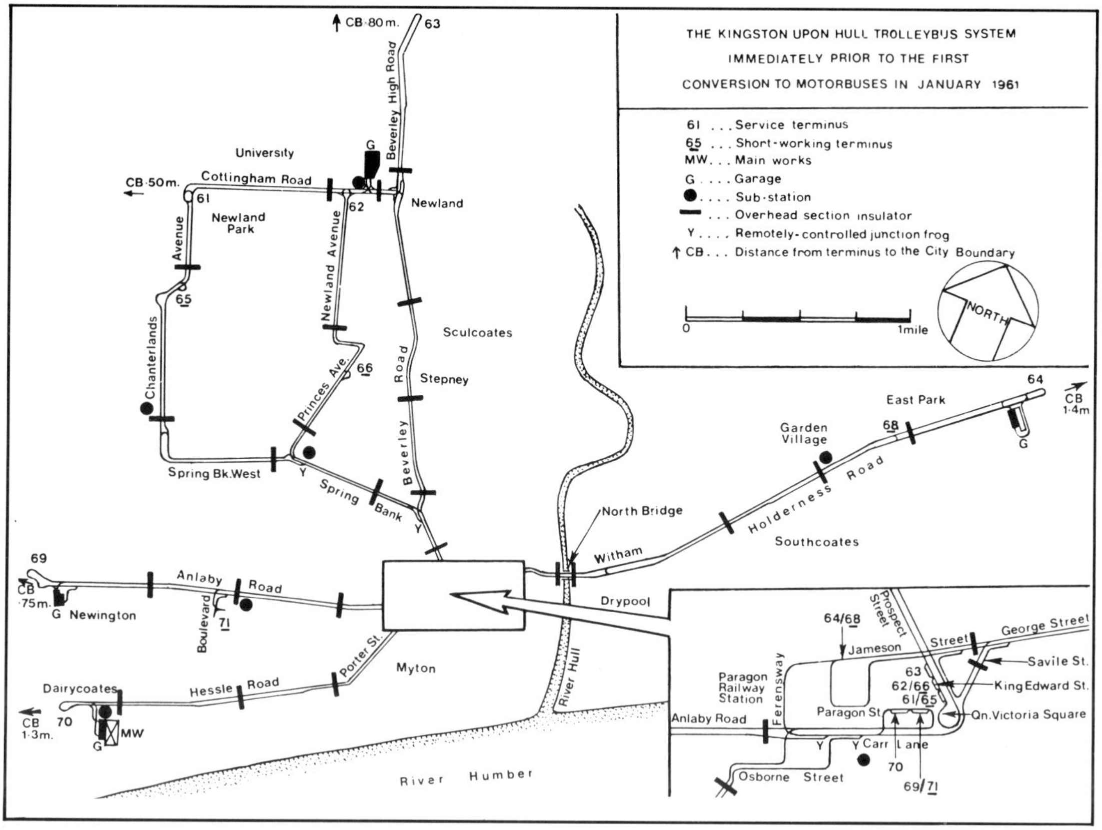

service commenced on 25 July 1937. This was followed on 3 October by the Newlands Avenue route, on which the tramcars had been temporarily displaced by motorbuses while the overhead was reconstructed. The initial fleet of 26 Weymann-bodied Leyland TB4s appeared in the new streamlined blue and white livery introduced on the buses a year earlier.

With the delivery of 20 Craven-bodied Crossleys in 1938, trolleybuses took over the Beverley Road route on 4 September, thus completing the replacement of tramways in the northern areas of the city. The next installation was along Holderness Road, where an added complication was North Bridge, a rolling-lift bridge across the River Hull; this necessitated the erection of troughs and knife contacts for the overhead at the lifting end of the bridge and of a system of flexible cables with pulleys and counterweight at the fixed end. This worked satisfactorily, but it required trolleybuses to keep to the centre of the roadway and cross the bridge at low speed. Because of wartime conditions the new service did not start until 18 February 1940.

The war also delayed further changeovers, but eventually the declining state of the remaining tramways and the fact that falling traffic meant that no new vehicles were needed, resulted in the introduction of trolleybuses on the Anlaby Road route on 6 September 1942. This also marked the introduction of trolley skates instead of the wheels which had been used since the start of the system, the change

Below:

Kingston-upon-Hull: Hull's first trolleybuses in 1937 were Weymann-bodied Leyland TB4s. This is No 1 in its pristine state. *Ian Allan Library*

proving so successful that the rest of the fleet was also converted. The final tramway conversion came when the Hessle Road route was taken over by 12 new semi-utility Sunbeams on 1 July 1945.

To assist in coping with increased postwar traffic, Nos 1-66 had their seating capacity raised from 54 to 56, while in 1946 a reverser (the only one on the system) was erected in Boulevard off Anlaby Road to provide for short-working rugby football specials. Also on the Anlaby Road route, a short extension was

Kingston-upon-Hull: Hull's last new trolleybuses in 1954/5 were dual-doorway Roe-bodied Sunbeam MF2Bs, of which No 102 is seen at the Commercial Motor Show of 1954. *Ian Allan Library*

Kingston-upon-Hull: On the Holderness Road route, a lifting bridge necessitated the installation of a special section of movable overhead. No 61 (a 1939 East Lancs-bodied Leyland TB7) has just negotiated the bridge. *V. C. Jones/Ian Allan Library*

brought into use on 30 March 1947 to reduce traffic congestion at the terminus. The fleet reached its maximum strength of 100 vehicles in 1948.

With a view to future fleet replacements, an advanced design of trolleybus for one-man operation was developed, and the prototype (No 101) entered service in January 1953. A Sunbeam MF2B, it had a 54-seat Roe body with front entrance and central exit, two stairways, and trolley retrievers. Although it was not in fact used as a one-man vehicle, such was its success that a further 15 of this 'Coronation' type were ordered for delivery in 1954/5. There were also proposals for another 10 similar vehicles, as well as the conversion of the Preston Road bus route to trolleybus operation, but these projects did not materialise.

By the late 1950s, the declining passenger traffic, coupled with the high cost of re-equipment and with plans for the redevelopment of the city (including new housing estates beyond the trolleybus termini), led to the decision in 1959 that the trolleybuses should be gradually replaced by motorbuses. The first closure took place on 28 January 1961 when the Hessle Road service was withdrawn. Other closures followed:

3 February 1962 — Anlaby Road.
28 July 1962 — Chanterlands Avenue.
21 September 1963 — Holderness Road.
16 November 1963 — Newlands Avenue.

The last route — Beverley Road — was withdrawn on 31 October 1964; the last trolleybus was appropriately the prototype 'Coronation' No 101, providing a reminder of what might have been.

References
'British Trolleybus Systems: No 17 — Kingston-upon-Hull; *Buses*, February and April 1973.

Leeds

To Leeds belongs the distinction of having operated the first public service of trolleybuses in Britain, for while both Leeds and Bradford officially inaugurated their trolley vehicle installations at the same time on 20 June 1911, Bradford did not begin a public service until 24 June, whereas the Leeds service began immediately after the opening. The Leeds route was also a much longer one: nearly 4 miles against only 1¼ miles of the Bradford line. Moreover, while Bradford's line was a suburban link, the Leeds route joined an outer suburb with the city centre. Yet while Bradford went on to develop its system into one of the largest in the country, in Leeds the trolleybus played no more than a minor role and finally succumbed as early as 1928.

With the intention of providing a service along a thinly-populated road where the cost of tramway construction would not have been justified, Leeds Tramways Committee examined the case for railless traction and visited Continental undertakings. As a result, it recommended the new system, and the Corporation applied for powers in the 1909-10 session to equip the Drighlington route for railless traction. The route ran from Aire Street, adjacent to the City Square, along Whitehall Road, through New Farnley, to the city boundary, a distance of about 4½ miles. However, the initial installation was only as far as Upper Moor Top, Farnley — a distance of about 3¾ miles. For almost a mile at the city end, the route ran along the same street as a tramway, and both tramcars and trolleybuses shared the same positive wires.

There were obviously few expectations about the likely profitability of the new system. In its 1911 description, *Tramway & Railway World* commented: 'It is not expected, for a time at least, that any substantial revenue will be earned, but it seems certain that the provision of travelling facilities will encourage the development of the district, and in time the route may prove not only self-supporting but remunerative.' It was noted that the new route was not merely a feeder to an outlying tramway, but was instead a cheaper option than a tramway to connect an outer suburb with the city centre.

Operations started at noon on 20 June 1911, at the same time as Bradford's installation, for work on the two had proceeded neck-and-neck and it was agreed that both cities should start their new trolleybuses simultaneously so that neither should claim precedence as the pioneer of the new mode. In Leeds, the Lord Mayor drove the first car, and among the early users of the line were visitors to the city for the Coronation celebrations.

The four vehicles (Nos 501-4) were single-deckers supplied by Railless Electric Traction with Siemens equipment and Hurst Nelson bodies. They were generally similar to the Bradford cars, but the bodies were of the front-entrance type and for the first few months the cars were one-man operated. Two 20hp motors were capable of providing a speed of 10mph. To enable the vehicles to obtain access to the depot in Kirkstall Road, a skate was fitted for use along the tram tracks.

In 1913 the Tramways Committee was proposing two extensions to the system: a branch off Whitehall Road along Lawns Lane and Chapel Lane; and a cross-suburban route from the Tong Road tramway, across the

Below:
Leeds: One of the pioneer Railless cars of 1911, No 503 poses for the photographer on the Farnley route soon after the opening.

Leeds

Fleet Nos	Registration Nos	Chassis	Electrical equipment	Body	In service	Withdrawn	Notes
501-4	U 8403-5	Railless	Siemens	Hurst Nelson B28F	1911	1916/21	a
505-9	U 8406-10	Railless	Siemens	Hurst Nelson B28F	1915/6	1926	
501/2	U 9431, NW 296	Railless			1921	1926	b
510	U 9745	Elec Traction Co	Elec Traction Co	Leeds City Tys H59ROS	1921	1925	
511/2	NW 2402/2734	Elec Traction Co	Elec Traction Co	Leeds City Tys H59ROS	1923	1928	
513	NW 5550	Trackless Cars		Olympia H34/30C	1924	1928	
514	NW 2755	Straker-Clough		B36C	1924	1928	
515	NW 7390	Straker-Clough		B40C	1924	1928	

Notes:

a No 504 withdrawn 1916 before registration

b Replaced original Nos 501/2.

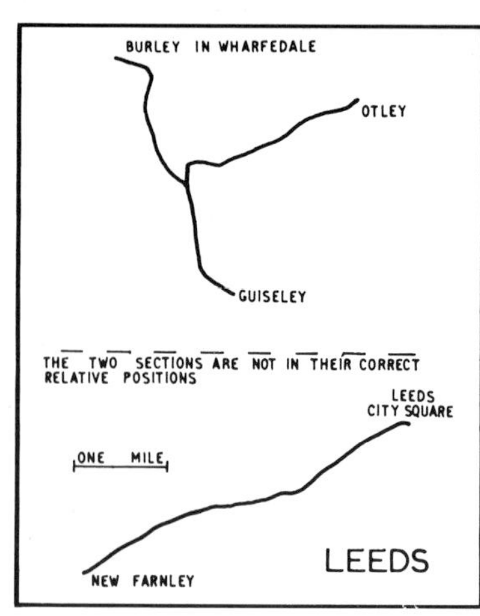

Above:
Leeds: On the inner section of the first Leeds trolleybus route, trackless cars shared road and overhead with tramcars. Railless No 504 of 1911 is bound for Farnley.

existing trackless route in Whitehall Road, then along Domestic Street, Hunslet Hall Road and Moor Road to Low Road in Hunslet. These proposals did not materialise, but after powers were sought in 1914 to operate on four additional routes, in 1915 two further routes were opened. In contrast to the Farnley route, these were both outside the municipal boundary and ventured nowhere near the city centre. They started at the terminus of the tramway from Leeds at the White Cross in Guiseley, and continued outward respectively to Otley (opened on 9 September) and to Burley-in-Wharfedale (opened on 22 October). Along the country roads traversed, Leeds Corporation did not consider that the construction of tramways would have proved worthwhile. Five further vehicles were added to the railless fleet; Nos 505-9 were Railless single-deckers. A low bridge on the Otley route precluded the operation of double-deckers.

The first double-decker (No 510), which made its appearance in 1921, was a remarkable front-wheel drive, low-loading vehicle, described by the contemporary press as a 'railless trolley tractor'. The front end was somewhat reminiscent of a steamroller, with the front wheels mounted on a fore-carriage pivoted on a turntable. 'The principle of the front drive', *Tramway & Railway World* explained, 'is that of a tractor, the driving wheels being on a fore-carriage, and the motors are carried fore and aft of the front axle, being supported at their outer ends by coil springs bearing on the fore-carriage frame. Each motor

drives one of the front wheels, the drive being direct through a pinion on the motor shaft and internal gear ring fixed in the wheels.' Steering was by worm and rack. The chassis frame dropped down behind the front assembly to permit a low floor and platform only 14in above the ground. The overall height of the 59-seat covered-top body was only 13ft 10in. A skate was fitted for use along tram tracks, and No 510 served on the Farnley route. The front-drive arrangement had previously been tried on one of the earlier single-deckers at the start of 1920. The success of No 510 was enough to encourage the introduction of two further similar double-deckers, Nos 511 and 512. 'These vehicles compare very favourably with the carrying capacity of our trams', the Tramways Manager commented. 'They are of the utmost stability, and absolutely irreproachable and certain in operation.'

Nevertheless, the trackless did not seem to prosper. Proposed extensions from Burley to Ilkley, and from Guiseley to Baildon Bridge (with a possible connection with the Bradford system) never materialised, and although the system had grown to some nine route-miles the fleet never exceeded a total of 15 vehicles. By the latter years of the 1920s the motorbus was offering a preferable alternative to the trolley vehicle on the routes concerned, with a through service paralleling trolleybus and tram between Ilkley and Leeds, and the last of the city's trolleybuses ceased operation on 26 July 1928.

References
'British Bus & Tram Systems; No 17: Leeds City Transport', by W. D. Wilson, *Buses Illustrated*, July-September 1956, October-December 1956, January-February 1957, March-April 1957.
'The Railless Trolley System at Leeds', *Tramway & Railway World*, 9 March 1911.

Llanelli

There have been only five trolleybus systems in the Principality of Wales, spanning the years 1913 to 1970 with a break in the middle years, and Llanelli was the fourth to open. It was one of the few company-owned systems in Britain; it ran for about 20 years and in that time the ownership passed through three distinct identities.

The first announcement of plans to replace the tramway system was made public in November 1929. The Llanelly & District Traction Co (a subsidiary of the Llanelly & District Electric Supply Co, one of the Balfour Beatty group) operated trams on three routes from the town centre, to Felin Foel, Pwll and Bynea. It laid a Bill before the House of Lords in January 1930 for powers to abandon the trams entirely in favour of trolleybuses and to cover several extensions. Royal Assent was given to the Llanelly District Traction Act 1930 on 10 July, and five years was allowed in which to complete the trolleybus system.

Economic depression caused the scheme to be delayed, and it was 26 December 1932 before seven trolleybuses had been delivered, and operations began that day on the Bynea route. Completion of the conversion was subject to further delays, and it was not until 13 February 1933 that the final inspection of the Pwll and Felin Foel routes was made, and full operation over the whole system began on 17 February. Thoughts of holding a formal opening ceremony had been discussed, but with various postponements the idea was quietly dropped.

A total of 14 vehicles was supplied in the initial Leyland batch (Nos 1-12, 14 and 15). In 1935 they were joined by three Guy BTX six-wheel double-deckers, two of which had formerly served as demonstrators, and these became Nos 16-18. A further three Guys, four-wheelers this time, were obtained in 1937. Wheel trolley heads were fitted to the collector booms.

The normal pattern of services was that each of the three terminal points was connected to the other two by services across the centre. Of the outer termini, only Loughor Bridge boasted a turning circle, Felin Foel and Pwll being equipped with only reversers initially, but in 1942 a new motor vehicle factory at Felin Foel gave rise to a turning circle at this point. There was also a turning circle at the station, and turning was also possible in the town centre. Additional reversers for short-workings were provided on the Loughor Bridge route at Pemberton and Bynea. Subsequently the Pemberton Arms was provided with a turning circle, and much later a turning circle was also provided at Llwyn Hendy for the Trostre steelworks. Total route mileage was 8.38. The Llanelly District Traction Act of 1936 gave powers for extensions beyond Pwll, westwards to Burry Port, and beyond to Pembrey, but these plans were not proceeded with.

Under the Electricity Act of 1947 the Government took powers to nationalise the

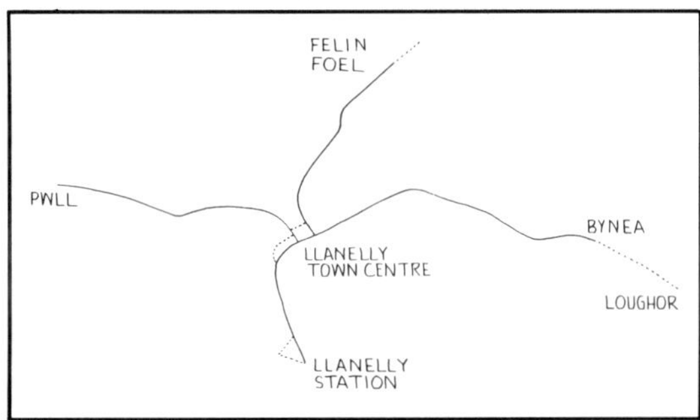

Llanelli

Fleet Nos	Registration Nos	Chassis	Electrical equipment	Body	In service	Withdrawn	Notes
1-12, 14, 15	TH 3004-17	Leyland TBD2	GEC	Leyland H26/24R	1932/3	1952	
16	OG 9886	Guy BTX	Rees-Stevens	Guy H32/28R	1935	1945	a
17	TH 5166	Guy BTX	Rees-Stevens	Guy H32/28R	1935	1945	b
18	TH 5167	Guy BTX	Rees-Stevens	Guy H32/28R	1935	1945	
33-5	TH 8906-8	Guy BT	Elec Con Co	Weymann H30/26R	1937	By 1952	
36	TH 8909	Guy BT	Elec Con Co	Weymann H30/26R	1939	By 1952	
37-40	CBX 530-3	Karrier W	BTH	Roe UH30/26R	1945	1952	c
41, 42	CBX 600/1	Karrier W	BTH	Brush UH30/26R	1945	1952	c
43-8	CBX 909-14	Karrier W	BTH	P/Royal UH30/26R	1946	1952	c

Notes:

a Ex-Birmingham No 19

b Ex-Birmingham No 18

c Nos 39 and 40 sold to Maidstone; chassis of Nos 37, 38 and 41-8 sold to Bradford

Above:
Llanelli: Nos 15 and 8, two of the 1932 Leylands, load at Llanelli station in 1951. *R. W. A. Jones*

electricity supply companies, and as a result on 1 April 1948 the South Wales Electricity Board (which had only come into existence on 1 January that year) became responsible for the Llanelly trolleybus system. The change of ownership coincided with a period of financial difficulty for the trolleybus undertaking, which was operating at a loss and thus became an embarrassment to the Electricity Board which in 1951 began negotiations to dispose of this encumbrance. With the consent of the Ministry of Transport, the sale to the South Wales Transport Co took place in February 1952 and was effective from 20 March 1952. The company's declared intention was to abandon the trolleybus system as soon as possible; after negotiation, the Llanelly District Traction Act of 1952 gave the South Wales Transport Co full powers to discontinue the system while in return Llanelly Corporation would be granted a fresh option to purchase the replacing bus services within a defined area on 31 December 1972. Within nine months of the change of ownership the trolleybuses were gone; the services operated for the last time on 8 November 1952.

The company stated that it had not been possible to meet rising costs while the level of fares remained fixed. Substantial wage awards on a national basis had occurred during the 1948-52 period of Electricity Board ownership, and it was also ironic that the sharp rise in electricity charges came on 1 July 1950 in the middle of that period of ownership.

References
'British Trolleybus Systems: No 18 — Llanelly', *Buses*, September 1975.
'Llanelly Trolleybus System', *Tramway & Railway World*, 16 February 1933.

London

The London system was the whale among the minnows. Even though it never attained its full projected size, with a total of 1,800 vehicles it owned about half of the total number of trolleybuses in Britain, more than all those owned by the local authorities put together, and it towered over its nearest challengers which could boast of only about 200 each. The vast network was practically all built up over a period of only about five years (1935-40); yet most of it saw no more than one generation of vehicles, and it was all dismantled again within the short space of three years (1959-62). Replacing an extensive tramway network, the electrical equipment of which was a major factor in determining the precedence of the trolley vehicle over the motorbus, it inherited the basic defect of the tramway layout in that it never penetrated across the central area of London, while few extensions were made beyond the confines of the old tracks.

Above:
London: In the heyday of the London United system, new No 61 of 1933 heads through Kingston for Hampton Court, followed by one of the original 1931 vehicles on the Dittons route. *Ian Allan Library*

Below:
London: The end of the road for the 'Diddlers', London's first trolleybuses, as withdrawn ex-London United vehicles await scrapping outside Poplar depot in 1949. *V. C. Jones/Ian Allan Library*

The first trolleybus to operate in London — and indeed the first in Britain — made demonstration runs in 1909 at the Hendon depot of the Metropolitan Electric Tramways (MET). In the following years various schemes were put forward in several parts of London, and trials were actually made during 1912 by the London County Council (LCC) between Eltham and Woolwich and by West Ham Corporation, as well as by the London United Tramways on its Haydons Road route in Merton between 1922 and 1924. In the event, it was to be the London United Tramways (LUT) which would put the trolleybus into service on London's streets.

Powers were obtained under the London United Tramways Act of 1930 for a scheme of considerable magnitude, involving almost 20 miles of routes and 60 vehicles. Trolleybuses were to take over from tramcars between Twickenham and Teddington, then on to Kingston, Surbiton and Tolworth, and to Wimbledon, while in Kingston a section of new wiring would connect formerly separate routes to complete a loop to Richmond Park. While the LUT had been introducing new tramcars on other routes, the routes involved in the conversion plans were held to be more suitable for trolleybus operation, since they were not the most heavily trafficked and they were plentifully encumbered with narrow roads and sharp corners.

Operation began between Twickenham and Teddington on 16 May 1931, when the Mayor of Twickenham inaugurated London's first public trolleybus service. The rest of the system was opened during the next few months: to Kingston, Richmond Park and Surbiton on 15 June, to Tolworth on 15 July, to the Dittons on 29 July, and finally to Wimbledon on 2 September, though for a time a few tramcars were kept running until all the new vehicles had arrived.

The LUT introduced 60 vehicles which were to become renowned as one of the classic trolleybus types. Six-wheel double-deckers, Nos 1-60 had AEC 663T chassis, with distinctive bodies

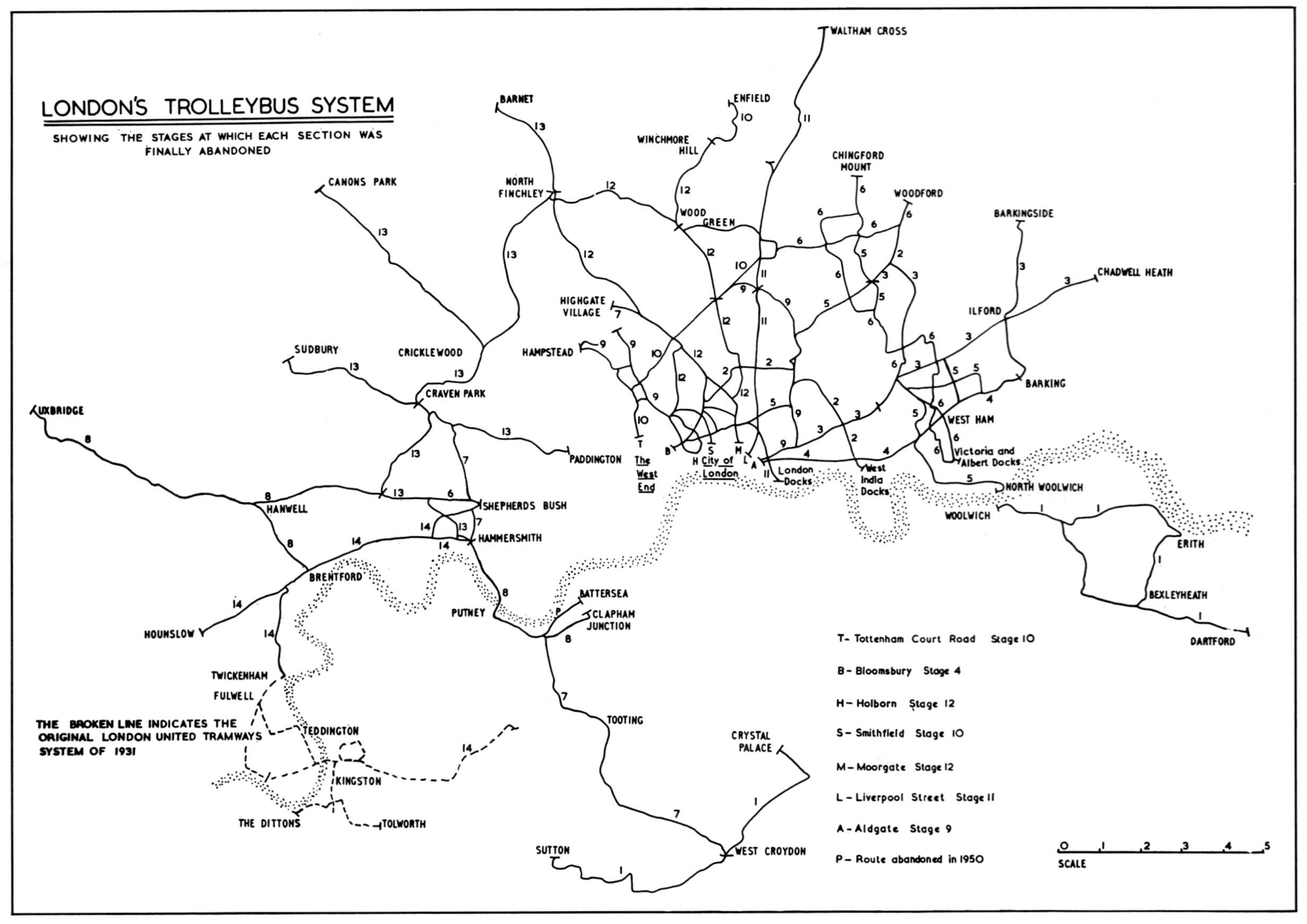
LONDON'S TROLLEYBUS SYSTEM
SHOWING THE STAGES AT WHICH EACH SECTION WAS
FINALLY ABANDONED
THE BROKEN LINE INDICATES THE
ORIGINAL LONDON UNITED TRAMWAYS
SYSTEM OF 1931
WALTHAM CROSS
BARNET
ENFIELD
WINCHMORE HILL
CHINGFORD MOUNT
WOODFORD
BARKINGSIDE
CANONS PARK
NORTH FINCHLEY
WOOD GREEN
CHADWELL HEATH
ILFORD
HIGHGATE VILLAGE
BARKING
SUDBURY
CRICKLEWOOD
HAMPSTEAD
WEST HAM
CRAVEN PARK
UXBRIDGE
PADDINGTON
The West End
City of London
London Docks
West India Docks
Victoria and Albert Docks
NORTH WOOLWICH
WOOLWICH
HANWELL
SHEPHERDS BUSH
HAMMERSMITH
ERITH
BRENTFORD
BATTERSEA
PUTNEY
CLAPHAM JUNCTION
BEXLEYHEATH
HOUNSLOW
DARTFORD
TWICKENHAM
FULWELL
TOOTING
TEDDINGTON
CRYSTAL PALACE
KINGSTON
THE DITTONS
TOLWORTH
SUTTON
WEST CROYDON
T- Tottenham Court Road   Stage 10
B- Bloomsbury   Stage 4
H- Holborn   Stage 12
S- Smithfield   Stage 10
M- Moorgate   Stage 12
L- Liverpool Street   Stage 11
A- Aldgate   Stage 9
P- Route abandoned in 1950
SCALE
0 1 2 3 4 5

Above:
London: Representative of the large number of trolleybuses put into service by the London Passenger Transport Board between 1935 and 1940 is No 142, an MCW-bodied AEC 664T of Class C1 of 1935. Note the rear wheel splasher covers, and the new 'Trolleybus' symbol on the front. *Ian Allan Library*

built by the Union Construction Co at Feltham, with half-cab and bonnet. They were 56-seaters with straight stairways (except No 60 which had a quarter-turn stairway and was planned as a 61-seater but failed the tilt test) and were of a pattern with the company's contemporary 'Feltham' type tramcars. Interior panels were in silver-grey wood with blue panelling, and the seats in the lower saloon were upholstered in green moquette while the upper saloon seats were in red Rexine. Except for the resistances, the traction equipment was mounted at the front, under the bonnet or in the cab. Electrical equipment for 35 of the vehicles was supplied by English Electric, and for the other 25 by British Thomson-Houston. As well as rheostatic braking, vacuum-assisted braking was also provided. A maximum speed of just on 30mph was attainable, and a speed of 20mph could be reached in 10 seconds from start. Notable features, reported the contemporary press, are 'smooth and quiet running, and rapid acceleration and deceleration'. Nos 1-60 were to become affectionately known as 'Diddlers'.

One addition was made to the LUT fleet in 1933. No less distinctive, it was of entirely different appearance, for No 61 was a central-entrance full-fronted 74-seater, built by AEC and English Electric with body built by the London General Omnibus Co (LGOC) at its Chiswick bus works, as an experimental unit to meet the growing need for a large-capacity trolley vehicle. 'It is no exaggeration to say that in appearance it is by far the most pleasing public service vehicle yet seen on the road', was the verdict of *Tramway & Railway World*. No 61 went into service on the Hampton Court-Wimbledon route on 27 March 1933.

Two extensions were soon made to the LUT system. A short section at Wimbledon, from St George's Road to the new Town Hall, was brought into use on 15 December 1932, while a loop of about a mile round was opened on 20 September 1933 at Tolworth from the original Red Lion terminus to the Kingston By-pass.

In 1933, however, the LUT ended its separate existence, for from 1 July of that year it became

part of the new London Passenger Transport Board (LPTB), though probably few of its originators could have foreseen that the company's system would form the nucleus of the greatest trolleybus network in the world. There was obviously a wide field, for while the LPTB took over only 61 trolley vehicles, it acquired a total of some 2,500 tramcars from the various company and municipal operators. In view of the pressing need for the renewal of many obsolete tramcars and much worn-out track, it was not long before the Board obtained powers under its Act of 1934 to convert some 90 miles of tramways to trolleybus operation. This was only the start: the 1935 Act provided for the conversion of another 60 miles of tramways, the 1936 Act for a further 50 miles, and the 1937 Act gave powers for the changeover of the remainder of the tramways.

To determine the type of vehicle best suited to the needs of such an ambitious scheme, two different models were delivered for trials in 1934. No 62 was a six-wheel AEC 663T with a Metropolitan-Cammell 73-seat body, while No 63 was a four-wheel AEC 661T with an English Electric 60-seat body. The larger vehicle was chosen, since its capacity more nearly matched that of the majority of the trams, and with its seating modified to a total of

70 seats, it was to become the standard for the rest of the coming fleet, in which No 63 was to remain the sole four-wheeler.

The first stage of the Board's conversions took place on 27 October 1935 with the introduction of trolleybuses in place of trams between Shepherds Bush and Hounslow and between Hammersmith and Hampton Court. Consequent on the new numbering scheme, these received route numbers 657 and 667 respectively. The original LUT routes numbered 1 to 5 were renumbered 601 to 605 respectively (601 Twickenham-Tolworth; 602 Dittons-Kingston loop; 603 Tolworth-Kingston loop; 604 Hampton Court-Wimbledon; 605 Teddington-Malden). Other conversions followed in fairly rapid succession, if sometimes in apparently bewildering geographical sequence.

10 November 1935: 698 Woolwich-Erith-Bexleyheath.
24 November 1935: 696 Woolwich-Dartford.

These two routes always remained physically isolated from the rest of the system. A new depot with a capacity for 60 vehicles was constructed at Bexleyheath; this was to be the only entirely new depot to be erected for trolleybuses.

8 December 1935: 654 Sutton-West Croydon.

This route was extended on 9 February 1936 to Crystal Palace, involving the negotiation of a 1 in 9 gradient on Anerley Hill, for which purpose the vehicles employed were equipped with runback brakes.

6 June 1936: 669 Stratford-Canning Town.
    687, 697, 699 Chingford Mount-Victoria & Albert Docks.
5 July 1936: 666 Hammersmith-Edgware.
2 August 1936: 660 Hammersmith-North

Finchley.
    645 Edgware-North Finchley.
23 August 1936: 662 Sudbury-Paddington.
    664 Edgware-Paddington.
18 October 1936: 623 Woodford-Manor House.

This included the first instance in the scheme of a section of trolleybus route to be introduced on a road previously unserved by trams: a link between Ferry Lane and Bruce Grove.

15 November 1936: 607 Shepherds Bush-Uxbridge.
6 December 1936: 655 Hammersmith-Hanwell.
17 January 1937: 685 Leyton-Walthamstow.
12 September 1937: 626 Acton-Hammersmith.
    628 Craven Park-Clapham Junction.
    630 Scrubs Lane-West Croydon.
    612 Battersea-Mitcham.
    689/690 Stratford circular.

This stage, the largest so far, saw incursions being made into former LCC tramway territory in which the conduit system of current collection had been used; hence streets in Battersea and elsewhere were now seeing overhead wires for the first time. The need for completely new overhead installations also increased the work involved in conversion, as well as its cost. Also with this stage came the 630: for long, vehicles bound for the Scrubs Lane terminus showed on their indicators the truthful if rather vague destination 'Nr Willesden Junction'.

6 February 1938: 691 Barking-Barkingside.
    692 The Horns-Chadwell Heath (Saturdays only).
    693 Barking-Chadwell Heath.

On the same date, the 669 was extended from Canning Town, via Silvertown, to North Woolwich, the longest section of new trolleybus route along roads not formerly served by trams.

6 March 1938: 609 Moorgate-Barnet.
    517/617 Holborn-North Finchley via East Finchley.
    521/621 Holborn-North Finchley via Wood Green.
    651 Barnet-Cricklewood.

This stage brought trolleybuses for the first time into the centre of London, with the linking of the former tram termini at Holborn and Farringdon to make a new terminal loop. Route numbers in the 500 series were also introduced to distinguish services traversing the loop in opposite directions.

8 May 1938: 625 Woodford-Wood Green.
629 Tottenham Court Road-Enfield.
641 Moorgate-Winchmore Hill.

With the introduction of this stage trolleybus route mileage now exceeded the tramways. More than 1,000 trolleybuses were running on almost 200 miles of route. Although tramcars were still in the majority (at some 1,670) they worked only 175 route miles.

1 June 1938: 645 was extended from Edgware to Canons Park over the former section of tramway which had been withdrawn in 1936, and also extended from North Finchley to Barnet in place of 651.
10 July 1938: 513/613 Hampstead Heath-Holborn-Parliament Hill Fields.
615 Parliament Hill Fields-Moorgate.
639 Hampstead Heath-Moorgate.
12 October 1938: 649 Ponders End-Stamford Hill.
679 Ponders End-Smithfield.
16 October 1938: 659 Holborn-Waltham Cross.
6 November 1938: 627 Tottenham Court Road-Edmonton.
5 February 1939: 643 Holborn-Wood Green.
647 Stamford Hill-London Docks.
649 extended from Stamford Hill to Liverpool Street.
683 Moorgate-Stamford Hill.

5 March 1939: 653 Aldgate-Tottenham Court Road.
11 June 1939: 555 Bloomsbury-Leyton.
557 Liverpool Street-Chingford Mount.
581 Bloomsbury-Woodford.
10 September 1939: 677 Smithfield-West India Docks.
5 November 1939: 661 Aldgate-Leyton.
663 Aldgate-Ilford.
10 December 1939: 611 Moorgate-Highgate.

Negotiating the steep Highgate Hill, this route also called for vehicles fitted with runback brakes.

9 June 1940: 565 Holborn-East Ham.
567 Aldgate-Barking.
665 Bloomsbury-Barking.

This brought a halt to the conversion programme. Trolleybuses had now almost entirely superseded trams in north, west and east London, although only a few inroads had been made into the south London network. The

trolleybus fleet now numbered about 1,700, compared with just over 1,000 tramcars, while their route mileage was up to 250 while the tramway mileage was down to little more than 100.

In most instances the trolleybus routes were virtually direct replacements for the old tramway routes, but useful extensions in east London served to join up the gaps left between the formerly separate municipal undertakings. The ring of termini on the periphery of the central area — Paddington, Tottenham Court Road, Bloomsbury, Holborn, Smithfield, Moorgate, Liverpool Street, Aldgate — also reflected the old tramway pattern. Like their predecessors, the trolleybuses were not permitted to traverse the city of London or the West End or to provide cross-town services, despite the Board's strenuous efforts to obtain permission to instal such facilities. The short extensions to Tottenham Court Road and the Holborn loop were primarily to permit turning facilities for the new vehicles.

As might be expected from such an extensive system, there were striking contrasts in the routes and the areas they served, from the packed housing and the docklands of east London, to the outer suburbs of Finchley, Hendon and Barnet, and the sylvan retreats of Hampton Court and Epping Forest. There were many lengthy routes: the record was claimed for the 655 peak-hour Acton-Clapham Junction working at 14.8 miles, but the 14½-mile 630 was a near contender, and there were runs of more than 11 miles to Barnet and over 13 miles to Waltham Cross. The busy 607 on the lengthy Uxbridge Road called for a daily allocation of 75 vehicles, while the 630 and the 653 required 50 each. By contrast, the quiet 602 between the Dittons and Richmond Park needed only five. The heaviest concentration of trolleybuses in the world was claimed on the road between Holloway and Manor House, with seven services each with an off-peak five-minute frequency.

Trolleybuses worked from 22 depots, all of which (with one exception — Bexleyheath) were based on former tram depots. The largest depot, Holloway, which accommodated 230 vehicles, continued to house tramcars until 1952. The pioneer Fulwell took 120 trolleybuses. Following reorganisation in 1950, the names of several depots were changed and the new names are given in brackets in the following table, which lists the depots in order of opening for trolleybus operation.

In outward appearance the fleet was almost completely standardised, with only apparent detailed differences, in spite of the numerous variations in classes, which ranged from A1 and A2 (the original, and non-standard, LUT

Depot	Date opened for trolleybuses	Date closed for trolleybuses
Fulwell	16 May 1931	8 May 1962
Hounslow (Isleworth)	27 October 1935	8 May 1962
Bexleyheath	10 November 1935	3 March 1959
Sutton (Carshalton)	8 December 1935	3 March 1959
West Ham	6 June 1936	26 April 1960
Hendon (Colindale)	5 July 1936	2 January 1962
Stonebridge	5 July 1936	2 January 1962
Acton	5 July 1936	26 May 1937
Finchley	2 August 1936	2 January 1962
Walthamstow	18 October 1936	26 April 1960
Hanwell	15 November 1936	8 November 1960
Hammersmith	12 September 1937	19 July 1960
Wandsworth	12 September 1937	30 September 1950
Ilford	6 February 1938	18 August 1959
Holloway (Highgate)	6 March 1938	25 April 1961
Wood Green	8 May 1938	7 November 1961
Edmonton	16 October 1938	18 July 1961
Stamford Hill	5 February 1939	18 July 1961
Leyton (Lea Bridge)	11 June 1939	14 April 1959
Hackney (Clapton)	10 September 1939	14 April 1959
Bow	5 November 1939	18 August 1959
Poplar	9 June 1940	10 November 1959

London

Class	Fleet Nos	Registration Nos	Chassis	Electrical equipment	Body*	In service	Notes
A1	1-35	HX 2756/5, 3984/ 3/5/6/8/7, 4217/ 20/19/18, 4305/6/ 4/3/78/77/76/75, 125, MG100-3/ 125-8/187/183-6/ 350	AEC 663T	E/Electric	Union Construction Co H32/24R	1931	a
A2	36-60	MG 349, MV 242- 51/335-8/409-17/ 1261	AEC663T	BTH	Union Construction Co H32/24R	1931	a
X1	61	AHX 801	AEC663T	E/Electric	LGOC H40/34C	1933	b
X2	62	AXU 188	AEC663T	Metrovick	MCW H40/33R	1934	
X3	63	AXU 189	AEC661T	E/Electric	E/Electric H32/28R	1934	
B1	64-93	CGF 64-93	Leyland	Metrovick	BRCWH32/28R	1935/6	
B2	94-131	CGF 94-131	Leyland	Metrovick	Brush H32/28R	1935	c
C1	132-83	CGF 132-83	AEC664T	E/Electric	Weymann (132-41) MCW (142-83)	1935	d
C2	184-283	CUL 184-283	AEC664T	E/Electric	MCW	1936	
C3	284-383	CUL 284-383	AEC664T	E/Electric	BRCW	1936/7	e
D1	384	CUL 384	Leyland	Metrovick	Leyland	1936	
D2	385-483	DGY 385-483	Leyland	Metrovick	MCW	1936-7	f
B3	484-8	DGY 484-8	Leyland	Metrovick	BRCW H32/28R	1936	
B1	489-93	DGY 489-93	Leyland	Metrovick	BRCW H32/28R	1936	
D3	494-553	DLY 494-553	Leyland	Metrovick	BRCW	1937	
E1	554-603	DLY 554-603	AEC664T	E/Electric/Metrovick	Brush	1937	g
E2	604-28	DLY 604-28	AEC664T	E/Electric/Metrovick	Weymann	1937	h
E3	629-53	DLY 629-53	AEC664T	E/Electric/Metrovick	P/Royal	1937	i
F1	654-753	DLY 654-753	Leyland	Metrovick	Leyland	1937	
X4	754	DLY 754	LPTB/AEC	Metrovick	LPTB H40/28D	1937	
H1	755-904	ELB 755-904	Leyland	Metrovick	MCW	1938	j
J1	905-52	ELB 905-52	AEC 664T	Metrovick/E/Electric	Weymann (MCW: 952)	1938	
N1	953	ELB 953	AEC/MCW	Metrovick/E/Electric	Weymann	1938	
L2	954	ELB 954	MCW/AEC	Metrovick/E/Electric	MCW	1938	
J2	955-1029	ELB 955-99, EXX 10, EXV 1-29	AEC664T	Metrovick/E/Electric	BRCW	1938	k
J3	1030-54	EXV 30-54	AEC664T	Metrovick/E/Electric	BRCW	1938	
K1	1055-1154	EXV 55-154	Leyland	Metrovick	Leyland	1938/9	l
	1255-1304	EXV 255-304	Leyland	Metrovick	Leyland	1938/9	
K2	1155-1254	EXV 155-254	Leyland	Metrovick/E/Electric	Leyland	1938/9	
	1305-54	EXV 305-54	Leyland	Metrovick/E/Electric	Leyland	1938/9	m

'Diddlers') to the last of the P1 class delivered in 1941. The prewar fleet was supplied on AEC and Leyland chassis, while bodywork came from a total of 10 different makers and although it was nearly all to the same general specification, there were detail differences. Notable also was the inclusion of some 200 chassisless vehicles, while other exceptions to the general run were the small number of short six-wheelers of 60-seat capacity primarily for use on hilly routes such as that to Crystal Palace. During the war, 61 vehicles damaged by enemy action were given new bodies, and a suffix letter was added to their fleet numbers.

There were also several notable experimental vehicles, classified X1 to X7. These included the sole four-wheeler No 63 as X3, and No 754 (X4) which was the first experimental chassisless trolleybus and was also distinguished by having a separate forward exit door. No 1379 (X5) was unique in having an offside rear door in addition to its normal nearside entrance. It was intended for working through the Kingsway tramway subway in which the two intermediate stations were situated between the up and the down tracks, making it necessary for the tramcars to load and unload by way of the front platform. The offside entrance of No 1379 was fitted with power-operated doors which would have been used at the

Class	Fleet Nos	Registration Nos	Chassis	Electrical equipment	Body*	In service	Notes
L1	1355-69	EXV 355-69	MCW/AEC	Metrovick/E/Electric	MCW	1939	n
L2	1370-8	EXV 370-8	MCW/AEC	Metrovick/E/Electric	MCW	1939	
X5	1379	EXV 379		Metrovick/E/Electric	MCW chassisless H40/28D	1939	
L3	1380-1529	FXF 388, FXH 381-529	AEC/MCW	Metrovick	MCW	1939/40	o
M1	1530-54	FXH 530-54	AEC/MCW	Metrovick/E/Electric	Weymann	1939/40	p
N1	1555-1644	FXH 555-644	AEC664T	Metrovick/E/Electric	BRCW	1939/40	q
N2	1645-69	FXH 645-69	AEC664T	Metrovick/E/Electric	P/Royal	1939/40	
X6	1670	FXH 670	E/Electric/AEC	Metrovick/E/Electric	E/Electric H40/28R	1940	
X7	1671	DTD 649		Metrovick	Leyland chassisless	1939	
K3	1672-96	GGP 672-96	Leyland	Metrovick/E/Electric	Leyland	1940	
P1	1697-1721	GGP 697-721	Leyland	Metrovick/E/Electric	MCW	1941	
SA1	1722-33	GGW 722, GLB 723-33	Leyland	GEC	MCW H40/32D	1941/2	r
SA2	1734-46	GLB 734-46	Leyland	Metrovick	MCW H40/32D	1942	r
SA3	1747-64	GLB 747-64	AEC664T	E/Electric	MCW H40/32D	1942/3	r
Q1	1765-1891	HYM 765-841, LYH 842-91	BUT	Metrovick/E/Electric	MCW	1948-52	s

Notes:

* All seating H40/30R unless otherwise stated

a Ex-London United Tramways 'Diddlers'. No 60 (H29/27R) in service 1932

b Ex-London United Tramways experimental. Rebuilt for pay-as-you-enter 1945

c No 99 destroyed in war; Nos 95 and 107 rebodied by Weymann 1942 and reclassified D2; Nos 97 and 98 rebodied by NCB 1946 and reclassified D2

d Nos 138, 142, 148, 175 and 183 sold to Georgetown, Malaya

e No 364 destroyed in war; No 378 rebuilt for pay-as-you-enter 1945

f Nos 386/7/94/8, 418/28/35/48 destroyed in war; No 406 rebodied by Weymann 1941; Nos 390/1/2/5, 405/7/9/12/51/70 rebodied by East Lancs 1945/6; Nos 385/8/9/96, 412/5/9/30 rebodied by NCB 1945/6

g Nos 575/8 and 602 rebodied by NCB 1946

h No 621 rebodied by Weymann 1942; Nos 623/6 rebodied by NCB 1946

i Nos 629/33/5/41/3 rebodied by NCB 1946

j Nos 787/91 and 812 destroyed in war; Nos 792/5, 808/61 rebodied by Weymann 1941/2; Nos 766/84/6/90/4/9, 801/4/8 rebodied by East Lancs 1946/7

k No 1001 rebodied by Weymann 1942; Nos 993, 1001A/7 rebodied by East Lancs 1947/8

l Nos 1123/8 and 1285 rebodied by Weymann 1941/2

m Nos 1244/7 rebodied by Weymann 1941

n No 1365 destroyed in war

o Nos 1387 and 1492 destroyed in war; No 1385 fitted with chassis and rebodied by East Lancs 1948. Reclassified N1

p Nos 1543/5 fitted with chassis and rebodied by East Lancs 1948

q Nos 1565/87 rebodied by Weymann 1942
Rebodied vehicles in above notes renumbered with suffix 'A' (Weymann), 'B' (East Lancs) or 'C' (NCB)

r Originally intended for service in South Africa: SA1 and SA2 in Durban and SA3 in Johannesburg

s In 1961, 88 of Q1 class sold to Spain and 16 to Bangkok

Preserved vehicles: Nos 1, 260, 796, 1201, 1253, 1348, 1521, 1768

stations. Trial runs were made through the subway in 1939, but the restricted clearances in the tunnels suggested that regular operation would have been impracticable. Also unique was No 1671 (X7) which had four-wheel steering and a single rear axle.

Following the halt to the conversion scheme, the last of the new vehicles ordered by the Board entered service in 1941, while in the same year came the first of 43 newcomers which had been destined for duty in South Africa but which because of war conditions were diverted for employment in London. Designated classes SA1, SA2 and SA3, they comprised 25 Leylands ordered for Durban and 18 AECs for Johannesburg, and although in appearance much like the Londoners, they differed in originally being fitted with front exit, while some had tinted glass in their windows to ease the glare of the African sun. They were also notable in being the first 8ft-wide vehicles in the London fleet; since the legal maximum was still only 7ft 6in, special permission had to be given for running them in the Ilford area where they spent their working lives. Between 1940 and 1942 Ilford also had the services of 18 Sunbeams hired from Bournemouth.

In 1948/9 came the first new postwar trolleybuses — Metropolitan-Cammell-bodied BUTs of the Q1 class intended as replacements for the original 1931 'Diddlers'.

They were followed in 1952 by a further 50 of similar type, and these proved to be the last new trolleybuses delivered to London. Though generally of a pattern with their prewar counterparts, they were of improved design and were 8ft wide. Vehicles of the same type were also delivered to Newcastle and Glasgow.

In 1946 it was announced that the trolleybus programme would not be resumed, and that instead motorbuses would be used to replace the remaining 900 tramcars. This work was carried out between 1950 and 1952, when London's last trams were withdrawn. In the course of the change, one trolleybus route became a casualty, when on 30 September 1950 the 612 was withdrawn in the interests of the integration of services with the new tram-replacement buses; this closure involved the removal of about two miles of wiring between Wandsworth and Battersea.

In 1954 it was announced that practically the whole of the trolleybus system was to be replaced by diesel buses. Since nearly all the fleet was nearing the end of its life, and since running costs of both types of vehicle were about the same, the change had been decided because the diesel bus offered advantages in mobility and flexibility, was not subject to holdups through dewirements or power failures, and its use would facilitate the integration of trolleybus routes with existing bus routes in the interests of economy and 'streamlining'. Even more fundamental to the case was the fact that distribution equipment was also nearing the end of its life and costly renewals would have been necessary. The exceptions to the plan 'for the time being' would be the Fulwell group of routes in the southwestern suburbs (the original LUT network) where the postwar trolleybuses were running; these would continue until the vehicles had 'completed their full life'.

The conversion programme started in 1959 and was carried out in stages over the next three years. In 1960 the southwestern routes were also condemned, and these too were to be converted to complete the elimination of the trolleybus; consequently the postwar Q1 class were withdrawn in 1960/1, following an opportunity for their sale overseas, and 125 out of the 127 went for further service to nine Spanish operators.

The first stage of the abandonment programme on 3 March 1959 saw the last trolleybuses run on the isolated Bexleyheath routes 696 and 698, as well as on the Sutton-Crystal Palace route 654, sections

Above:
London: London's only postwar trolleybuses were the Q1 Class of MCW-bodied BUTs delivered between 1948 and 1952. No 1779 stands at the Wimbledon terminus when still in new condition.
V. C. Jones/Ian Allan Library

Below:
London: Trolleybus comfort: the upper deck interior of the Q1 Class of 1948-52.   *V. C. Jones/Ian Allan Library*

Below right:
London: The first route casualty on the London system was the section of 612 between Wandsworth and Battersea, withdrawn in 1950. No 514 stands at the Battersea terminus during the last days of operation.   *V. C. Jones/Ian Allan Library*

which had been among the first in the prewar programme. Further stages followed in quick succession:

14 April 1959: 555, 581 and 677: This included services to Leyton, Woodford and West India Docks.

18 August 1959: 661, 663, 691, 693.
This stage saw the end of the local Barking services, which extended to the easternmost outpost of the system at Chadwell Heath, and used the South African vehicles, the last of which were now withdrawn.
10 November 1959: 567, 569, 665.
This stage marked the first full-scale entry into service of the Routemaster bus (RM) which had been developed in the preceding years primarily for trolleybus replacement. Now about 70 Routemasters took up their duties.

2 February 1960: 557, 669, 685, 689, 690.

26 April 1960: 623, 625, 687, 697, 699.
These two stages marked the end of trolleybus operation on the east London routes.

19 July 1960: 611, 626, 628, 630.
This stage ended operation on Highgate Hill, as well as on three of the routes which penetrated southward: 626 and 628 would have been considerably extended if the intended south London plans had gone ahead as originally envisaged.

8 November 1960: 607, 655.
This ended another lengthy route, the 607 to Uxbridge.

31 January 1961: 513/613, 615, 517/617, 639.
Services to both Hampstead and Parliament Hill Fields ended, together with the 10-mile U-shaped 653 between Aldgate and Tottenham Court Road.

25 April 1961: 627, 629, 659, 679.

18 July 1961: 543/643, 647, 649.
Trolleybuses ceased to run to the northern outpost of the system at Waltham Cross, while 647 was the last service in the dockland area.

7 November 1961: 521/621, 609, 641.
These further north London routes included the 11½-mile run to the country town of Barnet.

2 January 1962: 645, 660, 662, 666.
This stage marked the end of the former MET electric routes in the northwestern suburbs, including Canons Park, Edgware, Sudbury, Barnet and Finchley. It included the 13½-mile U-shaped 645 between Barnet and Canons Park, as well as the 662 to Paddington, which could claim to be the last trolleybus route to operate into 'central' London.

The final stage swept away routes 601, 602, 603, 604, 605, 657 and 667, appropriately including the original network of 1931. It was no less appropriate that trolleybus No 1 (since withdrawal, preserved as a museum piece) should be brought out of retirement on the final day of service, 8 May 1962, during which it made a ceremonial last run over its old routes. However, it was to be No 1521 which officially closed the system in the small hours of 9 May as it completed the last scheduled journey and entered Fulwell depot for the last time. So ended Britain's — and the world's — largest trolleybus system.

References
London's Trams and Trolleybuses by John R. Day (London Transport 1977).
The London Trolleybus (Dryhurst Publications 1961).
London's Trolleybuses by R. F. A. Neale (PSV Circle and Omnibus Society 1969).
'Trolleybuses on the London United Tramway Routes': *Tramway & Railway World*, 14 May 1931.
'London Passenger Transport Board Trolleybus Proposals': *Transport World*, 13 December 1934.

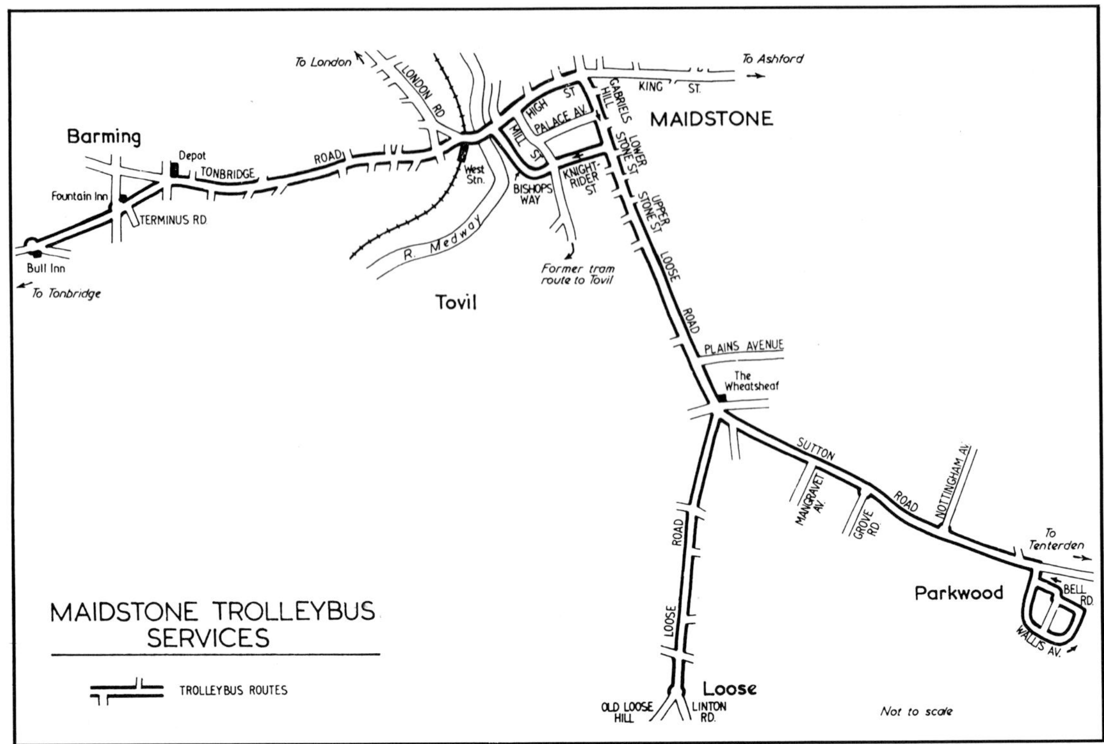

Maidstone

Maidstone Corporation's first trolleybus powers were obtained under its 1923 Act which authorised a route from the West Station to Penenden Heath. In the same year, an official delegation visited Birmingham to inspect the new trolley vehicles, while the Town's Tramways Manager was reporting that the main tram route — to Barming — would soon be in need of replacement. More visits followed, and as a result in 1927 a Provisional Order was obtained for the use of trolleybuses on all three tram routes (to Barming, Loose and Tovil) together with a new route of about 1½ miles along Sutton Road as far as the borough boundary.

Work on the conversion of the Barming route, from a terminus in the High Street and along the Tonbridge road, went ahead and eight six-wheel double-deckers were ordered from Ransomes Sims & Jefferies. With justifiable pride, the manager claimed these as 'in many respects the most luxurious vehicles of their type that have yet been constructed'. Service was inaugurated on 1 May 1928. Since the depot was situated towards the outer end of the route and still housed the remaining tramcars, tracks had to be retained over much of the route. As a result, the manager explained, 'the surface of the road leaves much to be desired, and although the trolley omnibuses are a great improvement over the old tramcars, still better results will be obtained when the surface and camber are reconstructed'.

Such was the success of the new mode of transport that it was soon decided to convert the Loose route to trolleybus operation, as well as to construct the new Sutton Road route to Grove Road, and the new services were brought into use on 12 February 1930, the day after the town's last trams had run (the Tovil route was taken over by motorbuses). At the same time a one-way system was introduced in the town centre with the wiring of Lower Stone Street for outward-bound trolleybuses, inward vehicles continuing to use the former tram route along Mill Street. To augment the fleet, English Electric six-wheelers were chosen.

In 1937 extension of the Barming route by about ½ mile to the Bull Inn was agreed, together with the installation of a new sub-station. However, war came before the plans could be implemented, and it was not until 22 May 1947 that this new section was brought into use. Meanwhile, the original fleet was being renewed by the influx of Sunbeam Ws.

Extensions of the Sutton Road route were now in contemplation, and the first part — to Nottingham Avenue — came into operation on

Above:

Maidstone: Ransomes, Sims & Jefferies supplied Maidstone's first trolley vehicles in 1928. One of the pioneer eight here poses for the camera before entering service. *Ian Allan Library*

Below:

Maidstone: Among the last additions to the Maidstone fleet was this ex-Hastings Weymann-bodied Sunbeam, No 88, photographed en route to Park Wood in 1962. *V. C. Jones/Ian Allan Library*

21 June 1954. To serve a new council housing estate at Parkwood, further extension took place to provide a loop around Wallis Avenue West, Brishin Lane and Bell Road, and this was opened on 4 May 1959. To meet further development, the wires were continued along Wallis Avenue East and Bell Road, this section being opened on 19 August 1963, the wires in Brishing Lane being removed. The system had now reached its maximum extent at just over seven route-miles. Another extension to Long Shaw Road, Selby Road and Bicknor Road was envisaged, but this did not materialise in view of the early stage of development of this part of the estate. Services on the expanded system were assisted by the purchase of secondhand vehicles from Brighton and Hastings.

In 1964 the decision was taken to replace the trolleybuses by motorbuses over a four-year period. By this time, the trolleybus operator was suffering acute problems regarding spare parts and the high cost of new vehicles, matters of especial concern to a relatively small undertaking with a fleet of only about two dozen vehicles in addition to its motor bus operations. A new terminal layout at Loose was installed in 1963, and the last change in the system saw the erection of wiring along the new central thoroughfare Bishops Way, brought into use on 13 December 1964, and the wires in Mill Street

Fleet Nos	Registration Nos	Chassis	Electrical equipment	Body	In service	Withdrawn	Notes
11-18	KO 8891/8543/4/ 8892-6	Ransomes D6	Ransomes	Ransomes H32/31R	1928	1946/7	
23-29	KR 351-7	E/Electric	E/Electric	E/Electric H30/26R	1930	1946-8	
54, 55	GKN 379/80	Sunbeam W	BTH	P/Royal UH30/26R	1943	1967	a
56-58	GKP 511-3	Sunbeam W	BTH	P/Royal UH30/26R	1944	1967	a
62-73	HKR 1-12	Sunbeam W	BTH	NCB H30/26R	1946/7	1965/7	
83, 84	CBX 532/3	Karrier W	BTH	Roe UH30/26R	1955	1960	b
51, 52	LCD 51/2	BUT 9611T	C/Parkinson/A/West	Weymann H30/26R	1959	1966/7	c
85-89	BDY 807/9/10/ 17/18	Sunbeam W	BTH	Weymann H30/26R	1959	1965-7	d

Notes:

a Rebodied by Roe H34/28R 1960

b Ex-Llanelli 39/40, new in 1945

c Ex-Brighton Corporation 51/52, new in 1947

d Ex-Hastings 32, 34, 35, 42, 43, new in 1947/48

Preserved vehicles: Nos 52, 56, 72, 86

were removed. During the transition period of the conversion programme, buses were gradually injected into the trolleybus services, and the final withdrawal came on 15 April 1967.

References

The Maidstone Trolleybus by D. J. S. Scotney (National Trolleybus Association), 1972.

'Maidstone Corporation's New Transport System', *Tramway & Railway World*, 12 May 1928.

Manchester

'Fine weather attended the official opening on 1 March of Manchester's first trolleybus services', according to the contemporary report in 1938. It needed to, for many storms had preceded the opening. 'The question as to whether Manchester should experiment with trolleybuses was discussed for some time before a decision was made', *Transport World* diplomatically explained. Replacement of the city's extensive tramway system by motorbuses had been proceeding for several years when in 1935 the City Council rejected the Transport Committee's proposal that tramcars on the Ashton Old Road services should be superseded by buses. Trolleybuses, their proponents argued, not only used home-produced fuel but were also *a la mode*. The Council therefore told the Committee to keep the trams going until the Corporation obtained powers to instal trolleybuses. This was done under the Corporation's Act of 1936, and the Council accordingly decided on the use of trolleybuses for Ashton Old Road, even though the Transport Committee still favoured motorbuses. Work was

had already in 1936 obtained powers to operate trolleybuses but was in fact never to do so.

With the new system satisfactorily in operation, proposals were announced early in 1939 for more conversions, involving the addition of another 77 trolleybuses. The next service to be taken over was a branch off the Ashton Old Road along Audenshaw Road to Guide Bridge, on which trolleybuses started on 16 October 1939. This service was extended on 22 March 1940 to Ashton, where it connected with the 'main line' again. On 6 April 1940 trolleybuses started service on the route to the University, and on 1 July 1940 between Guide Bridge and Denton, extended to Haughton Green on 9 December 1940.

Although World War 2 was now well under way, the system was still set for further expansion, even if not on the lines that had previously been envisaged. It had been antici-

therefore put in hand and tenders were invited for 43 trolleybuses.

In 1937, however, the Transport Committee recommended that it would make sense for the Ashton New Road tram services to be included in the conversion scheme, since their operation was closely linked with that of the Old Road. This was agreed, and orders were placed for an increased total of 76 trolleybuses, equally divided between six-wheelers and four-wheelers. Leyland supplied 10 four-wheelers and 28 six-wheelers, and Crossley 28 four-wheelers and 10 six-wheelers. All the bodies were supplied by Crossley to Manchester's 'streamlined' design, using Metropolitan-Cammell framing. The scheme also included a new depot in Rochdale Road, with accommodation for 115 vehicles, and this was opened on the same day as the new services. The trolleybuses ran to Ashton, where the Corporation already operated this mode of transport, and into the territory of the Stalybridge, Hyde, Mossley & Dukinfield Transport Board, which

Left:
Manchester: The newly-opened Rochdale Road depot in 1939, with an array of four-wheelers and six-wheelers. *Ian Allan Library*

Above right:
Manchester: Brand-new in 1940, No 1144 was one of a series of Crossley four-wheelers delivered between 1940 and 1943. *Ian Allan Library*

Right:
Manchester: Manchester's first postwar trolleybuses were of the Crossley 'Empire' type in 1949/50. No 1208 was photographed in course of delivery. *Ian Allan Library*

pated that the Hyde Road route would have been taken over on 3 September 1939 (the fateful day when the war began) but, although work had made progress and the SHMD Board was on the point of ordering a batch of Sunbeams, in fact it was to be more than 10 years before trolleybuses materialised on this route. Instead, new fields of conquest were found north of the city, where new arrivals of trolley vehicles were to take over from motorbuses to ease wartime fuel oil shortages.

First the wires were installed along Rochdale Road to Moston, to which point services started on 4 November 1940, followed early in the next year by a continuation along Moston Lane to Ben Brierley. A proposed extension from Moston to the Blackley estate, however, did not come into being. Next it was the turn of Oldham Road. Wires were strung along Oldham Road, to Newton Heath, then along Thorp Road and Kenyon Lane to join the Rochdale Road route at Ben Brierley, and continuing along Moston Lane to Nuthurst Road, to which point services started on 14 July 1941. Extension to Gardeners Arms was opened on 2 August 1941. Two years later, on 23 August 1943, a further short extension was brought into use to provide a peak-hour service to the A. V. Roe aircraft works at Chadderton (shown as 'Greengate' on the indicators) where both buses and trolley vehicles terminated at a private bus station. Traffic needs of the wartime expansion were met by the intake of Crossley and Leyland four-wheelers Nos 1100-1176.

While the Corporation had powers to operate trolleybuses on any former tramway, the outer sections of the Moston routes went beyond the old tram tracks, and since the Corporation did not therefore possess the necessary powers for this purpose, the new lines were installed under wartime emergency orders. This situation was

Above:
Manchester: The last new trolleybuses for Manchester were 62 Burlingham-bodied BUT 9612Ts, including No 1302 seen when new in 1955.
Ian Allan Library

not legalised until the Corporation's Act of 1946.

Postwar expansion development saw the extension in 1946 of the University route first to Moss Lane East on 14 January and then to Platt Lane (Greenheys) on 20 February. The major post-war expansion, and indeed the last new route, was the Hyde Road route, on which it had been planned to start trolleybus operation at the beginning of the war. A total of 54 Crossleys had been ordered for the purpose, but frustrated by delivery delays the Corporation took off the tramcars in 1948 and used motorbuses, until the new vehicles were available to enable them to begin their duties on 16 January 1950, a year after the city's last tramcars had been with-

Manchester

Fleet Nos	Registration Nos	Chassis	Electrical equipment	Body	In service	Withdrawn	Notes
1000-27	DXJ 951-78	Crossley TDD4	Metrovick	Crossley H28/26R	1938	1953-6	
1028-37	DXJ 979-88	Leyland TB4	Metrovick	Crossley H28/26R	1938	1951-5	
1050-61	DXJ989-93, ENB175-81	Crossley TDD6	Metrovick	Crossley H38/30R	1938	1950-6	
1062-87	ENB182-207	Leyland TTB4	Metrovick	Crossley H38/30R	1938	1950-6	
1100-36	GNA 18-54	Leyland TBS	Metrovick	E/Electric H28/26R	1940/1	1954-9	
1137-76	GNA 55-94	Crossley TDD4	Metrovick	Crossley H28/26R	1941-3	1953-6	
1200-37	JVU 707-44	Crossley TDD42/1 'Empire'	Metrovick	Crossley H32/26R	1949/50	1963	
1240-55	JVU 745-60	Crossley TDD64/1 'Dominion'	Metrovick	Crossley H36/30R	1951	1963	
1301-62	ONE 701-62	BUT 9612T	Metrovick	Burlingham H32/28R	1955/6	1962-6	

Preserved vehicles: Nos 1250, 1344

drawn. The route between Piccadilly and Hyde, Gee Cross, followed Hyde Road out of the city to Denton, where it crossed the Ashton-Haughton Green route, then continued in SHMD territory through Hyde to Gee Cross.

It was not long before the whole future of the system was under review. In 1952 it looked as though there could have been substantial expansion; a report by the general manager identified routes which could have gone over to trolleybuses, amounting to about one-third of the city's motorbus network. However, the economic advantage in favour of the trolleybus was only marginal. The report concluded that any extensions should be deferred, but that meanwhile 62 new vehicles should be obtained to maintain the existing routes. Accordingly, orders were placed in 1953 with BUT and the first of the newcomers appeared in 1955. These proved to be the city's last new trolleybuses, for only five years after the Hyde Road service had started, the first closures were under way.

On 24 April 1955 the last trolleybuses ran on the Rochdale Road route to Moston, followed on 7 August of the same year by the closure of the Oldham Road route to Gardeners Arms. Prompting the changeover was the imminent need for new vehicles and for the renewal of the overhead. Rebuilding in the city centre and the consequent need to alter the terminus hastened the closure of the Platt Lane route on 31 May 1959. Next to go, on 3 July 1960, was the out-of-town Haughton Green route; new housing development in the area would have demanded extensions of the wiring, so instead motorbuses were introduced.

Examining the remainder of the system, a 1961 report foresaw its complete cessation by 1967, thus keeping overhaul and renewal costs to the minimum. Moreover, Ashton (engaged in town-centre rebuilding which made overhead wiring an embarrassment) was urging an end to trolleybus operation. The end did indeed come by 1967. The Hyde Road services were withdrawn early in 1963, with the last trolleybuses to Gee Cross running on 28 April, after which only the BUTs remained on duty. The Guide Bridge route was withdrawn on 10 October 1964, leaving only the original two routes to Ashton. Manchester Corporation withdrew its workings from Ashton Old Road on 1 May 1966, although Ashton Corporation still continued to run some trolleybuses over the route. The final closure took place on 30 December 1966, when both Manchester and Ashton ended trolleybus operation, although on the following day two enthusiasts' specials (preserved Manchester No 1344 and Rotherham No 44) made a farewell tour.

The Manchester system suffered from its somewhat half-hearted beginnings. Though it grew to require the duties of some 150 vehicles, it never approached the size or extent of the tramcar fleet of more than 900 cars, since the official view favoured the flexibility of the motorbus. There was an absence of cross-city routes and a surfeit of scattered central-area termini, while the lack of interest in the trolleybus shown by neighbouring operators (with the exception of Ashton) with whom many Manchester routes were integrated, prevented the full development of a co-ordinated system, though in fact the joint working between Manchester and Ashton demonstrated what could have been achieved.

References
Manchester's Trolleybuses by D. M. Eyre, C. W. Heaps and C. Taylor (Manchester Transport Museum Society, 1967).
'First Trolleybuses in Manchester', *Transport World*, 10 March 1938.
'Trolleybus Extension in Manchester', *Modern Transport*, 25 February 1950.

Mexborough & Swinton

(See also map on page 126)
Already operating a tramway from Denaby, through the Yorkshire industrial towns of Mexborough and Swinton, and then into Rotherham over that corporation's tracks, the Mexborough & Swinton Tramways Co in 1912 sought powers to run trackless trolleys in order to supplement its tramcars. Five routes were

Below:
Mexborough & Swinton: Well loaded at Manvers Main, this AEC was put into service in 1922.
Ian Allan Library

Mexborough & Swinton

Fleet Nos	Registration Nos	Chassis	Electrical equipment	Body	In service	Withdrawn	Notes
21-3		Daimler/Brush	Brush	Brush B28R	1915	1922	
24		Daimler/Brush	Brush	Brush B28R	1917	1922	a
25/6	WY2743, 3059	AEC 603	Brush	Brush B36R	1922	1929	
31		AEC 603	Brush	Brush B36R	1924	1929	
34-9	WW4688-93	Garrett O	BTH	Garrett B32C	1928	1945-50	
40-8	WW7872-80	Garrett O	BTH	Garrett B32C	1928	1945-50	
49-60	WW8790-8801	Garrett O	BTH	Garrett B32C	1929	1945-50	
61-3	WX4440-2	Garrett O	BTH	Garrett B32C	1930	1945-50	
64-9	RB5568-73	E/Electric	E/Electric	E/Electric B32F	1937	1945-50	b
70-5	DY5118/31, 5640, 5579/80	Guy BTX	Rees-Stevens	Ransomes B32C	1942	1945	c
1-6	EWT 478-80, 513-5	Sunbeam W	BTH	Brush B32C	1943	1954	d
7-24	FWX 891-908	Sunbeam W	BTH	Brush B32C	1947	1960	
25-36	FWX 909-20	Sunbeam F4	BTH	Brush B32C	1947/8	1961	e
37-9	JWW 375-7	Sunbeam F4	BTH	Brush B32C	1950	1961	e

Notes:

a Ex-Stockport

b Ex-Notts & Derby Nos 300-5

c Ex-Hastings Nos 16, 29, 47, 48, 52 and 53. Only Nos 71, 74
and 75 ran in service

d Sold to Doncaster 1954

e Nos 25-33 and 35-7 sold to Bradford; Nos 38 and 39 sold to
Teesside

---

envisaged: from the Woodman Inn on the tramway at Swinton, to Wath-upon-Dearne; from Wath to West Melton; from Wath to Goldthorpe; from the tram terminus at the Old Toll Bar at Denaby to Conisbrough; and from Mexborough to the colliery at Manvers Main. Because of opposition from local councils (who entertained thoughts of building their own tramway or trackless system) the Mexborough & Swinton Tramways Railless Electric Traction Act of 1913 bestowed powers for only the last two of the five proposed routes.

These two routes were opened on 31 August 1915. There was no physical connection between them; the Manvers Main route ran from the tramway at Mexborough, along Wath Road for just over a mile to the colliery, while the Conisbrough route extended from the Old Toll Bar tram terminus, along the Doncaster Road to Station Road and The Dale at Conisbrough, a distance of nearly 2 miles. A depot was built at Old Toll Bar to house the trolley vehicles, together with a few trams. To reach the Manvers Main route, trolleybuses had to use a skate along the tram tracks, and a similar procedure appled when they were required to go for repairs at the main depot at Rawmarsh. Thus began the first company-operated trolleybus system in Britain.

To work the services the company obtained

three single-deck Daimlers with 28-seat bodies by Brush (Nos 21-3). To these was later added a secondhand purchase from Stockport, to become No 24. This had originally worked on the 'Bremen' overhead-wire system, and it had to be converted by its new owners to conform to more conventional overhead. Because of low bridges, the company's trolley vehicles were always to be confined to single-deckers; in fact the road under a bridge at Manvers Main had to be lowered before even single-deckers could negotiate it.

Wartime traffic to and from the collieries made heavy demands on the services, but shortage of staff and problems in obtaining spares eventually led to the complete suspension of service on both routes. Even after the war, operation remained spasmodic. Trolley vehicles resumed on the Manvers Main route at the end of 1919 but disappeared again after a few months, while the Conisbrough service ran for a few weeks early in 1921 before the vehicles were transferred to Manvers Main, and Conisbrough did not see them again until April 1922. In 1922 the small fleet was strengthened by the coming of Nos 25 and 26, AECs with Brush bodies with the luxury of upholstered seats, followed by another similar vehicle in 1924.

The company started its first motorbus route in 1922, but it still had visions that its own tramways might eventually link with the Doncaster system, as well as with the newly-constructed Dearne District Light Railways which were opened in 1924. Such a scheme would have involved converting the existing trolleybus routes to tramways. However, when such prospects began to fade, the company sought powers to replace its tramways by trolleybuses. Rotherham Corporation, although itself a trolleybus operator since 1912, objected at first to the idea of the company's vehicles coming into its territory, but in 1926 agreement was reached whereby Rotherham would convert its section of tramway to enable the company's vehicles to enter the town, while Rotherham's trolleybuses would be permitted to run through to Mexborough termini. The company's Act was consequently passed in 1927.

In addition to replacing the tramway, trolley buses were also to be extended at the Conisbrough end along Low Road to Brook Square ('Conisbrough Low') where they could meet the Doncaster wires if they ever got that far, and also beyond the original Dale Road terminus and up the hill to a new housing estate at Conanby ('Conisbrough High'). Talks had also been taking place with the Dearne District Light Railways on the construction of a route from Manvers Main to Bolton.

To enable the overhead to be renewed in preparation for the extensions, trolleybuses were withdrawn from Conisbrough on 1 January 1928. Two months later, work was so far advanced that a Doncaster double-decker was able to make a trial run over the two new routes, perhaps reviving visions of the anticipated through service to Doncaster. Linking the formerly separate routes for the first time, the company introduced new services between Manvers Main and Conisbrough Low and between Mexborough and Conisbrough High.

The section of tramway between Mexborough and the Woodman Inn at Swinton was next converted and, after the Ministry of Transport inspection on 9 November 1928, by 11 November the trolleybus services were running between Swinton and Conisbrough Low and between Manvers Main and Conisbrough High. On the final section of tramway between Swinton and the boundary with Rotherham, the company's cars ceased on 9 March 1929, and on the following day the through trolleybus service was inaugurated between Rotherham and Conisbrough Low. A short terminal branch in Kilnhurst Road allowed for short workings to Ryecroft. To operate its new services, the company (which in 1929 changed its name to the Mexborough & Swinton Traction Co) brought in a fleet of central-entrance Garretts.

In February 1931 a new turning circle was

Below left:
Mexborough & Swinton: A new delivery of O-type Garretts parades outside the depot in 1929.
Ian Allan Library

Below:
Mexborough & Swinton: Postwar re-equipment was with a fleet of Brush-bodied Sunbeams. No 18 arrived in 1947. *Ian Allan Library*

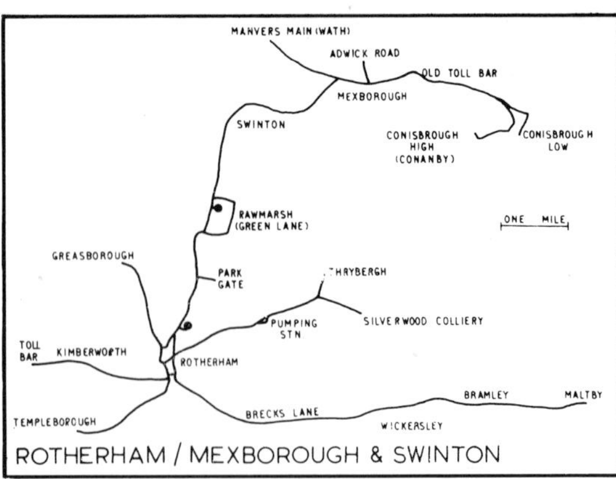

ROTHERHAM / MEXBOROUGH & SWINTON

Above:
Mexborough & Swinton: Joint working: standing at the Rotherham terminus in 1950 on joint service to Mexborough, Rotherham Corporation No 28 is followed by a Mexborough & Swinton Brush-bodied Sunbeam. *C. Carter*

installed at Conisbrough High in place of the original loop around the Crescent, while on 28 June of the same year an extension was opened along Adwick Road, Mexborough, as an intended first step towards a northward expansion. On 28 February 1932 trolleybuses began to use the newly-built road at Warren Vale in place of the old narrow and hilly road. The last extension to the company's system was opened on 15 October 1934; this was a loop from the main route at Rawmarsh, along Green Lane to join the Kilnhurst Road branch. Although so near to Rotherham and served from the town centre, service round the loop was provided by company vehicles.

In 1937, six English Electric vehicles of 1930 vintage were purchased from the Notts & Derby Traction Co, while during the war another six single-deckers were bought from Hastings Tramways. In 1943 came six new vehicles in the shape of Sunbeams with Brush utility bodies, and when the war ended these were the first to be attired in the new green livery. Postwar renewal was by 33 Brush-bodied Sunbeams of generally similar design to the wartime examples though with more rounded outlines. Delivered between 1947 and 1950, they enabled the veteran Garretts which had given such sterling service to be retired. A new section of wiring to permit one-way operation in the narrow roads around Conisbrough Castle was brought into use in 1948, but a proposed ½-mile extension of the Adwick Road branch to the Windhill estate was never installed.

The first contraction in the system came when the Green Lane loop went over to buses on 27 September 1954. With the further development of bus services to serve growing areas beyond the wires, and the desirability of co-ordinating all services, the company obtained powers in 1960 to discontinue trolleybus operation entirely. On 1 January 1961 trolleybuses ceased on the Manvers Main-Conisbrough High route, and on 26 March 1961 the last public services ran on the Rotherham-Conisbrough Low route. The replacement 72-seat double-deck Atlanteans, in contrast to the 35-seat single-deck trolleybuses, emphasised the economics of the changeover. A ceremonial closure procession of four trolleybuses (including one with the top removed and carrying a brass band) took place on the day after public service ceased and marked the end of the last company-operated trolleybus system in Britain.

References
54 Years of Public Service 1907-1961 — Mexborough & Swinton Traction Co, 1961.
'British Bus & Tram Systems No 33: The Mexborough & Swinton Traction Company' by C. C. Hall; *Buses Illustrated* November and December 1961, January 1962.
'A History of the Barnsley, Dearne, Mexborough and Rotherham Tramway Conurbation' by C. C. Hall; *Tramway Review*, No 51-58, 1967-9.

Newcastle upon Tyne

Newcastle came near to introducing trolley vehicles as early as 1912, for powers to operate such a form of transport were sought in the Corporation's Bill of 1911. However, the cost of road maintenance on the suburban highways where it was proposed to run, led to the plans being dropped, and instead the Corporation opted for petrol-electric buses. In the event, it was 1934/5 before Newcastle obtained powers to operate trolleybuses in place of its tramways, following the decision that, when tracks became worn out, consideration should be given to replacing tramcars by another form of transport. Then things moved rapidly and the city's first trolleybuses started service on 1 October 1935.

The route was a cross-city one, about 9½ miles in length, from Denton Burn to Wallsend. For most of the distance it followed the tramway it superseded, but at the western end it continued beyond the old tram terminus along West Road to Denton Burn, with an extensive loop via Whickham View and Fox & Hounds Lane. In the city centre, a loop was provided via St Nicholas Street for terminal workings from either direction. Traffic was varied, from workmen's services to and from the Wallsend shipyards, to business services to and from the residential western suburbs.

The initial fleet included 30 vehicles of varying types; of the chassis, all six-wheelers, 10 each were supplied by AEC (Nos 10-19), Guy (Nos 30-39) and Karrier (Nos 20-29), while 20 of the bodies came from Metropolitan-Cammell and five each from English Electric and Brush. The bodies were of a standard design, with a seating capacity of 60. They featured a rear

Above:
Newcastle upon Tyne: Included among the city's first trolleybuses in 1935 was No 38, a Guy BTX with Metropolitan-Cammell-Weymann body of the standard forward-exit design adopted for the Newcastle fleet. *Ian Allan Library*

entrance, with a forward exit with air-operated folding door, and two stairways. For years, a rear entrance and front exit system had been in use on the Corporation's tramcars. An attractive new livery of yellow with brown waistband was adopted.

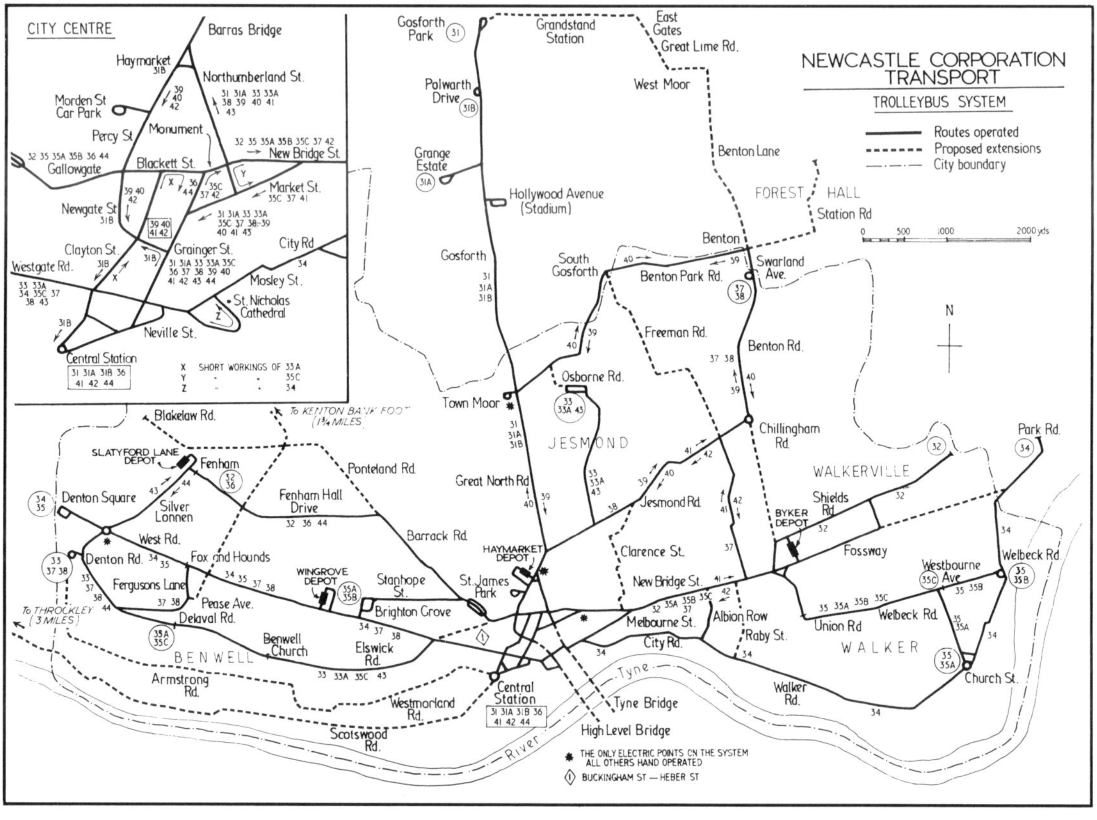

A further six vehicles (Nos 41-46) were added in 1936, and by 1937 *Transport World* was able to report that 'the new system has been remarkably successful, and traffic has increased to a very gratifying extent'. Indeed, at times motorbuses had had to be pressed into service to augment the trolley vehicles.

In 1937 came 32 additional members of the fleet, together with the next stage of the programme, when on 19 September trolley-buses took over another cross-city tram route, between Brighton Grove and Walker via Stanhope Street. The year 1938 saw further substantial expansion. On 24 April the original Denton Burn route was extended to the city boundary at Denton Square, and then on 1 August conversion took place on the route from Central Station to Fenham, Netherley Drive. On 2 September it was the turn of the route to Osborne Road and to Wallsend boundary. Another 32 vehicles were taken into stock to serve the new needs, and by this time the fleet had reached the 100 mark.

Nor was it intended that this should be the limit. In 1939 the Transport Committee was proposing that the remaining tram routes (with the exception of the private right-of-way through Gosforth Park) should be converted to trolleybus operation, but the intervention of World War 2 brought a necessary postponement. While much of the plan materialised later, proposals which did not come into being included lines in Two Ball Lonnen and along the former sleeper-track tramway to Westerhope. At the time it was also envisaged that trolleybuses would cross the Tyne into Gateshead, where the Gateshead & District Tramways Co was preparing for the conversion of its own tram routes.

Nevertheless wartime conditions did not

Newcastle upon Tyne

Fleet Nos	Registration Nos	Chassis	Electrical equipment	Body	In service	Withdrawn	Notes
10-14	BVK 800-4	AEC 664T	E/Electric	E/Electric H33/27D	1935	1949/50	
15-19	BVK 805-9	AEC 664T	E/Electric	Brush H33/27D	1935	1948-50	
20-29	BVK 810-9	Karrier E6A	Metrovick	MCCW H33/27D	1935	1949/50	
30-39	BVK 820-9	Guy BTX	BTH	MCCW H33/27D	1935	1949	
40-43	CVK 52, DTN 141-3	Karrier E6A	Metrovick	MCCW H33/27D	1936	1949/50	
44-46	DTN 144-6	Guy BTX	BTH-E/Electric	MCCW H33/27D	1936	1949	
47-56	ETN 47-56	Karrier E6A	Metrovick	MCCW H33/27D	1937	1949	
57-66	ETN 57-66	Guy BTX	BTH-E/Electric	MCCW H33/27D	1937	1948/9	
67-77	ETN 67-77	AEC 664T	E/Electric	MCCW H33/27D	1937	1949/50	
78	FBB 78	Guy BTX	BTH-E/Electric	Roe H34/26D	1938	1949	
79-84	FVK 79-84	AEC664T	E/Electric	Roe H34/26D	1938	1950	
85-98	FVK 85-98	Karrier E6A	Metrovick	MCCW H33/27D	1938	1949	
99-108	FVK 99-108	Guy BTX	BTH-E/Electric	MCCW H33/27D	1938	1949	
109	FVK 109	Guy BTX	BTH-E/Electric	NCB H33/27D	1938	1949	
112	DHP 112	Daimler CTM6	Metrovick	MCCW H33/27D	1938	1950	
113-8	HVK 113-8	Karrier E6A	Metrovick	Roe H34/26D	1939/40	1950	
119-24	HVK 119-24	Karrier E6A	Metrovick	MCCW H33/27D	1940	1950	
1-9, 0	KW9461/3/53-5, 6063, 9460, 6656/5, 9464	E/Electric E11	E/Electric D/Kerr	E/Electric H30/26R	1943	1948	a
125	JTN 955	Karrier W4	Metrovick	E/Electric H30/26R	1944	1953	
126-36	JTN 956-66	Karrier W4	Metrovick	P/Royal UH30/26R	1944	1953/6	
137/8	JVK 277/8	Karrier W4	Metrovick	Weymann UH30/26R	1945	1953	
139-42	JVK 279-82	Karrier W4	Metrovick	P/Royal UH30/26R	1945	1953	
(In 1946, Nos 10-142 renumbered 310-442)							
443-78	LBB 43-78	Sunbeam F4	Metrovick	MCCW H30/26R	1948/9	1961-3	
479-98	LTN 479-98	BUT 9641T	E/Electric	MCCW H40/30R	1948/9	1964/5	
499-528	LTG 499-528	Sunbeam S7	Metrovick	NCB H39/31R	1948/9	1963-5	
529-53	LTN 529-53	Sunbeam F4	Metrovick	NCB H30/26R	1949/50	1963/4	
554-78	LTN 554-78	BUT 9611T	E/Electric	NCB H30/26R	1949	1964	
579-628	NBB 579-628	BUT 9641T	E/Electric	MCCW H40/30R	1950	1965/6	

Note:

a Ex-Bradford No 9 had Park Royal body. Nos 6, 8, 9 and 0 did not enter service

Preserved vehicles: Nos 501, 628

Above:
Newcastle upon Tyne: Postwar deliveries included this line of Metropolitan-Cammell-bodied BUTs in 1948. Similar vehicles went to London and Glasgow.
Ian Allan Library

prevent the extension of the Fenham route from Netherby Drive to Springfield Gardens on 23 November 1941 to serve new housing development. Heavy wartime traffic demands on the system resulted in the purchase of 10 English Electric four-wheelers from Bradford, as well as the hire of four AECs from Brighton and nine Sunbeam six-wheelers from Bournemouth. In 1943, 12 Park Royal-bodied Karriers (Nos 125-136) entered service as the first of the Corporation's own four-wheelers. Another nine Karriers (Nos 137-142) were acquired to inaugurate operation in place of tramcars on the Elswick Road route on 11 June 1944; the wires were extended beyond the erstwhile tram terminus at Benwell to connect with the Benton loop.

Complete renewal of the fleet took place between 1948 and 1950 with the introduction of a total of 186 new vehicles. These came from Sunbeam and British United Traction and comprised both four-wheelers and six-wheelers, with bodywork by Metropolitan-Cammell and Northern Coachbuilders, a notable feature being the absence of the forward exit which had characterised the prewar design. At the same time further conquests were being made: along the Great North Road to Gosforth Park on 18 April 1948, then on 1 November 1948 along Jesmond Dene Road and Benton Park Road, which had never been served by tramcars, to provide new circular services. A short branch followed on 28 October 1951 from the Gosforth Park route to serve Grange Estate. The last extension to the system was made in 1956, when wires were installed along Silver Lonnen to connect the Fenham and Denton routes, and to provide access to the new Slatyford depot which was opened on 10 July 1956; the service started on 21 October.

The Corporation's last tram route — along Scotswood Road — was taken over in 1949 by motorbuses rather than trolleybuses. Tramcars of Gateshead & District continued to work into Newcastle until 1951; an earlier plan had envisaged that these would be replaced by trolleybuses. The Gateshead & District company, with which Newcastle Corporation operated several joint tram services, had obtained powers in 1938 to operate trolleybuses in replacement of its trams, but war came in 1939 before the changeover could be effected. After the war, altered circumstances (including the possible purchase of the undertaking by Gateshead Corporation or its nationalisation in the proposed Area Scheme under the 1948 Transport Act) led the company to relinquish its trolleybus powers under its 1950 Act, whereby instead it obtained powers to adopt motorbuses to supersede the tramcars, the last of which ran in 1951. Had the original scheme gone ahead, trolleybuses would have crossed the Tyne to serve the Gateshead termini of Heworth, Wrekenton, Low Fell, Saltwell Park, Bensham and Dunston, and indeed so imminent did the conversion appear even after the war, that Newcastle's new trolleybuses included Gateshead destinations on their indicator blinds.

The Newcastle system was not long to remain at its zenith, for in 1963 it was announced that abandonment was to take place by 1968. The trolleybus, it was claimed, was less mobile than the motorbus, and moreover was costing something above 6d more per vehicle-mile to run. Its fixed wiring was further alleged to cause difficulties with the reconstruction of the central area road layout.

The closure took place in four stages. The first involved the long-established Denton-Walker-Wallsend route, on which the last trolleybuses ran on 2 June 1963; this, the only route to reach Wallsend, had been the first trolleybus route of 1935. Its choice as the first candidate for closure was influenced by the work of road reconstruction being carried out at the junction of City Road and Pilgrim Street. The second stage of the changeover covered the more recently completed routes to Gosforth Park as well as the South Gosforth and Benton circulars, and these were operated by trolleybuses for the last time on 1 February 1964, after which they were replaced by revised motorbus routes.

The third stage saw the last trolleybuses run on 29 May 1965 to Fenham, Osborne Road and Wallsend boundary, as well as on the Jesmond Road and Heaton Road circular services. It also marked the end of trolleybus operation from Slatyford depot, the remaining 38 vehicles then being concentrated at Byker depot. The final day of trolleybus operation was 1 October 1966, when the last routes serving Denton, Elswick Road, Brighton Grove and Walker made their last runs and ended without official ceremony.

References
The Trolleybuses of Newcastle upon Tyne by T. P. Canneaux and N. H. Hanson (Trolleybooks 1974).
'Newcastle Trolleybuses' (*Buses Illustrated*, November 1965, January 1966, May 1966).
'Newcastle Trolleybus Installation' — *Transport World* 10 October 1935.

Nottingham

Nottingham's first powers to operate trolleybuses were sought in the Corporation's 1913 Bill, which in addition to tramway extensions and motorbus routes, proposed a trolley vehicle route from the Market Place via Arkwright Street to Trent Bridge, and thence to West Bridgford. The Urban District Council of West Bridgford objected to this latter part, but powers were granted for a route between the Market Place and Trent Bridge. Powers were also obtained to seek Provisional Orders for the operation of trolleybuses on any of the existing tram routes as required.

Early in 1924, following an official visit to

Top:
Nottingham: New in 1930 was No 18, a product of Ransomes, Sims & Jefferies. *Ian Allan Library*

Above:
Nottingham: No 27 was the prototype Karrier-Clough of 1930 with Park Royal body, forerunner of a batch of modified design purchased in 1931/2.
Ian Allan Library

Below:
Nottingham: The modified design adopted for the Karrier-Clough E6 is exemplified by No 25, photographed in 1932. *Ian Allan Library*

Above:
Nottingham: Seen at Wollaton Park in the summer of 1932, No 44 was a Brush-bodied Ransomes.
Ian Allan Library

Birmingham to look at the trolleybus installation in that city, it was recommended that this new mode of transport should be introduced in place of the single-track tramway routes in Nottingham, and a Provisional Order was obtained for the conversion of the sections in Nottingham Road, Wilford Road and St Anne's Well Road. In 1925 the Corporation's Act gave powers to operate trolleybuses on Nottingham Road, and an order was placed with Railless for 10 double-deckers with Short bodies.

The new service was inaugurated on 10 April 1927. The route was about 2½ miles in length and ran from a city terminus, comprising a loop around King Street, Queen Street and Upper Parliament Street, along Nottingham Road to New Basford, where it met the Bulwell tram route at Vernon Road. 'Generally speaking, the route is well populated', according to a contemporary report, while 'the vehicles represent all that is up to date and efficient in railless traction'. Railless Nos 1-10 were each powered by two 35hp English Electric motors, and their open-stair double-deck Short bodies seated 26 on each deck. The success of the new venture was such that further vehicles were needed, and these were ordered from Ransomes, Sims & Jefferies.

In 1929 orders were given for six trolleybuses each from English Electric and Ransomes, Sims & Jefferies in order to take over the tramway between Wilford Road and St Anne's Well Road, and this new 3-mile route was inaugurated on 23 February 1930. A short extension was made beyond the former tram terminus at St Anne's Well Road, along the Wells Road to Kildare Road. The process of conversion now seemed to be getting well under way, and with the object of deciding the most suitable types to be used in further changeovers, in 1931 four different vehicles were hired: from AEC, Guy, Karrier and Thornycroft. The Karrier was the one chosen, but while the first batch of Karrier E6s made their debut in 1931/2 and were followed by others in 1934, they shared honours with additional Ransomes vehicles.

An extensive network was envisaged in the Corporation's 1930 Bill, which proposed not only the conversion of the remaining tramways, but considerable extensions to be served by trolley vehicles. These included a connection between the Carlton and Mapperley termini, as well as a continuation beyond Mapperley to

109

Spring Lane and Mansfield Road; a connection between the Carlton and Mapperley routes via Thornywood Lane and Porchester Road; an extension of the Bulwell route to Bulwell Hall Estate; and new routes to Attenborough and Beeston. However, the routes which would have gone beyond the city boundary were struck out of the Bill, following opposition by Nottinghamshire County Council and Trent Motor Traction.

The introduction of further trolleybus services took place in succeeding years:

29 November 1931 — Wollaton Park (taking over from motorbuses on Ilkeston Road).
20 March 1932 — Carlton (with service linked with Wollaton Park).
25 July 1933 — Cinderhill-Nottingham Road.
5 October 1933 — The trolleybuses of the Notts & Derby Traction Co started running into Nottingham over the Cinderhill-Nottingham section.

The company's trolleybuses followed the route along Nottingham Road and Mansfield Road, instead of the former tram route along Radford Road and Alfreton Road. From 10 October 1933 the Corporation also operated a part-day service to Cinderhill, but generally the Valley Road-Cinderhill section remained a company preserve. There were proposals for a joint Corporation/company service extending beyond the boundary to Kimberley, but this did not materialise.

13 May 1934 — Bulwell and Bulwell Hall Estate; Arkwright Street to Trent Bridge.
2 June 1935 — Colwick Road, London Road-Trent Bridge.

This latter proved to be the last extension to the system. In 1936 the two remaining tram routes — to Mapperley and Arnold — were replaced by motorbuses, following opposition by residents and the rejection of the Bill seeking powers to run trolleybuses. 'The majority of the public have expressed desire for speed; in Nottingham the motor omnibus meets that desire', the General Manager explained. 'When the trolleybus programme was drawn up, the heavy-oil vehicle was nowhere near its present stage of perfection, and accurate comparisons were not possible.' As early as 1938 it was being recommended that the trolleybuses should be abandoned, but the question was deferred until the following year. Early in 1939 an increase in the price of electricity prompted further consideration of a possible changeover, but again this was postponed.

Above:

Nottingham: Hauled by a Fordson tractor on the way to enter service in 1934 is No 87, a later Ransomes with Brush body. *Ian Allan Library*

Below:

Nottingham: On test just after delivery in 1935 is MCW-bodied Leyland No 132. *Ian Allan Library*

In 1939 the fleet was renumbered by having 300 added to the original numbers, and in 1940 trolley wheels were replaced by skids to eliminate flashing during the wartime blackout. Increased traffic during the war called for additional vehicles, and these included visitors from other systems: four AECs from Cleethorpes (Nos 437-40 in their new home), two English Electrics from Southend (Nos 302 and 303), six single-deck Guys from Hastings, and No 441, a Daimler demonstrator which had been operating in Hull. The first utility-bodied trolleybuses arrived in 1942 in the shape of Weymann-bodied Sunbeams Nos 447-51; originally intended for service in South Africa, but frustrated in their departure because of the war, they were the first 8ft-wide vehicles in the fleet. They were followed by further utility models between 1943 and 1945.

Plans for extensions were under consideration in 1943, during the wartime period when oil shortages emphasised the value of electric-powered transport. The Corporation was proposing an extension of the Carlton route for more than a mile to provide a circle around Main Street, Burton Road, Conroy Road and Station Road, to Post Office Square. Powers were also being sought for an extension to Wollaton, but since this would have involved joint operation with the companies, the plan did not materialise. Following this, the Notts & Derby company made application for powers to introduce a route through Wollaton, to connect its Ilkeston routes with its Nottingham route and running under Corporation wires between Middleton Boulevard and the city, but these proposals were withdrawn after objection by the Corporation. The subject arose again in 1947, when both the Corporation and the company sought powers for a route to Wollaton; but each opposed the other, and in the event neither scheme reached fruition.

Postwar fleet renewals included the arrival in 1949 of the first 70-seat Brush-bodied BUT six-wheelers, the first new six-wheelers to be taken into stock since the mid-1930s and the largest-capacity vehicles so far in service.

Nottingham

Fleet Nos	Registration Nos	Chassis	Electrical equipment	Body	In service	Withdrawn	Notes
1-10	TO 5002-11	Railless	E/Electric	Short H26/26ROS	1927	1934/5	a
11, 12	TO 8621/2	RS&J D6	RS&J/BTH	RS&J H26/26R	1928	1936	
13-18	TV 743-8	RS&J D6	RS&J/BTH	RS&J H32/28R	1930	1946	
19-24	TV 749-54	AEC/E/Electric	E/Electric	E/Electric H30/26R	1930	1946	
25-36	TV 4463-74	Karrier-Clough E6	BTH	P/Royal H30/30R	1932	By 1950	b
37-49	TV 4475-87	RS&J D6	RS&J/BTH	Brush H32/28R	1932	By 1950	
50		Karrier-Clough	BTH	P/Royal H30/26R	1930	By 1952	c
1	TV 8473	Karrier E6A	BTH	Brush H30/26R	1933	By 1952	d
51-60	TV 9313/5/2/0/1/6/ 7/4/08/09	Karrier E6	E/Electric	M/Cammell H34/30R	1934	By 1952	
61-85	TV 9327-33/18-26	Karrier E6	E/Electric	Brush H34/30R	1934	By 1952	
86-106	TV 9343-63	RS&J D6	RS&J/BTH	Brush H34/30R	1934	By 1952	
107-36	ATV 170-99	Leyland TTB4	GEC	MCW H34/30R	1935	By 1952	

(In 1939 fleet renumbered by adding 300 to original numbers)

Fleet Nos	Registration Nos	Chassis	Electrical equipment	Body	In service	Withdrawn	Notes
437-40	FW 8995, AFU 153-5	AEC 661T	E/Electric	P/Royal H30/26R	1940	1952	e
302/3	JN 60/1	E/Electric	E/Electric	E/Electric H30/26R	1940	By 1952	f
441	GTO 741	Daimler CTM4	Metrovick	Weymann H28/26R	1941	1952	g
304-9	DY 5111/20/1/6, 5483, 5578	Guy BTX	Rees-Stevens	RS&J B32C	1941	1946	h
442-5	GTV 42-5	Karrier W	E/Electric	Weymann UH30/26R	1943/4	1960/2	
447-51	GTV 47-51	Sunbeam MF2	BTH	Weymann UH30/26R	1942	1957/8	
452-4	GTV-652-4	Karrier W	E/Electric	P/Royal UH30/26R	1944	1957-62	
455-8	GTV 655-8	Karrier W	E/Electric	Weymann UH30/26R	1944	1960	
459-65	GTV 659-65	Karrier W	E/Electric	Roe UH30/26R	1945	1962-5	
466-8	GTV 666-8	Karrier W	E/Electric	Brush UH30/26R	1945	1962-5	
469-78	HAU 169-78	Karrier W	BTH	P/Royal H30/26R	1946	1962-5	
479-82	KTV 479-82	Karrier W	BTH	Roe H30/26R	1948	1965	
483-95	KTV 483-95	BUT 9611T	E/Electric	Roe H30/26R	1948	1963-5	
500-24	KTV 500-24	BUT 9641T	E/Electric	Brush H38/32R	1949/50	1965/66	i
525-601	KTV 525-601	BUT 9641T	Note j	Brush H38/32R	1951/2	1965/6	j

Notes:

a After accident, No 9 replaced by Karrier E6 chassis with Brush body ex-Thornycroft demonstrator No 28 and this became No 1 in 1933 (TV 8473)

b The first Nos 25-28 in 1930 were demonstrators by AEC, Guy, Karrier-Clough and Thornycroft respectively; Nos 25 and 26 and chassis of No 28 were returned to makers, No 27 was taken into stock as No 50

c Ex-demonstrator No 27

d See Note a

e Ex-Cleethorpes Nos 59, 60-62

f Ex-Southend-on-Sea Nos 110 and 111

g Demonstrator of 1938, intended for Kingston-upon-Hull

h Ex-Hastings Nos 9, 18, 19, 24, 40 and 51

i 8ft wide

j 7ft 6in wide. Nos 525-34, 565-71 equipped by Crompton-Parkinson; Nos 535-64, 587-601 by Metrovick; Nos 572-86 by English Electric

Preserved vehicles: Nos 466, 493, 502, 506, 578

Above:
Nottingham: A 1940 photograph of No 439, one of four Park Royal-bodied AEC 661Ts just purchased from Cleethorpes Corporation and the only AEC trolleybuses in the Nottingham fleet.
Ian Allan Library

Further deliveries enabled the last prewar trolleybuses to be withdrawn by 1952, in which year the last new trolleybuses entered service. At its maximum size the fleet numbered 155 vehicles.

The first contraction of the network came when the Notts & Derby company's trolleybuses on the Nottingham-Ripley route were withdrawn on 25 April 1953. Following this, the Corporation's services along Nottingham Road were re-organised to cover the former company service between Cinderhill and the city. Abandonment of the Corporation's system was decided in 1961, when it was expected that the process would be complete by 1968. The first stage of conversion was the replacement of the 45 service between Trent Bridge and Wollaton Park, via London Road and Derby Road, by buses after 3 November 1962.

Replanning of the city centre stimulated an acceleration of the programme, and practically the whole of the remainder of the system ceased operation during 1965. Service 43 between Trent Bridge and Bulwell Market was converted to buses on 1 April and Trent Bridge depot was closed, followed on 1 May by service 41 (Cinderhill and Trent Bridge), marking the end of the former Notts & Derby route as well as the last service to Trent Bridge. Then on 1 June, service 44 between Bulwell Hall Estate and Colwick Road went over to buses. Service 39 (Wollaton Park and Carlton) was withdrawn on 30 September, and services 40 and 47 (Wilford Bridge, Kildare Road and Ransome Road) on 9 October. The final day of operation was 30 June 1966, when the last trolleybus ran over the original 1927 route along Nottingham Road. An official closure ceremony took place on the following day.

References
A History of Nottingham City Transport 1897-1959 by R. Marshall (Nottingham City Transport 1960).
'British Bus & Tram Systems — No 20: Nottingham City Transport' by J. Wyndham (*Buses Illustrated* No 34, November-December 1957).
Nottingham's Trolleybus System by C. F. Riley (Omnibus Society 1966).

Notts & Derby

The trolleybus system of the Nottinghamshire & Derbyshire Traction Co was one of the most intriguing 'might have beens' in the history of this mode of transport. If the trolleybuses had

Top:
Notts & Derby: An impressive line-up outside the depot in 1932 of new arrivals Nos 306-315, AEC 662Ts with English Electric bodies. *Ian Allan Library*

Above:
Notts & Derby: The first double-deckers in the Notts & Derby fleet were Nos 317-331, AEC 661Ts with MCCW bodies complete with bonnet and radiator. They were delivered in 1933. *Ian Allan Library*

inherited the whole of the 80-mile tramway network originally envisaged, and if they had materialised on other routes proposed later, this would have been one of the great empires of the trolley vehicle. Nevertheless, the system as it came into being was by no means negligible; it joined up two former unconnected tramways, its total route mileage of over 22 miles put it in the ranks of the larger British undertakings, and its principal route was one of the longest and fastest.

In 1913 the Nottinghamshire & Derbyshire Tramways Co's tramway from Cinderhill, in the suburbs of Nottingham, was completed to the town of Ripley in Derbyshire, a distance of some 11 miles. At Cinderhill the company's tracks met those of Nottingham Corporation and company cars ran the further three miles into the centre of Nottingham. In 1916/17 the company took over the Ilkeston Corporation tramways, though there was no physical connection with the Nottingham-Ripley route. In 1928 the company obtained powers to abandon the tramways and to operate trolleybuses, not only over the tram routes but also on roads between Ilkeston and Heanor, thus connecting the two separate systems. At the same time it changed its name to the Nottinghamshire & Derbyshire Traction Co.

In 1931 the company replaced the Ilkeston tramways by motorbuses, until on 7 January 1932 the first trolleybuses were put on between Cotmanhay and Hallam Fields. On 1 August 1932 the trolleybuses were extended via Shipley to Heanor, including also a new route bypassing Cotmanhay, and then on to Loscoe and Ripley in replacement of trams on this part of

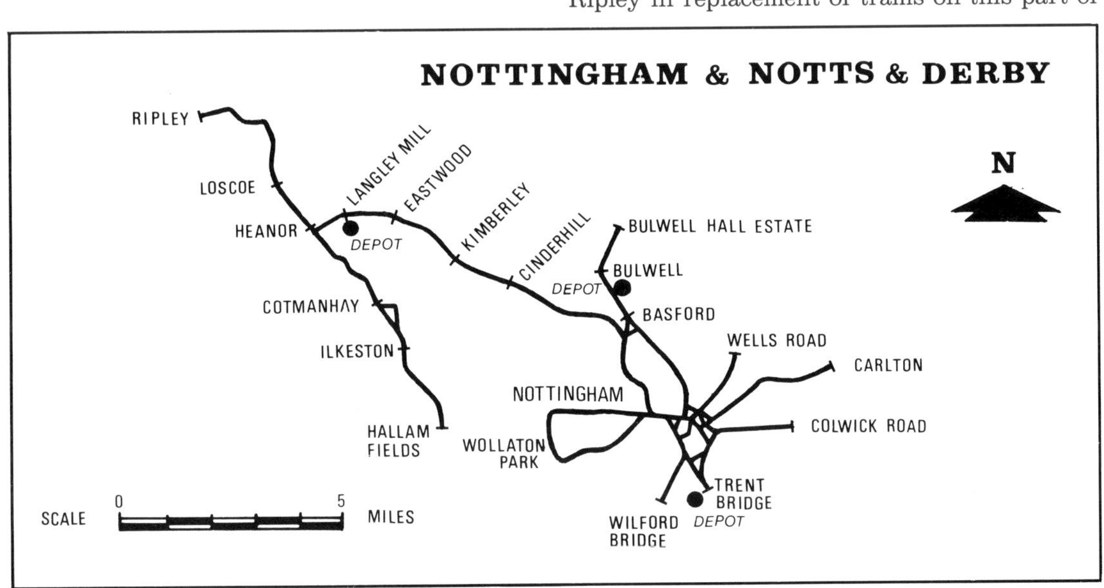

Notts & Derby

Fleet Nos	Registration Nos	Chassis	Electrical equipment	Body	In service	Withdrawn	Notes
300-5	RB 5568-73	E/Electric	E/Electric	E/Electric B32F	1932	1937	a
306-15	RB 6613-22	AEC 662T	E/Electric	E/Electric B32F	1932	1949	
316	UK 9601	Guy BT32	E/Electric	Guy B32F	1932	1949	b
317-31	RB 8951-65	AEC 661T	E/Electric	MCCW H31/24R	1933	1949	
300-5/32	ORB 616-22	AEC 661T	E/Electric	Weymann H30/26R	1937	1953	c
333-7	HNU 826-30	AEC 661T	E/Electric	Weymann H30/26R	1941	1953	c
338-42	HNU 970-4	AEC 661T	E/Electric	Weymann H30/26R	1942	1953	c
343-57	NNU 224-38	BUT 9611T	E/Electric	Weymann H30/26R	1949	1953	c

Notes:

a Sold to Mexborough & Swinton as Nos 64-69

b Ex-Guy demonstrator of 1930

c Nos 300-5, 332-57 sold to Bradford as Nos 580-96 and
760-74 respectively

Right:
Notts & Derby: One of the 1937 Weymann-bodied AEC 661Ts, No 332 negotiates a low bridge on the long Ripley-Nottingham route. *Ian Allan Library*

the Nottingham-Ripley route. Meanwhile work was undertaken to replace the remaining tramway between Heanor and Cinderhill, motorbuses being used as an interim measure. At last on 5 October 1933 the Notts & Derby trolleybuses started up on the full route from Ripley to Cinderhill and into Nottingham. The Corporation had by now extended its own wires to Cinderhill as an extension of its Nottingham Road route (the city's first trolleybus route of 1927) and Notts & Derby vehicles thus ran under some three miles of Nottingham Corporation wires, via Basford, Nottingham Road and Mansfield Road (a different route from that followed by the trams) to a terminus in the city centre at the junction of King Street and Queen Street. With the new Nottingham-Ripley service, the company now worked a route some 15 miles long, giving it a claim to the longest through trolleybus route in Britain.

For its first trolley vehicle operations in 1932 the company put into service a fleet of four-wheel single-deckers, some with English Electric chassis (among the last chassis of this manufacturer) and the others with AEC 662T chassis; all had English Electric front-entrance bodies but those on the AECs had half-cabs with bonnet and 'radiator'. For the Nottingham-Ripley service in 1933 a batch of double-deckers was obtained; these were AEC 661Ts with MCCW bodies, again of the half-cab design, and probably the first with all-metal bodies.

New double-deckers acquired in 1937 (replacing single-deckers sold to Mexborough & Swinton) were also on AEC 661T chassis, but this time with Weymann bodies of the more conventional full-fronted design. Further double-deckers were ordered before the war, but were not available until 1941 and 1942. Postwar members of the fleet were Weymann-bodied BUT 9611Ts obtained in 1949, replacing the 1933 AEC double-deckers. The single-deckers had been withdrawn from service by this time, though several had continued running during the war. Trolley wheels were in use until the end of operation. On the company's exposed and elevated routes, frost was a problem in winter, and special frost-cutting trolley wheels (with milled inside surfaces) were employed on the first vehicles out in the morning.

The system was operated basically as three services:

A1: Nottingham-Ripley.
A2: Heanor-Cotmanhay-Ilkeston-Hallam Fields.
A3: Heanor-Heanor Road (bypassing Cotmanhay)-Ilkeston, Rutland Hotel.

On all these routes numerous short-workings utilised the various reversing places.

Over the years there were several proposals for extensions, the most important of which was for a direct route between Ilkeston and Notting-ham via Wollaton. There were also plans for the joint working of Corporation vehicles under Notts & Derby wires to Kimberley.

The advantages of integrating services with Midland General, plus the need for replacement of time-expired equipment, sealed the fate of the trolleybuses, which in their final years had been undergoing changes in ownership. The Midland Counties Electricity Supply Co (owners of Notts & Derby and, in turn, controlled by Balfour Beatty), as an electricity undertaking, was nationalised in 1948, when the trolleybuses came into the ownership of the British Electricity Authority. In 1949 they were transferred to the British Transport Commission. Abandonment was finally authorised under the Nottinghamshire & Derbyshire Traction Act of 1952, and the last services operated on 25 April 1953. The whole of the fleet was sold to Bradford for further service.

References
'British Trolleybus Systems: No 19 — Notts & Derby' *Buses* January 1977.

Pontypridd

'The first modern trolleybus system in Wales' was the proud claim when Pontypridd Urban District Council's new undertaking was formally inaugurated in 1930. As in so many other towns, by the late 1920s Pontypridd's tramways were in need of renewal, while additional problems resulted from mining subsidence and local trade depression. Powers were obtained in 1929 to operate trolleybuses on the council's tram routes to Trehafod, Treforest and Cilfynydd. However, the neighbouring Rhondda

Tramways Co, with which Pontypridd worked a through service to Porth, after considering conversion decided not to adopt trolleybuses for its part of this route between Trehafod and Porth. So in the event Pontypridd's trolley vehicle operations were confined to the route from Treforest, through the town, to Cilfynydd, a distance of 3.3 miles.

During 1930 driver training took place on the new vehicles, using a skate in the tram track, and by September the work of converting the overhead was complete. At the Cilfynydd terminus a turning circle was provided, while at Treforest, where the depot was located, a triangular reverser was installed. Service commenced on 18 September 1930. For a time after this, trams continued to run, together with motorbuses, to augment the trolley vehicles at

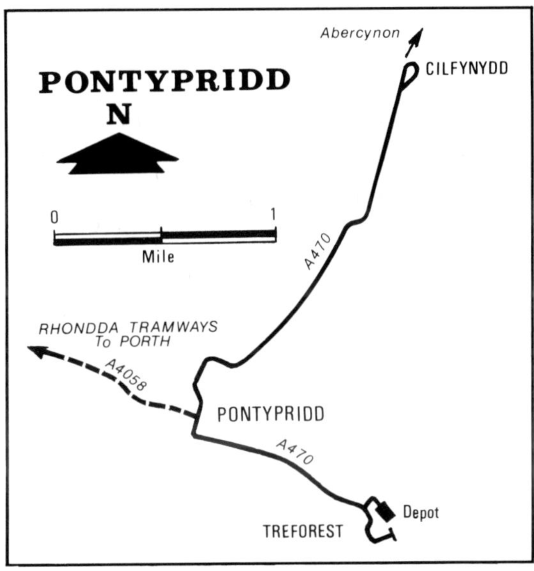

Pontypridd

Fleet Nos	Registration Nos	Chassis	Electrical equipment	Body	In service	Withdrawn	Notes
1-7	TG 379/81/3/5/7/ 9/91	E/Electric SD6W TB	E/Electric	E/Electric B32C	1930	1946	a
8	UK 8948	Guy BTX	Rees-Stevens/BTH	Guy H30/29R	1931	1946	
9	HY 2391	Bristol	BTH	Beadle H32/28R	1931	1947	
10, 11	FNY 983/4	Karrier W	BTH	Weymann UH30/26R	1945	1957	b
12, 13	FTG 284/5	Karrier W	BTH	P/Royal UH30/26R	1945	1957	c
14, 15	FTG 697/8	Karrier W	BTH	Roe UH30/26R	1946	1956	d
8, 9	GNY 301/2	Karrier W	BTH	P/Royal UH30/26R	1946	1957	e

Notes:

a Sold to Cardiff as Nos 231-7

b Sold to Doncaster as Nos 351/2

c Sold to South Shields as Nos 238/9

d Sold to Walsall as Nos 301/2

e Sold to South Shields as Nos 236/7

Above:
Pontypridd: Against a background of Welsh hills, 1946 Karrier No 8 stands poles down at the Cilfynydd terminus while companion No 11 negotiates the turning circle on an enthusiasts' special. *C. Carter*

peak periods. The trolleybuses made the round journey in 48 minutes, compared with the trams' scheduled one hour.

The first fleet consisted of seven six-wheel English Electric 32-seat central-entrance single-deckers. An indication of the traffic they had to handle is given by the fact that the seats 'are provided with easily-detachable covers, which are slipped over the normal upholstery when workmen are travelling to and from their work'. These vehicles were joined in 1931 by two double-deck demonstrators, one a Guy and the other a Bristol, the latter being one of only two trolleybuses produced by the Bristol company. Further variety in rolling stock was added during the war, when to assist with the heavy traffic Kingston-upon-Hull's Leylands Nos 1-4 were obtained on loan. They returned home in 1942, when their place was taken by a quartet of six-wheelers from Portsmouth; Nos 212-5 in their native city, they comprised two AECs and two Sunbeams. They remained in Pontypridd until 1946, by which time the council's own fleet had been renewed by the receipt of eight Karrier Ws. The newcomers also made redundant the original fleet, in which nearby Cardiff soon displayed interest; the single-deckers were purchased in 1947 for use on the city's Bute Street route on which double-deckers could not be used.

Extensions to the system had been considered in 1939/40 but were rejected, and by the 1950s such a small trolleybus undertaking as Pontypridd's could hardly remain viable. Operation ended without ceremony on 31 January 1957. Two of the Karriers had earlier gone to Walsall, while the rest now also found new homes in Doncaster and South Shields. Pontypridd was the last Urban District Council to run trolleybuses, and also the last operator in Britain to use trolley-wheel collectors.

References
'Pontypridd's New Trolleybus Route', *Tramway & Railway World*, 16 October 1930.
'Cilfynydd to Treforest' by D. Kain: *Trolleybus Magazine*, July 1970.
Passenger Tramways of Pontypridd by R. Large (Oakwood Press 1977).

Portsmouth

Although as early as 1923 Portsmouth had considered installing trackless trolley vehicles along Copnor Road in preference to extending the tram route, it was not until Portsmouth Corporation Act of 1930 that powers were obtained to operate trolleybuses. In that year the Tramways Committee examined the possibility of establishing a route from Southsea, along Waverley Road, Fawcett Road, Bradford Road and Greatham Street, past the Guildhall, and along Unicorn Road to the Unicorn Gate at the dockyard. However, it was 1933 when the Council approved the gradual replacement of the tramways by trolleybuses, and 15 vehicles of different types were acquired in order to determine which would best suit the needs of the proposed system. Nos 1-4 were AECs, Nos 5-7 were Leylands, Nos 8 and 10 were Sunbeams, and Nos 9 and 11 were Karriers; all of these were six-wheelers. The other four were four-wheelers: Nos 12 and 15 were AECs and Nos 13 and 14 Sunbeams.

The first service was officially inaugurated on 4 August 1934 between South Parade Pier and Cosham via Fawcett Road, Fratton Road and London Road. More than a year later, on 3 November 1935, services were extended from South Parade Pier via Festing Road, Albert Road, Blackfriars Road to Guildhall, then northward via Twyford Avenue into Northern Parade (a road not previously covered by trams) to join the original Cosham route again at Hilsea and so to establish the first of numerous links that were to characterise the system. Another nine vehicles were now added to the stock.

To complete the changeover from trams, another 76 four-wheel AECs were ordered and these became Nos 25-100. On 1 October 1936 trolleybuses began operating over the section between the Guildhall and Clarence Pier, together with workings to the 'Red Lion' at Cosham, while on 1 November they took over

Above:
Portsmouth: No 211 (originally No 11) was a member of the first fleet in 1934. A Karrier E4, it had a Metropolitan-Cammell body and continued in service until 1951. *V. C. Jones/Ian Allan Library*

Various extensions were proposed in 1947. These included several links in the city network: about 2½ miles of route between Milton and Hilsea via Copnor; Gladys Avenue; Unicorn Road; Stubbington Avenue; and from Copnor to Tangier Road and Stanley Avenue. Two other proposed extensions would have greatly increased the northern scope of the system in the developing area on the 'mainland', and could well have been significant in the light of later experience. These would have taken the wires nearly two miles beyond Cosham, through Drayton to Rectory Avenue at Farling-ton, as well as nearly 2½ miles from Northern Road in Cosham along a new link road and through the Paulsgrove estate to Porchester. In anticipation of the extension to Farlington, on 18 May 1947 service 1/2 between Clarence Pier and Cosham was replaced by buses which continued on to Farlington. This was the first trolleybus service to be taken over by buses.

services from Copnor via Lake Road to the Dockyard and through the Old Town to the Floating Bridge, where a triangular reverser was installed. The final conversion was effective a few days later, on 10 November 1936, when the last trams were followed by the first trolleybuses on the Milton and Eastney circular services. In 1938 the fleet was renumbered from 1-100 to 201-300.

During the war, apart from interruptions of service due to air raid damage, services were cut back from South Parade Pier and Clarence Pier and others were reduced. However, reduced traffic demands made it possible to send four trolleybuses (Nos 212-5) on loan to Pontypridd, where they did duty from 1942 to 1945.

These two northern extensions were never constructed, but others did materialise. The Milton-Copnor-Hilsea route was opened on 25 May 1952, and the extensions along Gladys Avenue and Chichester Road (the latter replaced the earlier proposed Stubbington Avenue route) on 27 September 1953. Meanwhile, the route to the Floating Bridge through the narrow streets of the Old Town ceased on 29 September 1951 and was replaced by buses.

The resultant network allowed for consider-able complexity of routeings, a tradition inherited from the tramways, and permitted the operation of circular and out-and-back services and even 'figure eights'. Services were numbered in pairs, each number being applied

Portsmouth

Fleet Nos	Registration Nos	Chassis	Electrical equipment	Body	In service	Withdrawn	Notes
1-4	RV 4649-52	AEC 661T	E/Electric	E/Electric H26/24R	1934	1951-8	
5-7	RV 4653-5	Leyland TBD2	GEC	E/Electric H26/24R	1934	1951	
8	RV 4656	Sunbeam MF2	BTH	E/Electric H26/24R	1934	1952	
9	RV 4657	Karrier E4	E/Electric	E/Electric H26/24R	1934	1951	
10	RV 4660	Sunbeam MF2	BTH	M/Cam H26/24R	1934	1952	
11	RV 4661	Karrier E4	BTH	M/Cam H26/24R	1934	1951	
12	RV 4658	AEC 663T	E/Electric	E/Electric H32/28R	1934	1938	
13	RV 4659	Sunbeam MS3	BTH	E/Electric H32/28R	1934	1951	
14	RV 4662	Sunbeam MS3	BTH	M/Cam H32/28R	1934	1951	
15	RV 4663	AEC 663T	E/Electric	M/Cam H32/28R	1934	1951	
16-24	RV 6374-82	AEC 661T	E/Electric	E/Electric H26/24R	1935/6	1950-6	
25-100	RV 8307-36/9106-45/49-54	AEC 661T	E/Electric	Craven H26/26R	1936/7	1951-63	

(Fleet renumbered 201-300 in 1938)

| 301-15 | ERV 926-40 | BUT 9611T | E/Electric | Burlingham H28/24R | 1950/1 | 1961/3 | |

Preserved vehicles: Nos 201, 313

to only one direction. Numerous changes took place over the years to meet changing traffic demands and the impact of paralleling bus services. The complexity of the network, with its many complicated junctions, was later to be advanced as a factor militating against the retention of trolleybuses.

To revitalise the fleet, 15 Burlingham-bodied BUTs (Nos 301-15) entered service in 1950/51, but these were to prove the last new vehicles to be taken into stock. In 1954 the Transport Committee was proposing the purchase of a further 15 trolleybuses as replacements, but by this time doubts were being raised about the future of the system and motorbuses were ordered instead.

Trolleybuses were still working some 40% of the Corporation's total mileage, carrying some 33 million passengers a year compared with 36 million on the buses. But for several years an air of uncertainty hung over the trolley vehicles. The 21-year co-ordination agreement between Portsmouth Corporation and Southdown Motor Services came into operation in 1946 and set up a joint committee to handle operations within an area extending beyond Portsmouth itself and well into the hinterland where extensive residential and industrial development was taking place. This arrangement brought Portsmouth buses out to housing estates at Paulsgrove and Leigh Park, but it also brought some reductions in trolleybus services consequent on the rationalisation of the bus services of both Southdown and the Corporation.

From Cosham, in particular, trolleybus services were reduced in the face of paralleling buses which continued northward to the expanding hinterland, while, moreover, Southdown buses could take part in local services within the city. Nevertheless, the scheme still envisaged that an extension of trolleybuses from Cosham to Paulsgrove should take over from buses on this route, which already called for a six-minute peak-hour headway.

Recommendations that the trolleybuses should not be extended, but rather that they should be replaced by buses in the interests of economy, were advanced in 1956 by the general manager and the Transport Committee. These were accepted by the Council, and reaffirmed in 1957. Special attention turned on the main north-south routes which were paralleled by both Corporation and Southdown buses operating on the longer distance services. If the trolleybus system were to remain viable it would need to be extended to such areas as Paulsgrove and Leigh Park, but the cost of such extensions would place a heavy burden on the under-

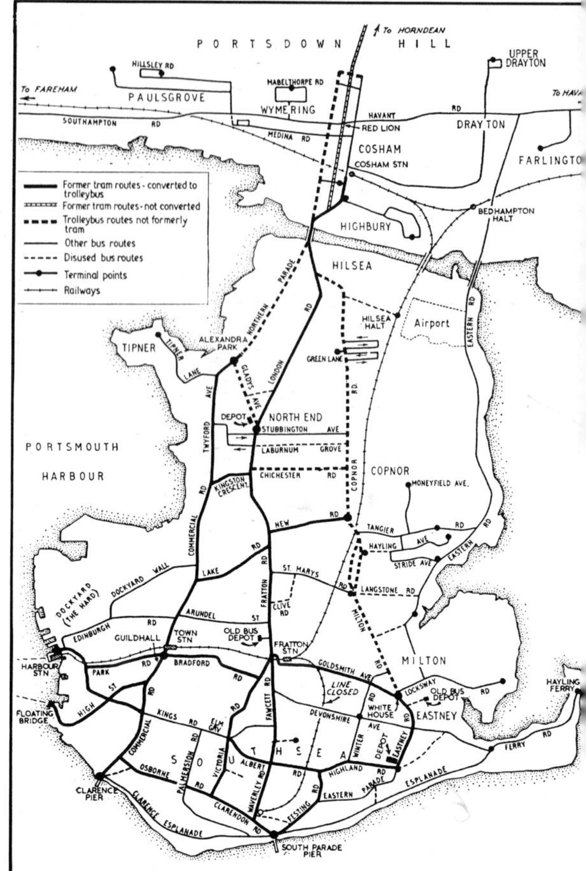

taking. Moreover, much of the existing fleet was now badly in need of renewal.

However, all was not yet over, for when the actual details of the changeover were put forward in 1955 they were rejected and the Council decided that an independent investigation should be made. Consultants were therefore called in to examine the transport undertaking, including the role of the trolleybus and the working of the co-ordination agreement.

The consultants' report, published in 1959, confirmed the abandonment as 'sound'. The greatest objection to the trolleybuses was that they were 'routebound and inflexible'. Their routes were based largely on the original tram routes, which were designed to serve a self-contained city, and could not extend beyond Cosham. Now that longer distance traffic was increasing, the services terminating at Cosham were largely redundant. Extending the trolleybuses 'would not be expedient', since flexibility was of the utmost value in catering for changing needs. The consultants believed that the agreement with Southdown should con-

tinue, since the two parties already had wide freedom to modify its terms to adapt to new circumstances.

On 8 September 1959 the City Council approved the Transport Committee's proposal to abandon the trolleybuses, and the changeover took place in five stages:

1 May 1960 — 15/16 Eastney-Copnor-Gladys Avenue-Alexandra Park.
    19/20 Milton-Eastney-Twyford Avenue-Cosham.
17 September 1960 — 3/4 Cosham-North End-Fratton-Green Lane.
2 December 1961 — 7/8 Clarence Pier-Fratton-Green Lane and 11/12 Dockyard-Green Lane.
22 June 1963 — 17/18 Dockyard-Eastney-Milton.

Above left:
Portsmouth: Photographed in 1950 on the turning loop at Cosham Compound, No 214 (originally No 14) was a Metropolitan-Cammell-bodied Sunbeam MS3 dating from 1934. *V. C. Jones/Ian Allan Library*

Left:
Portsmouth: A member of the postwar series of trolleybuses for Portsmouth, No 312 was a 1950 BUT 9611T with Burlingham body. *Ian Allan Library*

Below:
Portsmouth: No 237 was the last of the series of Cravens-bodied AEC 661Ts of 1935. *Ian Allan Library*
Ian Allan Library

The last day of trolleybus operation was 27 July 1963, when the final runs were made on service 5/6 between the Dockyard, Southsea, Eastney, Copnor and Cosham.

References
Portsmouth City Transport by A. F. Milton and L. T. A. Bern (Authors 1977).
The Tramways of Portsmouth by S. E. Harrison (Light Railway Transport League 1963).
The Portsmouth Joint Scheme — *Modern Transport*, 24 September 1955.

Ramsbottom

In the small group of pioneer operators who were too willing to put their trust in trolleybuses or trackless cars before World War 1, Ramsbottom stands out as being bolder than the others. Having wrestled for years with the difficulties of meeting the requirements of its 1903 Tramways Act, the Urban District Council decided to break with tradition and begin its public transport system using railless traction. It is interesting to note, however, that the Ramsbottom Urban District Railless Traction Act 1912 indicated clearly that the trackless routes might later be converted to tramway operation. The route authorised was from Holcombe Brook railway station (on the electrified line to Bury) via Bolton Road West, Bolton Street, Market Place, Ramsbottom Lane, Stubbins Lane, Bolton Road North, Bury Road, to Market Place, Edenfield, terminating (as the Act picturesquely describes it) at 'the fingerpost in that street'. A short spur diverged from the Market Place, Ramsbottom, via Bridge Street to Ramsbottom railway station.

An order was placed with Railless Electric Traction for four cars, the first of which arrived from Leeds towed by a motorwagon on 10 August 1913. The following day a private party, including the Chairman of Ramsbottom UDC, the Tramways Manager of Bury Corporation and representatives of Railless, took a trial run. After the Board of Trade inspection, public service was begun on the evening of 14 August 1913. It is believed the second car arrived the following day and the remaining two the following week.

The four cars were powered by two 20hp English Electric motors connected to a Siemens hand controller. The chassis had been supplied to RET by David Brown of Huddersfield while the rear-platform bodies were built by Milnes Voss, initially with seating for 28 passengers on transverse seats covered with rattan cane. The fare for the through journey was 3d. The use of the spur to the railway station was short-lived; it was abandoned on 5 October 1914, though the overhead was not removed until some 10 years later.

The granite setts of the town are likely to have caused severe vibrations on the vehicles, and by 1915 arrangements were necessary for the bodies to be replaced. To this end, two additional cars (Nos 5 and 6) were supplied by RET in 1915 with bodies built at Leeds by RET's neighbour Lockwood & Clarkson. Rebodying of the first four cars was carried out by the same company between 1915 and 1917, and during this period the cars originally numbered 2 and 3 became 3 and 2 respectively.

Below:
Ramsbottom: One of the RET cars at the time of the opening in 1913.

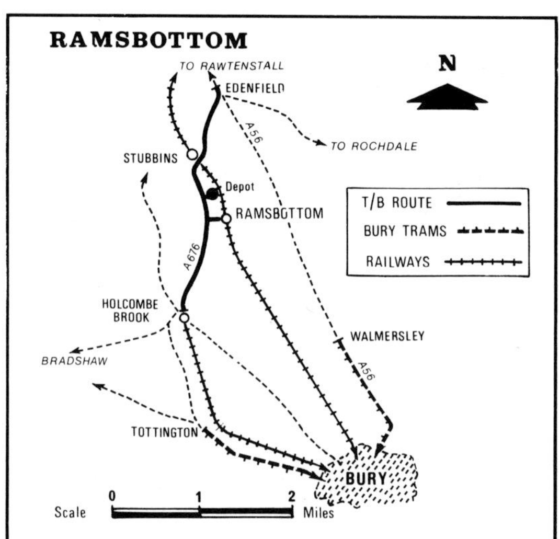

By the time car No 7 was purchased RET had been taken over by Short Brothers and manufacture was carried out by Railless Ltd at Rochester. The vehicle was demonstrated at Dover on 6 and 7 July 1922, and eventually began trials with its rightful owner on 20 July 1922. The 26-seat Short Brothers body had an enclosed rear platform. The chassis is believed to have been supplied by Thornycroft, and the single 42hp motor was still linked to a tramcar-type hand controller. The vehicle carried the registration number TD48. Meanwhile No 6 had been given registration TD47 and cars 4 and 5 were TB8572 and TB8573. Further rebuilding took place during 1923 and 1924; this involved new chassis for Nos 3 and 6 in 1923, followed by a complete rebuild on Nos 2 and 4 in 1924. New chassis were nominally supplied by Railless, and the new bodies were probably actually built by Short. It is also believed that No 6 received some attention at the Roe works in 1923, and that either No 1 or No 3 received its third body from Roe in 1924.

In 1925 the Council decided to promote a Bill to obtain powers to run motorbuses, and this was passed as the Ramsbottom UDC Act 1926. Effectively it was the beginning of the end for the trolleybuses. A through bus service between Bury and Rawtenstall began in November 1926, thus overshadowing the little trolleybus route. By October 1929 the trolleybus service was operating for only part of the day; only two vehicles remained licensed, and by March 1930 this was reduced to one. This sole survivor continued to run until 31 March 1931.

References
'British Trolleybus Systems: No 21 — Ramsbottom': *Buses* August 1979.
'Railless Traction in Lancashire: Inauguration of the Ramsbottom Installation': *Tramway & Railway World*, 11 September 1913.

Reading

In 1931 Reading Corporation set up a Tramways (Future Policy) Subcommittee to consider what type of vehicle should replace the town's tramcars when the time came, and after visits to various trolleybus systems it was decided that the trolley vehicle was the answer. Accordingly it was proposed to obtain a Provisional Order to enable conversion of the Caversham-Whitley route, but since the Corporation was already promoting an electricity supply Bill it was agreed that this should also seek trolleybus powers to cover all the tram routes, and these were in due course obtained in the Reading Corporation Act of 1935.

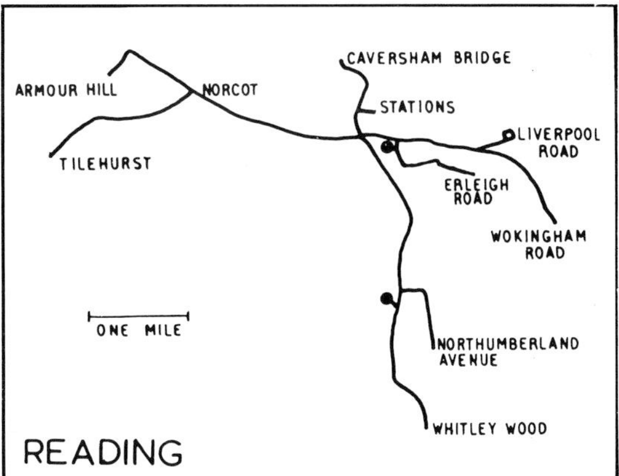

Above:
Reading: Reading's first trolleybus, a Sunbeam MF2A with lowbridge Park Royal body, is seen on driver-training duties on the Erleigh Road route before services commenced in 1936. *Ian Allan Library*

In preparation for the introduction of the new mode of transport, in May 1936 a Sunbeam demonstrator of 1933 (taken into the fleet as No 1) was used for driver training on the erstwhile Erleigh Road tram route on which trolleybus wires were strung for the purpose. Ironically this route, on which motorbuses had already taken over from trams, was never to have a regular trolleybus service, though on certain occasions during this initial period passengers were carried free of charge so as to taste the delights to come. No 1 was fitted with a skate so that it could run over the tram tracks.

Meanwhile, the conversion of the Caversham-

Whitley route was proceeding. Trams ceased on 15 July and buses were used while the overhead was completed. Then on 18 July 1936 Reading's first trolleybus service was officially opened, with No 1 driven by the Mayor. For purposes of comparison six different vehicles were utilised. Apart from Sunbeam No 1, these were respectively an AEC 661T, a Guy BT, a Leyland TB4, a Ransomes and a Sunbeam MF2A, all with lowbridge 52-seat bodies by Park Royal.

A Provisional Order of 1936 provided that trolleybuses should be extended beyond the limits of the existing 'main line' tram route, which ran from Oxford Road to Wokingham Road with a branch to London Road. The trolleybuses would continue beyond the Oxford Road terminus to the 'Bear' at Tilehurst, and along Wokingham Road to the 'Three Tuns' at Earley. Work was under way in 1938. When it was ready, the Tilehurst section was used for driver training in preparation for the final changeover. On 20 May 1939 the last trams ran, and on the following day the new services started, worked by a fleet of 25 new AEC 661Ts

Above right:
Reading: With the Mayor and the official party, No 1 takes part in the opening ceremony of Reading's trolleybus system in 1936. *Ian Allan Library*

Right:
Reading: The second experimental trolleybus in 1936 was No 2, an AEC 661T with Park Royal body, seen at the Caversham terminus when new.
Ian Allan Library

Reading

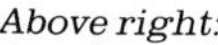

Fleet Nos	Registration Nos	Chassis	Electrical equipment	Body	In service	Withdrawn	Notes
1	RD 8085	Sunbeam MF2A	BTH	P/Royal L24/26R	1936	1949	a
2	RD 8086	AEC 661T	E/Electric	P/Royal L26/26R	1936	1950	a
3	RD 8087	Guy BT	E Constr	P/Royal L26/26R	1936	1949	a
4	RD 8088	Leyland TB4	GEC	P/Royal L26/26R	1936	1949	a
5	RD 8089	Ransomes	Crompton	P/Royal L26/26R	1936	1949	a
6	RD 8090	Sunbeam MF2A	BTH	P/Royal L26/26R	1936	1950	a
107-31	ARD 670-94	AEC 661T	E/Electric	P/Royal H30/26R	1939	1958-61	b
132-7	BRD 797-801/14	Sunbeam W	E/Electric	P/Royal UH30/26R	1943	1950	
138-57	DRD 124-43	BUT 9611T	E/Electric	P/Royal H30/26RD	1949	1966-8	
158-69	VH 6757/53/51/ 59/55/52/61/60/ 54/50/58/56	Karrier E6	Metrovick	Brush H34/30R	1948-51	1955/6	c
170-81	ERD 141-52	Sunbeam S7	BTH	P/Royal H38/30RD	1950	1967/8	
182-93	VRD 182-93	Sunbeam F4A	BTH	Burlingham H38/30F	1961	1968	d

Notes:

a Nos 1-6 renumbered 101-6 in 1938

b No 126 withdrawn after accident in 1952

c Ex-Huddersfield, new in 1934

d Nos 183-6 and 192 sold to Teesside

Preserved vehicles: Nos 113, 144, 174, 181, 193

(Nos 107-31). Trolleybuses were at first housed in the East Garage until the new Mill Lane depot, which was to replace the old tram depot, was completed in 1939. Between 1952 and 1958, trolleybuses also shared accommodation with buses at Bennett Road, where a former aircraft hangar was erected for the purpose.

Wartime brought a halt to further expansion, until in 1944 sanction was obtained for an extension along Oxford Road, from the Norcot junction with the Tilehurst route, to Kentwood, a distance of nearly a mile, so that a bus service could be replaced in the interests of saving fuel oil. This was brought into use on 31 July 1944, aided by a recent intake of half-a-dozen utility-bodied Karrier Ws. On the other hand, service on the Caversham-Whitley route, which was paralleled by buses, was reduced and later suspended altogether.

Postwar developments saw the Caversham-Whitley route projected southward to Northumberland Avenue on 5 June 1949, followed on 7 August of that year by the useful short branch to Reading stations and by another southward route to Whitley Wood, this last again being a replacement for a bus service. To meet growing traffic needs, a dozen six-wheel Karriers were purchased from Huddersfield (though only six actually entered service) and the first new postwar trolleybuses (and the first 8ft wide vehicles in the fleet) were 20 BUTs with Park Royal bodies fitted with platform doors (Nos 138-57). They were followed in 1950 by a dozen six-wheel Sunbeam S7s with similar style bodies but with a seating capacity of 68. The last additions to the fleet entered service in 1961; 12 Sunbeam F4As (Nos 182-93) — their Burlingham bodies were the first in the fleet to have forward entrances.

In the meantime, the Kentwood route was extended to Armour Hill on 4 August 1958, and then on 14 January 1963 came the final extension, of the Northumberland Avenue route to Whitley Wood Road. Little more than two years later, the process of contraction was under way, the first section to go being Caversham Bridge on 10 July 1965 as an 'economy measure'. In 1966 the decision was taken to replace the entire system, and consequently the Whitley Wood route was withdrawn on 8 January 1967, Northumberland Avenue and the branch to the stations on 31 December 1967, and Liverpool Road and Armour Hill on 3 March 1968. Finally the Tilehurst and Wokingham Road route was withdrawn on 3 November 1968, when No 144 made the last journey.

Below left:
Reading: Negotiating the reverser at Whitley Wood terminus in 1951 is No 153, one of the Park Royal-bodied BUTs of 1949.   *V. C. Jones/Ian Allan Library*

Below:
Reading: Representative of the last new trolleybuses obtained by Reading is No 192, a Sunbeam F4A with forward-entrance Burlingham body, dating from 1951. No 192 was later sold to the Teesside Railless Traction Board.
V. C. Jones/Ian Allan Library

References
Reading Transport 75th Anniversary 1901-1976 — Reading Transport 1976.
The Tramways of Reading by H. E. Jordan (Light Railway Transport League, 1957).
'British Bus & Tram Systems: No 26 Reading Corporation Transport' by M. J. C. Dare; *Buses Illustrated*, April and May 1959.

Rhondda

The Rhondda system was not a success. It had the doubtful distinction of being in operation for only a few weeks and was the shortest-lived system in Britain. The Rhondda Tramways Co (a subsidiary of the National Electric Construction Co — NECC) leased its tramways from the Rhondda Urban District Council and by 1912 had developed two routes with several branches, including one from Penygraig to Williamstown. However, in an area where transport for coal mines needed to be flexible enough to keep pace with the opening of new mining shafts, it was found that a tramway system was too expensive to extend or divert as required. Therefore, when in 1911/12 more pits were developed in the vicinity of Gilfach Goch, consideration was given to a service of motorbuses to connect with the terminus at Williamstown. However, the Rhondda Tramways Manager and Engineer, H. J. Nisbett, became interested in railless traction, having visited the new Rotherham system in 1912, and he persuaded the Council that this was the answer.

A Bill for the necessary powers was submitted during the 1913 session of Parliament, and following the insertion of clauses concerning responsibility for road maintenance, it received the Royal Assent on 15 August 1913. The route was detailed as follows: from the tramway terminus at the UDC boundary on the Penrhiwfa Road, proceeding south to Tonyrefail, then southwest along Gilfach Road, thence north along Gelliaroch Road past Gilfach Station, then northwest along Llewelyn Terrace and Nicholl's Terrace to the parish boundary of Llantrisant with Rhondda UDC. This took the form of a letter U and covered a distance of 4¾ miles.

Attention was now directed to comparing the merits of the three systems of trackless trolleys. At the end of October 1913 a report presented to the company by the Chief Engineer of the NECC, P. E. Stanley, ruled out the Cedes-Stoll system and concluded that the Lloyd-Kohler system (as used at Stockport) was better than the RET. It was decided to adopt the report and to order six cars from Brush, coupling the order with one for three or four similar cars for the Mexborough & Swinton Tramways Co. These were built on Daimler chassis with Brush rear-entrance bodies. Fleet numbers 55-60 in the tramway fleet are believed to have been allocated. Delays in delivery meant that the system was not ready for a trial run until December 1914.

The orthodox Lloyd-Kohler system, with its trolley running on the wires and a flexible connection to the cars, was not acceptable to the Rhondda company, since it wished to have the facility for running the trackless cars along its tramways, using a current-return skate. It therefore persuaded Brush to modify the system of current collection to resemble the RET system with two horizontally-parallel wires and two trolley poles on each car.

The exact date when the public service began has been difficult to confirm, although it is generally accepted as 22 December 1914, based

Below:
Rhondda: Rhondda Tramways trackless car No 56 comes to grief in 1915 after running away down a steep hill. *Ian Allan Library*

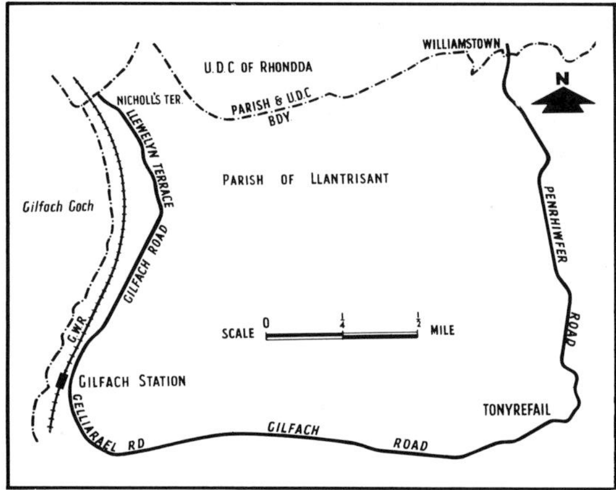

on official returns. Only four weeks later, the Rhondda Tramways minutes had noted reports of the very bad state of the Gilfach Road and expressed concern at the damage this was causing to the cars. By 4 February 1915 it was feared that the service would have to cease, but on assurance from Llantrisant Council that repairs were being put in hand, it was agreed to continue to operate.

The route included some steep gradients, and in March 1915 car No 56 went out of control when descending a hill and crashed into a house. This seems to have been the last straw, and the *Mid-Rhondda Gazette* of 17 March reported that Rhondda tramcars were carrying notices to the effect that the railless car service was suspended until further notice, but that it was hoped to resume when the road repairs were completed. However, the railless cars never ran again on the Rhondda system. There were proposals for an extension of the tramways, but eventually a service of motorbuses began over the route in January 1921. Meanwhile, in May 1920 the company sold the six cars for £2,800 to Clough Smith; they were repurchased by the Teesside Railless Traction Board, where they became Nos 11-16 in that operator's fleet.

Reference
'British Trolleybus Systems: No 22 — Rhondda', *Buses*, April 1982.

Rotherham

Only the fourth system to start operation in Britain, the Rotherham undertaking earned a well-merited reputation for smartness and speed with its distinctive fleet of sleek single-deckers. Outstanding among the routes was the 7-mile run to Maltby, incorporating the first rural trolleybus operation in Britain and still to the end maintaining an individual character. In the town centre were also to be seen the equally distinctive single-deckers of the Mexborough & Swinton Traction Co, with which Rotherham Corporation worked joint services to outlying destinations at Mexborough and Conisbrough. Then, during the final few years of the Rotherham system, when the trolleybuses seemed doomed to an early demise, a transformation took place as the long-established Corporation single-deckers were metamorphosed into double-deckers, their greater earning capacity serving to defer the ultimate closure for almost another 10 years.

As early as 1910, after sending 'a small deputation' to the Continent to see trolley

Top:
Rotherham: Railless car No 43 of 1913 in service on the Maltby route.   *Courtesy R. Brook*

Above:
Rotherham: Newly-delivered in 1937, Guy BTX No 13 had a Craven body.   *Ian Allan Library*

vehicle installations, Rotherham Corporation was seeking Parliamentary powers to operate its own trolleybuses over a wide area in extension of the town's tramways: to Wickersley, Bramley, Maltby and Tickhill; to Whiston, Aughton, Aston and Swallownest; to Brinsworth, Tinsley, Catcliffe and Treeton; to Brampton, Laughton and Dinnington; to Thorpe Hesley; and from Kimberworth to Blackburn. In

Top:

Rotherham: Caught on a service to Wickersley in 1940, No 70 was the first of a new batch of Sunbeam MS2Cs with bodies by East Lancashire.
Ian Allan Library

Above:

Rotherham: Postwar re-equipment of the Rotherham system was with East Lancashire-bodied Daimlers, of which No 9 was new in 1950.
Ian Allan Library

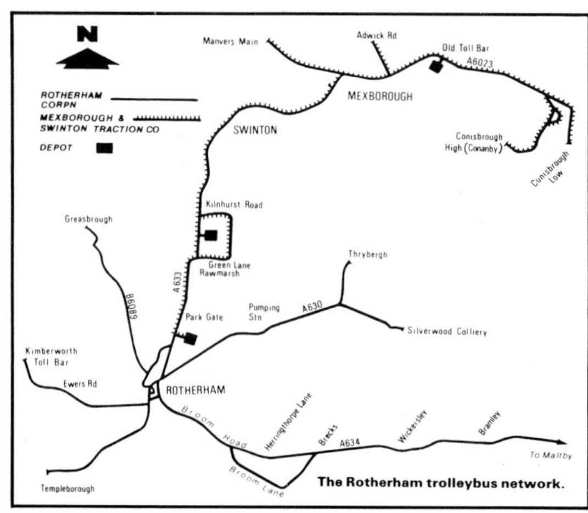

the event, powers were obtained for routes to Thorpe Hesley, Treeton and Maltby, and in 1911 the Council decided to go ahead with the proposed route from the Broom Road tram terminus to the outlying town of Maltby. The contract for the installation was placed with the RET Construction Co.

The Board of Trade inspection was made on 30 September 1912, and the formal opening took place on 3 October amid due ceremony, with the Tramways Committee chairman officiating and the occasion graced by the presence of the mayor and almost 180 guests. The latter included the Leeds Tramways chairman, who diplomatically acknowledged that the new installation was 'far and away better' than the one inaugurated in his own city only the previous year.

The route ran from the Stag Inn at Herringthorpe Lane (on the outskirts of the town and the terminus of a new extension of the Broom Road tramway), via Bramley and Wickersley, to the mining town of Maltby, a distance of about 4¾ miles, of which more than 4 miles was outside the municipal boundary. Rotherham thus became the first local authority to operate trolleybuses outside its municipal boundaries. The three original vehicles supplied by RET (Nos 38-40) were single-deckers powered by two 20hp motors, and with 28-seat, Roe-built bodies divided into two compartments and with open rear platform. According to a contemporary account, 'the vehicle rides very easily on comparatively poor roads, and a speed of 12mph may be easily attained up the steepest gradient'. Traffic must have justified expectations, for a further three vehicles of the same type (Nos 41-43) were obtained from RET in 1913. The six vehicles were renumbered T1 to T6 in 1916 with the arrival of new trams in the fleet.

During World War 1 operation suffered from maintenance problems with the rolling stock, and there were occasions when the service had to be suspended completely. No doubt such interruptions, backed by the evident traffic potential, gave heart to those who still favoured the tramcar, for the Corporation's 1915 Act included powers for the extension of the Broom Road tramway to Maltby. After the war, in February 1919, the Council agreed that it was 'most desirable' that the tramway should be extended along the trolleybus route, at least as far as Wickersley. However, this never came to pass. Instead, during 1923 the trolley wires were extended over the tramway along Broom Road to College Square, and in January 1924 trolleybuses began to operate a through service between Maltby and the town centre. Hitherto

Rotherham

Fleet Nos	Registration Nos	Chassis	Electrical equipment	Body	In service	Withdrawn	Notes
38-40		Railless	Siemens	Roe B28R	1912	1920-2	a
41-3	ET1923-5	Railless	Siemens	Roe B28R	1913	1922?	a
38	ET2337	S/Clough		Roe B26C	1920	1933	b
39	ET3217	S/Clough		Roe B26C	1922	1936	c
40		S/Clough		Roe B26C	?	?	
41-3	ET3340/1/?	S/Clough		Roe B32C	1924/5	1933	d
44/5	ET2840/4	S/Clough		Roe B26C	1923	1933	
46-8	ET4818-20	S/Clough		Roe B32C	1925	1936	e
49	ET4828	Railess		Roe B32C	1925	?	f
50	ET5968	RS&J	RS&J/E/Electric	RS&J B35C	1929	1929	g
46	ET4933	Guy BTX	R/Stevens	Roe B32C	1928	1942	h
43-5	ET5284-6	Guy BTX	R/Stevens	Roe B32C	1928	1936	
51	ET6020	Guy BTX	R/Stevens	Guy B32C	1930	1942?	
55, 56, 19-38	ET6607-28	RS&J	RS&J	Craven B32C	1931	1939-50	i
52-4, 57, 58	ET7880-4	Guy BT32	E/Electric	Craven B32C	1933/4	1949/50	j
39-42, 59	ET7885-9	Guy BT32	E/Electric	Roberts B32C	1933/4	1949/50	k
15-18	ET9230-3	Guy BT32	E/Electric	Craven B32C	1935	1951-6	l
60-5	ET9615-20	Guy BTX	E/Electric	Craven B39C	1936	1956	m
14, 47-50, 66	AET901-6	Guy BTX	E/Electric	Craven B39C	1937	1950-6	n
67-9, 58-60	AET907-12	AEC664T	E/Electric	Craven B39C	1937	1950-6	o
13	AET913	Guy BTX	E/Electric	Craven B39C	1937	1956?	p
57	AET914	AEC664T	E/Electric	Craven B39C	1937	1950	q
19-22	CET80-3	Guy BTX		E Lancs B38C	1939	1950-3	r
23-6	CET84-7	AEC664T	E/Electric	E Lancs B38C	1939	1950?	s
70-7	CET480-7	Sunbeam MS2C	GEC	E Lancs B38C	1940	1950?	t
82-9	CET607-14	Sunbeam MS2	GEC	E Lancs B38C	1942	1950-6	u
75-94	FET335-50, 471-4	Daimler CTC6/ CTE6	C/Parkinson/ E/Electric	E Lancs B38C	1949/50	1954-65	v
1-24	FET601-24	Daimler CTC6/ CTE6	C/Parkinson/ E/Electric	E Lancs B38C	1950/1	1954-65	v

Notes:

a Nos 38-43 renumbered T1-T6 in 1916

b Later renumbered 52

c Later renumbered 50. Sold to Darlington 1937

d Later renumbered 53, 42, 43

e Later renumbered 47-49. Sold to Darlington 1937

f Later renumbered 51

g On loan from St Helens where No 109

h Later renumbered 54

i Later renumbered: 55 to 39 then 19; 56 to 40; 20 to 29; 21 to 30; 22 to 31 then 78 then 17; 23 to 32; 25 to 33 then 16; 26 to 37 then 31 then 22; 28 to 15; 31 to 34 then 79 then 18; 32 to 35 then 80; 33 to 37; 34 to 20; 35 to 21; 37 to 81; 38 to 23

j Later renumbered: 54 to 26; 57 to 33; 58 to 44

k Later renumbered: 39 to 45; 41 to 24; 42 to 25; 59 to 43

l Later renumbered: 15 to 27 then 59; 16 to 28; 17 to 29 then 61; 18 to 30 then 62

m Later renumbered: 60 to 66 then 36; 61 to 31; 62 to 32; 63 to 33; 64 to 34; 65 to 35

n Later renumbered: 13 to 52; 14 to 46 then 37; 47 to 38 then 63; 48 to 39 then 64; 49 to 40; 50 to 41; 66 to 51 then 42

o Later renumbered: 67 to 48; 68 to 49; 69 to 50 then 66; 58 to 45; 59 to 46; 60 to 47

p Later renumbered 43 and 65

q Later renumbered 44

r Later renumbered: 19 to 55; 20 to 56 then 69; 21 to 57 then 70; 22 to 58 then 71

s Later renumbered: 23 to 51; 24 to 52; 25 to 53; 26 to 54

t Later renumbered 59-66 respectively

u Later renumbered 67-74 respectively. Later Nos 67 and 73 were renumbered 73 and 74 respectively

v Rebodied Roe H40/30R 1956/7 and renumbered as follows: 75 to 29; 78 to 35; 79 to 30; 80 to 38; 81 to 27; 82 to 39; 83 to 25; 85 to 26; 91 to 34; 92 to 36; 93 to 33; 7 to 28; 8 to 40; 11 to 41; 12 to 32; 14 to 42; 15 to 31; 16 to 43; 17 to 37; 18 to 44. Renumbered 1956: 76 to 7; 77 to 8; 84 to 2; 94 to 4; 6 to 3; 9 to 5; 10 to 6; 24 to 1.
Sold to Cadiz, Spain: Nos 1-5, 19-22, 23, 86-90.
Sold to Tolosa, Spain: 2 (ex-84), 1 (ex-24).

Preserved vehicles: Nos 37 (ex-17), 44 (ex-18)

their depot workings between Herringthorpe Lane and the Rawmarsh Road depot on the other side of town had involved the use of the tramways manager's ingenious contrivance which incorporated a steering arm guided by the tracks. On 14 December of the same year, the Maltby terminus was changed from Hall Estate to the Queen's Head hotel. In spite of the fact that the trolleybuses now ran through to the centre of Rotherham, it was not until 10 June 1929 that the last tramcar ran on the Broom Road tracks.

Meanwhile, the initial six vehicles had been replaced by six Straker-Cloughs with similar tram-type bodies, again by Roe but with enclosed rear platforms. They were followed by three more Straker-Cloughs, again with Roe bodies but of a greatly improved design with new-style windows and rounded roof. Some rebodying was also done in the depot workshops, including conversions to the central entrance layout which was to be favoured for single-deckers to the end.

The next incursion of trolleybuses into Rotherham resulted from the conversion plans of the Mexborough & Swinton Traction Co, which had since 1915 been operating two short routes as feeders to its Mexborough-Rotherham tram service. Now it was linking its two separate trolley routes and extending the wires in order to replace the tramcars entirely, so bringing the company's trolley vehicles into the centre of Rotherham. It was not until 1926 that the Corporation, over whose tracks the company tramcars entered the town, agreed to instal trolleybus wires over its section of route to permit this through working. Finally on 10 March 1929 through trolleybus services started between corporation and company, with Rotherham Corporation vehicles working to the company's termini at Mexborough and Conisbrough, employing Guy six-wheelers with 32-seat Roe bodies (including Nos 43-45) while the company's single-deck Garretts became a familiar sight in the town. A formal ceremony marking the commencement of the new services took place on 12 March.

Further expansion of Rotherham's own system came in 1931. In view of proposed road reconstruction on the Thrybergh route, it was decided that this should be replaced by trolleybuses rather than that the tram tracks should be relaid. In 1930 it was also decreed that the conversion of the Kimberworth tram route should be made at the same time. Accordingly, trolleybus operation on a through service between Kimberworth and Thrybergh started on 17 May 1931, utilising a new batch of 32-seat Craven-bodied Ransomes (originally numbered 39, 40 and 19-38), the Corporation's largest order so far.

At Kimberworth the wires were continued a short distance beyond the old tram terminus to the Colin Campbell Inn, while at Thrybergh the wires were installed along Old Gate Lane and Park Lane instead of following the former tramway on Whinney Hill along the main Doncaster road. A branch about 1 mile in length was brought into use on 2 June 1931 to serve Silverwood Colliery, to which point it had earlier been proposed that the tramway should be extended.

Back in 1928, proposals to replace the Thrybergh trams by trolleybuses had envisaged the wires continuing along the Doncaster road to connect with the Mexborough company's wires at Conisbrough, thus completing an extensive circle, but this plan was destined

Left:
Rotherham: Rotherham Corporation Daimler No 93 coyly hugs the wall at the Conisbrough Low terminus of the Mexborough & Swinton system.   *C. Carter*

Below left:
Rotherham: A scenic section of the Rotherham system on the branch to Silverwood. Double-decker No 30 was originally single-decker No 79.   *C. Carter*

Above:
Rotherham: A profusion of Daimlers in the centre of Rotherham in the early 1950s. No 84 on the right was soon to be given a new Roe double-deck body and become No 26.   *R. Brook*

never to reach fruition. Other earlier proposals which did not materialise would have seen the trolley wires projected from Conisbrough to meet those of Doncaster Corporation, conjuring visions of a through Rotherham-Doncaster service.

Of Rotherham's remaining tramways, it was decided that the Canklow route should be replaced by motorbuses rather than trolleybuses, and this change was effected on 10 July 1934. Meanwhile, on the Thrybergh route, in order to provide a turning point at the Pumping Station a loop around Mowbray Street and Herringthorpe Valley Road was brought into use during 1933, mainly for colliery extras to and from Silverwood, and a turning circle was also installed at the end of Mowbray Street. A new section of route, brought into operation on 28 March 1935, branched off the Maltby route and ran along Broom Lane and Bawtry Road, to join the existing service at the Brecks. Another new route, to Greasbrough, was opened on 1 July 1936; years before, this had been proposed as a tramway but had never been constructed.

Meanwhile, the fleet had been growing, with 1933/34 deliveries including 10 Guy BT32s (five with Craven bodies and five with bodies by Charles Roberts) all of which were 32-seaters and originally numbered respectively 52-54, 57 and 58, and 39-41 and 59. These were followed by six 1936 Craven-bodied Guys Nos 60-65. Further acquisitions during the later 1930s included six-wheelers on AEC 664T and Guy BTX chassis, some bodied by Cravens and others by East Lancashire. Wartime deliveries brought Sunbeams into stock; Nos 70-77 were MS2Cs obtained in 1940 and Nos 82-89 were MS2s of 1942, all with bodies by East Lancashire.

Rotherham's last tram route, the busy main line through Templeborough to Sheffield, had been considered as a likely candidate for conversion to trolleybuses. However, this depended on Sheffield, with whom the through service was operated jointly, and Sheffield did not favour the introduction of trolley vehicles. The outcome was that the trams continued to run, and in 1934/35 for its share of the joint service Rotherham introduced a series of new single-ended tramcars which looked more like double-deck trolleybuses than conventional trams. In 1939, with the coming of increased wartime traffic, Rotherham decided to extend the trolleybus wires along the tramway as far as Templeborough, the municipal boundary with Sheffield. This was done in March 1940, when services were operated to this point from other termini (including Maltby, Thrybergh and Kilnhurst Road on the Mexborough system) to give cross-town facilities to cater for workers to and from the steel works in the area. However, the trolleybus workings later became somewhat spasmodic, although the tramcars continued to run from Rotherham to Sheffield until 1948 and to Templeborough until 1949, when services ceased on 13 November.

Only the previous year, on 2 May 1948, the Kimberworth route had been extended about ½ mile to the Toll Bar. This proved to be the last route extension and was destined for a short life, for in September 1953 service was cut back to Ewers Road. With other withdrawals during the early 1950s, including Greasbrough in May 1951 and Broom Lane a few weeks later, the trolleybus was apparently on the way out in favour of the motorbus. Rising costs were telling against the relatively low earning capacity of the single-deckers.

The pioneer route to Maltby ran for the last time on 2 May 1954, although trolleybuses continued to work as far as Wickersley until 1963. The showpiece of the system, the Maltby route had long enjoyed a reputation for speed. A table published in *Tramway & Railway World* in 1927 showed that of 16 systems then in operation, Rotherham (which then comprised only the Maltby route) was the fastest, with an average speed of 10½mph. The slowest was Ramsbottom at 6½mph, while Wolverhampton averaged just over 8mph. As early as 1931 the Ministry of Transport had approved a maximum speed of 30mph, which was believed to be the first instance where such a high speed had been sanctioned for trolley vehicles. The 1949 schedule for the 14-mile round trip, including layover, was only 58min, while at peak times a 6min frequency was provided.

The impression of speed on the Rotherham system was heightened by the exclusive use of single-deckers until the final years, and of these the best remembered were the postwar Daimler six-wheelers. Models CTC6 and CTE6 chassis with stylish East Lancashire bodies, the first went into service in 1949 as the first postwar additions to the fleet and the prototype of the new Daimler range. Rotherham ordered a total of 44 to complete the replacement of prewar vehicles, including some of the 1931 veterans. Nos 75-94 were put into service in 1949/50, followed by Nos 1-24 in 1950/51, comprising both type CTE6 (with English Electric equipment) and CTC6 (with Crompton-Parkinson equipment). The three-axle chassis with Kirkstall rear bogies carried 38-seat bodies, the central entrance having jack-knife doors and only a single step from road level to the main saloon.

Before long, however, economic circumstances were telling against the use of single-deckers, and in 1955 the new General Manager, I. O. Fisher, suggested that larger-capacity double-deckers would be better able to deal with peak loads, as well as to alleviate the staff shortage. Since the Daimlers still had years of useful life left in them, it was decided that 14 of them should be rebuilt with new 70-seat double-deck bodies. The first of these, with Roe-built bodies, appeared in 1956, and subsequently a total of 20 vehicles were so transformed, to be renumbered 25-44. At the same time, eight vehicles were retained as single-deckers and these were renumbered 1-8. The remaining Daimlers were sold to Spain for further service, and were also joined by No 1.

The new double-deckers, which took over the Kimberworth-Thrybergh service on 7 May 1956 and Wickersley on 1 February 1957, succeeded in making operation more remunerative and so staved off the eventual demise for a time, but in the light of sustained losses in the face of mounting costs, it was decided in 1962 that the trolleybuses should eventually be replaced by diesel buses. Already, with the final abandonment of the Mexborough company's system, the last services between Rotherham, Mexborough and Conisbrough had run on 26 March 1961, ending the joint operations. This marked the end of the last of the few instances of joint municipal/company operation, as well as the demise of the last company-owned system in Britain.

In Rotherham itself, the Brecks and Wickersley services ended on 14 January 1963. The remaining Kimberworth-Thrybergh cross-town route, with its peak-time extension to Silverwood Colliery and short workings to the Pumping Station, survived until 1965, with the final closure on 2 October ending 53 years of 'trackless' operation.

References
Rotherham Transport History by John Attridge (Hendon Publishing Co, 1984).
'A History of the Barnsley, Dearne, Mexborough and Rotherham Tramway Conurbation' by C. C. Hall, *Tramway Review*, Nos 51-58, 1967-69.
'British Trolleybus Systems: No 23 — Rotherham', *Buses*, September 1985.

St Helens

'The general appearance of the body is extremely pleasing, and the interior finish of bird's eye maple contrasted with teak and red upholstery, gives a very charming effect.' So *Tramway & Railway World* described the first trolleybuses in St Helens in 1927. The observer would have had to go some 2 miles out of the town to see in action these four single-deck

St Helens

Fleet Nos	Registration Nos	Chassis	Electrical equipment	Body	In service	Withdrawn	Notes
1-4	DJ 3243-6	Garrett	Bull/Garrett	RS&J B35C	1927	1938	a
5, 105-9	DJ 3684, 4081-4, ET 5968	RS&J	Ransomes/E/Electric	RS&J B35C	1928/9	1938/40	b
110-4	DJ 4845-9	RS&J	Ransomes/E/Electric	RS&J L32/28R	1931	1945	b
116-20	DJ 6051-5	RS&J	Ransomes/E/Electric	Brush L24/26R	1934	1945-50	
121-5	DJ 6106, 6120-3	Leyland TBD2	GEC	Brush L24/26R	1934	1952	c
126-36	DJ 6453-63	Leyland TBD2	GEC	Massey L24/26R	1935	1952	d
137-44	DJ 6863-7, 7236-8	RS&J	Ransomes/ C/Parkinson/ Alan West	Massey L24/26R	1936/7	1949-52	
101	DJ 7428	Leyland TBD2	Ransomes/ C/Parkinson/ A/West	Massey L24/26R	1937	1956	e
102-4	DJ 7429-31	Leyland TBD2	Metrovick	Massey L24/26R	1937	1956	e
145-56	DJ 8120-31	RS&J	Ransomes/ C/Parkinson/ A/West	Massey L24/26R	1938	1950-2	
157-66	DJ 9005-14	Sunbeam MF2	BTH	Massey L24/26R	1942	1952-6	f
105-14	DJ 9183-92	Sunbeam W	BTH	Roe UL24/26R	1945	1956-8	g
174-81	BDJ 74-81	Sunbeam F4	BTH	E/Lancs H29/26R	1950/1	1958	h
182-9	BDJ 82-9	BUT 9611T	E/Electric	E/Lancs H30/26R	1950/1	1958	i

Notes:

a Renumbered 101-4 in 1929. Nos 101/3/4 renumbered 161/3/4 in 1937

b No 5 renumbered 100 in 1929. Nos 100 and 110 renumbered 110 and 115 respectively in 1934

c Rebodied by East Lancs in 1945-7

d Rebodied by East Lancs in 1944-8

e Rebodied by East Lancs in 1947-8; renumbered 301-4 in 1955

f Renumbered 357-66 in 1955

g Renumbered 305-14 in 1955

h Renumbered 374-81 in 1955; sold to South Shields in 1958 as Nos 201-3/5/6-9

i Renumbered 382-9 in 1958; sold to Bradford in 1958 as Nos 794-801

Below:
St Helens: New 1931 Ransomes No 111 demonstrates the necessity for its lowbridge body.   *Ian Allan Library*

Garretts with their central-entrance Ransomes bodies, for their route started at the somewhat unprepossessingly named terminus of 'Rainhill Mental Hospital' (later referred to as Nutgrove) and ran for about 2½ miles through Rainhill to Prescot. At each end of their journey the vehicles connected with tram services, while to travel to and from their depot in the town centre they used a skate in the tracks.

The new trolley route had itself previously been a tramway, but the need to provide a better service than was possible over the worn-out single track led to the decision to adopt trolley vehicles, the installation of which would cost substantially less than the reconstruction of the tramway. Moreover, the trolleys scored over the motorbuses (which had been serving the route since the tramcars had been withdrawn in 1923) in that they retained a useful load for the municipal power station. The service started on 11 July 1927 and was soon announced as 'proving very popular' with a 'decided increase' in receipts.

The next changeover took place on the other

side of town, when on 30 July 1929 trolleybuses were inaugurated on the route to Parr, on which motorbuses had been working since the trams were withdrawn at the end of 1928 to enable the overhead to be installed for the trolley vehicles. The wires were also extended beyond the former tram terminus along Derbyshire Hill Road to Waring Avenue, and for the first time trolleybuses now served the town centre. An additional six vehicles were obtained from Ransomes, again single-deckers with central entrance.

Double-deckers made their debut in 1931 with the introduction on 21 June of trolleybuses in place of tramcars on the route to Haydock, where they met the wires of the South Lancashire Transport Co which had been extending its trolley activities westwards. The link-up at Haydock enabled a lengthy through service to be operated jointly by the company and St Helens Corporation between St Helens and Atherton via Haydock, Ashton-in-Makerfield and Hindley. For its share the corporation employed five six-wheelers (they were to remain the only such in the fleet) built by Ransomes with lowbridge 60-seat bodies, presumably to match the capacity of the six-wheel double-deck Guys used by the SLT.

It was nearly 3 years later that the next new route commenced, when on 16 May 1934 trolleybuses began to operate to Windle and Moss Bank, taking over from buses which in their turn had replaced the trams to Windle in 1932. In the same year, on 4 July 1934, the isolated original route between Rainhill and Prescot was at last connected to the town centre and the rest of the growing system when trolleybuses were extended along Prescot Road to the Toll Bar to meet the existing wires at Nutgrove, and a new through trolleybus service was inaugurated between St Helens and Prescot via Rainhill. The fleet was enlarged by the addition of the first four-wheel double-deckers, of which five came from Ransomes and five from Leyland, all of them having lowbridge bodies. Two further conversions were made in 1935: to St Helens Junction on 1 May and to Dentons Green on 29 May.

The only tramcars still left in action were those on the main route to Prescot via St Helens Road, and with the completion of the wiring on the final 2 miles between the Toll Bar and Prescot these were withdrawn and replaced by a trolleybus service on 1 April 1936, making use of five more Ransomes double-deckers. With the connection of the wiring to the Rainhill route at Prescot, a circular service could be operated between St Helens and Prescot.

The corporation's fleet now amounted to some

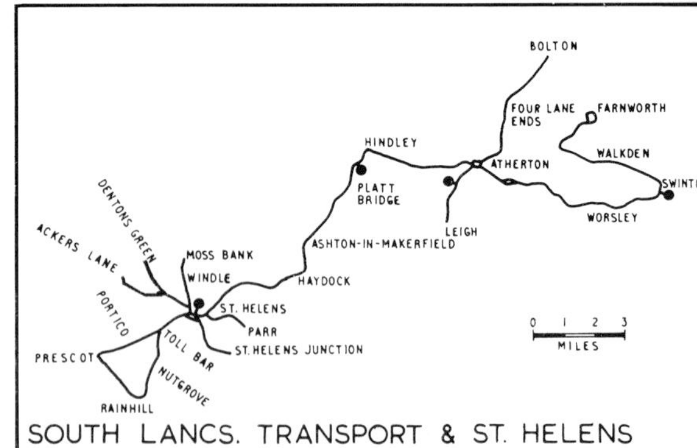

SOUTH LANCS. TRANSPORT & ST. HELENS

Above:

St Helens: En route to Haydock in 1952, No 129 was one of the 1935 Leyland TBD2s rebodied by East Lancashire between 1944 and 1948.
V. C. Jones/Ian Allan Library

40 vehicles on about 17 miles of routes. The linking of cross-town services, and an extensive one-way layout in the town centre, avoided the need for turning loops in the central streets.

By 1938 the trolleybuses were carrying almost 16 million passengers a year, while their efficiency was indicated by the fact that their ratio of working expenses to receipts was only 70% compared with 90% for the motorbuses. Their routes approached the optimum for trolley vehicle operation in that they were generally short and heavily loaded, and the intention was obviously to keep them in this happy situation. As *Transport World* reported in 1938, 'the policy governing development of facilities is that trolleybuses will be intensified in frequency of service as required on existing routes, whereas buses will be used to develop new districts in outlying areas'. Not until the late 1940s did the size of the motorbus fleet exceed the trolleybus fleet.

Acts of 1935 and 1939 authorised several extensions totalling some 5 miles. These included links which would have created circular routes: Boardman's Lane on the Parr route to Redgate on the Haydock route; Denton Green to Windle; and Denton Green and Toll Bar to Ackers Lane (this latter not yet a trolleybus route). There would also have been extensions or branches on the Parr, Rainhill and Junction routes, while a 'blanket' authorisation for any extension of less than half a mile was included in an Act of 1948. However, the only extension actually made came in 1943, when on 29 June trolleybuses took over from buses on the Ackers Lane route, which had never been a tramway. This conversion was made practicable by the accession to stock of 10 wartime-grey Sunbeam MF2s which had been destined for Johannesburg in South Africa. These were not only the first 8ft-wide vehicles in St Helens, but among the first in Britain and the only lowbridge 8ft-wide trolleybuses. Just after the war, delivery was taken of 10 utility-bodied Sunbeam Ws.

In 1950/51 highbridge double-deckers were placed in service for the first time when eight Sunbeam F4s and eight BUT 9611Ts arrived. They were to be the last newcomers to the trolleybus ranks. Their normal field of activity throughout their lives in St Helens was the St Helens-Rainhill-Prescot loop, but just in case one should have happened to stray, a special safety device was arranged to prevent it attempting to negotiate the bridge at Peasley Cross on the St Helens Junction route which was too low. At the approach to the bridge, the overhead wires were splayed several feet apart so that the nearside wire was almost over the footpath. The consequent outward and downward movement imparted to the nearside trolley pole caused it to actuate a switch to cut the power to the vehicle before it could decapitate itself under the bridge. At the same time a warning sign was illuminated in the driver's cab.

Even before the newcomers had had time to find their feet, the decision had been taken to discontinue the whole trolleybus system. The first major step taken in this direction on 2 February 1952 saw the withdrawal of the routes to Dentons Green, St Helens Junction, Ackers Lane and Moss Bank. Regular service on the Parr route ceased on 12 November 1955, but peak period workings continued for another year, until 9 November 1956. Also in 1956, with the neighbouring SLT also engaged in trolleybus replacement, came the withdrawal on 11 November on the joint route between St Helens and Atherton. Finally, services ceased on the St Helens-Prescot-Rainhill loop on 30 June 1958, followed on the next day by a ceremonial closure when the Mayor and Transport Committee made a special journey in No 374 to mark the end of the town's trolleybuses. The 16 vehicles of 1950/51 were sold for a further spell of duty elsewhere, the eight Sunbeams going to South Shields and the eight BUTs to Bradford.

References
The Trolleybuses of St Helens by Geoffrey Sandford (Reading Transport Society).
'St Helens Corporation Transport' by John G. E.Nye; *Omnibus Magazine*, October 1957.
'Municipal Transport Undertakings: 2 — St Helens; *Transport World*, 10 November 1938.
St Helens Tramways by E. K. Stretch (St Helens Corporation 1968).
'Trolleybuses in St Helens' — by E. K. Stretch; *Trolleybus Magazine*, July 1973.

South Lancashire Transport

(See map on page 132)
The trolleybus system operated by the South Lancashire Transport Co was one of the most extensive in Britain, but while it embraced a route mileage of more than 30 miles, the fleet amounted to only about 70 vehicles. This was no ordinary urban network of short intensive services, but a widespread interurban undertaking with routes which could claim to be among the longest in Britain in their course between strings of towns and colliery villages. In addition the vehicles made up for their comparative scarcity by establishing something of a record for longevity.

If all the early visions had materialised, the company's system might well have been very much more extensive than it actually was. Its origins went back to the turn of the century, when the South Lancashire Tramways Co opened its first tramways in 1902 and within the next few years constructed lines which met those of Bolton, Salford, Wigan and St Helens, so that the company occupied a strategic position in the network which traversed this busy industrial area. Many other proposed lines, however, were never built.

Under its Act of 1929, the company changed its name to the South Lancashire Transport Co and obtained powers to replace its tramways by trolleybuses. The first trolleybuses were intro-

duced on 3 August 1930 in place of tramcars between Atherton and Ashton-in-Makerfield. On 21 June 1931 they were extended to Haydock, the boundary with St Helens Corporation, which had itself by this time taken off its tramcars and installed wires to enable a through trolleybus service to be introduced between Atherton and St Helens, a distance of nearly 14 miles, and the company and St Helens Corporation worked the service jointly. The company's vehicles for this route were stationed at the former tram depot at Hindley.

The next conversion saw three tram services replaced by one long and curiously-shaped trolleybus route, when on 19 August 1931 trolley vehicles started to run between Atherton and Farnworth, by way of Worsley, Swinton, Walkden and Little Hulton. This was a trek of more than 14 miles, although the two termini were only about 5 miles apart as the crow flies. Service was operated from the former tram depot at Swinton, but was soon shared with the main depot at Howe Bridge (Atherton) which was brought into full trolleybus use when on 17 December 1933 trolleybuses took over the route between Leigh, Atherton and Bolton. The section of the company's tramway south of Leigh to Lowton, however, was replaced by motorbuses.

For the 3 miles between Four Lane Ends and the centre of Bolton, the company's trolley vehicles ran in Bolton Corporation territory (no through tickets were issued) and the corporation continued to work a tram service on this

section, until on 29 March 1936 it was replaced by additional trolleybuses. For its part, Bolton Corporation now became the owner of four trolleybuses, although this fact was not obvious since they were not distinguished from the company's vehicles in any way, they were operated by the company and they were housed in the company's depot. Although the corporation from time to time had hankerings after installing a complete system of its own, this was to remain the limit of its involvement with the trolleybus.

The company's fleet started in 1930 with 10 Guy BTX six-wheelers with Roe bodies, followed in 1931 by 20 more of similar type. For service on the Leigh-Bolton route, 16 Guy BT four-wheelers were acquired, again with Roe bodywork. All these were of the lowbridge type, in view of restrictive bridges on the Atherton-St Helens and Atherton-Farnworth routes. However, all later additions were of highbridge design, and so were mostly kept to the Leigh-Bolton route. The 12 1936-38 vehicles again were six-wheelers with Roe bodies, but this time on Leyland chassis; they included in 1936 the four vehicles for Bolton Corporation (Nos 48-51). An odd one out was No 47, a Guy six-wheeler with Guy body, acquired in 1935.

South Lancashire Transport

Fleet Nos	Registration Nos	Chassis	Electrical equipment	Body	In service	Withdrawn	Notes
1-10	TF 2072-81	Guy BTX	Metrovick	Roe L25/31R	1930	1956	a
11-30	TF 5792/3/5240/ 5794-6/5241/ 5797-5805/ 6951	Guy BTX	Metrovick	Roe L27/29R	1931	1956-8	a
31-46	TJ 3320-30/2969/ 3331/2/4/5	Guy BT	GEC/Electric Construction Co	Roe L22/26R	1933	1956-8	a
47	JW 5370	Guy BTX	GEC	Guy H27/29R	1935	1955	b
48-59	ATE 792-5, BTE 951/2, DTC 261-6	Leyland TTB4	Metrovick	Roe H35/29R	1935-8	1956	a, c
60-63	FTD 452-5	Karrier W	GEC	Weymann UH30/26R	1943	1958	
64, 65	FTE 152/3	Karrier W	E/Electric	Weymann UH30/26R	1944	1958	
66-71	HTD 863-8	Sunbeam MS2	Metrovick	Weymann H34/30R	1947-8	1958	

Notes:

a The following were rebuilt in varying degrees in 1950-55:
Nos 1, 5, 6, 7, 8, 10, 11, 12, 14, 16, 17, 18, 20, 22-25, 27-30,
31, 32, 40-42, 44 and 48. Nos 1-10 original seating L29/31R

b Ex-demonstrator

c Nos 48-52 were owned by Bolton Corporation

Wartime deliveries consisted of six Weymann-bodied Karrier Ws, while the last new vehicles to be added were six Sunbeam MS2 six-wheelers in 1948. Withdrawals did not begin to thin the ranks until the mid-1950s, and several of the original 1930 batch were still doing duty at the final closure in 1958.

While the continued existence of such vintage machines added character to the fleet, further variety was imparted by the numerous modifications which were made to individual vehicles in their later years, until it could ultimately be claimed that among the original 46 lowbridge vehicles, no two were exactly alike. The most noticeable change made to several of them comprised the fitting of a new and more modernistic front end which completely transformed their frontal aspect.

Strangely enough, the company continued to be responsible for about 3 miles of tramway until as late as 1944, although services on these lines were maintained by Bolton Corporation cars. From Moses Gate, there were two routes: to Farnworth and to Walkden. The company obtained powers in 1948 to operate trolleybuses over these routes to connect with its existing routes, but it did not exercise them. Although there had once been thoughts of an extension from Worsley to the Salford boundary at Winton, and from Farnworth to Pendlebury, in fact no further extensions were ever made to the system.

While the company's system comprised three routes, one of these was in effect three-in-one, and numerous short workings supplemented the basic service on all three. Perhaps not surprisingly, no through fares were offered on the Atherton-Swinton-Farnworth route (none but the enthusiast would have wanted to ride 14 miles by trolleybus rather than 5 miles by bus) and a layover was taken at Swinton. As well as turning facilities at Worsley, Walkden and Tyldesley, reversing triangles were provided at Mosley Common, Boothstown, Swinton and Sandhole colliery, at all of which points short workings could terminate to supplement the basic 15-20min headway. At Farnworth the original triangle was superseded in 1936 for normal service by a terminal loop around Market Street, Brackley Street and Albert Road. Overbridges at Worsley and Little Hulton restricted services east of Worsley to lowbridge vehicles, until 1957 when it was found that in fact highbridge trolleybuses could just manage to squeeze through.

The Leigh-Bolton route usually carried the company's most intensive service, and included the Bolton local workings to Hulton Lane and Four Lane Ends. The jointly-operated Atherton-St Helens route also had its share of short workings, with reversing triangles at Hindley Green, Hindley and Ashton, as well as at Haydock, partly for St Helens Corporation's own services. An unusual (and probably unique) feature near Platt Bridge was a short section of private road which had formerly been a length of tramroad. The tracks remained in position to the end, ensuring a somewhat

Above:

South Lancashire: On trial on the South Lancashire system in 1951 is Glasgow Corporation's experimental 'transit type' single-decker No TB35, which also underwent trials in Nottingham and Walsall
Ian Allan Library

narrow and bumpy passage for the trolley vehicles. This route also had its quota of low bridges: at Dangerous Corner (near Atherton), Platt Bridge, and Redgate in St Helens. The worst offender (at Dangerous Corner) was later removed, and then again as late as 1956 it was found that St Helens highbridge trolleybuses could negotiate the others. In Atherton, the St Helens route terminated at a reversing triangle, while the other services at this focal point of the SLT system traversed a layout of one-way streets through the town.

After plans for closure were announced in 1955, the first contraction involved the withdrawal on 25 March 1956 of the Bolton local service and its replacement by Corporation buses, although SLT trolleybuses continued to run into Bolton. In connection with St Helens Corporation's conversion plans, the St Helens-Atherton service was withdrawn on 11 November 1956. The whole of the rest of the SLT system ceased operation on the same day, 31 August 1958, on which date the company ceased to exist as a separate entity and was absorbed into the parent company, the Lancashire United Transport Co, of which it had been a wholly-owned subsidiary since 1906. On the following day, 1 September, a specially repainted trolleybus (No 71) lettered 'Lancashire United Transport', made a ceremonial journey between Atherton and Leigh. This was the first and only LUT trolleybus working.

References
'South Lancashire Trolleybuses'; *Modern Transport*, 1 November and 6 December 1958.
'South Lancashire Recollections' by E. K. Stretch; *Trolleybus Magazine*, May, July and September 1968.
South Lancashire Tramways by E. K. Stretch (Manchester Transport Museum Society, 1972).

Southend-on-Sea

The Southend system was one that never quite made it. The trolleybuses did not take over all the main tram routes, and their own routes included sections which were destined to be little used, while proposed extensions failed to materialise. Nevertheless, the Corporation acquired an interesting collection of unusual (and even unique) vehicles which offered pleasant rides in a contrasting environment of quiet residential roads and seaside bustle.

During the early 1920s, Southend Corporation was considering the need for additional transport facilities to meet the requirements of the expanding town, and the place of the trolleybus was examined in addition to the possible construction of sleeper-track tramways. The municipal tramway system already served the main London Road to Leigh-on-Sea, as well as the seafront and the coast road to Thorpe Bay. In 1923 the Light Railways Committee received a report from the electrical engineer on the best means of providing an improved service on the Prittlewell route. This was a single track tramway, and in order to handle the growing traffic and provide a better service, the track would need to be doubled and extended. Alternatively, a different form of transport would have to be adopted. Members of the Committee, who had recently visited the Birmingham installation, were favourably inclined towards the introduction of trolleybuses. After further consideration, it was agreed that trolleybuses should be employed as an experiment over a period of 12 months, and arrangements were made for Railless to lend two single-deck vehicles and to instal the overhead.

In due course, operation started on 16 October 1925 along the Victoria Avenue tramway of about ¾-mile between Victoria Circus and Prittlewell, with the new vehicles supplementing the tramcars. The installation incorporated a turning circle at Victoria Circus and a triangular reverser at the West Street terminus at Prittlewell.

The new trolley vehicles 'are not to be compared in any way with the converted

Above:
Southend-on-Sea: At Victoria Circus in 1932, new No 115 (an AEC 661T with lowbridge English Electric body) is followed by single-decker No 103.
Ian Allan Library

motor-omnibus type of vehicle which is often put forward for railless work', the contemporary transport press commented. They were 'built on the low-loading principle in accordance with Railless Limited's patent methods, and consist of a single-deck body with central entrance, mounted on a low-frame chassis'. Each was fitted with a 35hp Dick Kerr motor and a foot-operated cam-type controller of English Electric design. Although generally similar to cars already supplied to Ashton-under-Lyne, Oldham and West Hartlepool, an obvious difference was 'the remarkably neat design of the open driver's cab, which has the effect of eliminating the "boxy" appearance present in closed-cab types'. The appearance of the cars was 'greatly enhanced by the exterior finish in two shades of green'. Originally

Southend-on-Sea

Fleet Nos	Registration Nos	Chassis	Electrical equipment	Body	In service	Withdrawn	Notes
1, 2	HJ 5065, 5382	Railless	E/Electric	Short B34C	1925	1933	a
103	NW 9583	AEC 603	BTH	Strachan B30F	1927	By 1936	b
104	HJ 7363	Garrett OS	E/Electric	Garrett L30/25ROS	1928	1939	
105-9	HJ 8925-9	Garrett OS	E/Electric	Garrett H32/28R	1929	1939	
110/1	JN 60/1	E/Electric	E/Electric	E/Electric H30/26D	1930	1940	c
112-5	JN 2112-5	AEC 661T	E/Electric	E/Electric L24/24R	1932	1948-54	d
116	JN 2086	AEC 663T	E/Electric	E/Electric H31/24D	1932	1951	e
117-21	JN 2817-21	AEC 661T	E/Electric	E/Electric L24/24R	1933	1948-54	f
122	JN 3822	Gloucester TDD	Crompton-West	Gloucester L54C	1934	?	
123	JN 4373	AEC 'Q' 761T	E/Electric	E/Electric L26/30F	1935	1950?	
124-9	BHJ 194-9	AEC 661T	E/Electric	Strachan H30/26R	1939	1954	
130	BHJ 827	Sunbeam W	BTH	Brush UH30/26R	1945	1953	g
131-8	BHJ 828/9/98-903	Sunbeam W	BTH	P/Royal UH30/26R	1945	1953	g
139-43	VN 9434-8	Leyland TB3	GEC	Massey B32R	1946	1953	h
144-9	BOA 364-9	Sunbeam MF2	BTH	P/Royal H28/26R	1950	1954	i
150-2	BJW 171/3/5	Sunbeam MF2	BTH	P/Royal H28/26R	1950	1954	i

Notes:

a Renumbered 101/2 by 1930

b Registered and on loan in Leeds 1927

c Sold 1940 to Nottingham, where Nos 302/3

d Nos 113/4 later rebuilt with conventional front ends

e English Electric demonstrator; rebuilt later with full front

f Nos 119-21 later rebuilt with conventional front ends

g Sold to Doncaster, where Nos 384-92 and rebodied

h Ex-Teesside Nos 9-13 of 1936

i Ex-Wolverhampton Nos 264-9, 271/3/5 of 1938

numbered 1 and 2, the pair were later renumbered 101 and 102.

Such was the success of the experiment that the Corporation decided to purchase the two Railless vehicles, and the tramcars on the route were withdrawn on 4 March 1927. The small fleet was strengthened by the purchase of a single-deck AEC which had been running in Leeds (this became No 103) and by the first double-decker, Garratt OS No 104. By early 1929 a short extension had been brought into use from Prittlewell to Priory Park.

An extension towards the sea was also put in hand along roads not traversed by trams. The route along White Gate Road as far as Bankside, where a triangular reverser was installed, was opened on 12 December 1928, but here a low railway bridge brought a temporary halt. Powers for a further ½ mile along Seaway to the Marine Parade and the Kursaal were obtained in May 1929, and the work of lowering the roadway under the offending bridge and erecting the wires was pushed ahead with alacrity, in order that the new service could be available to carry trippers to and from the seafront by the coming August Bank Holiday. It was done just in time. The Ministry of Transport inspection took place on Thursday 1 August, and on the next day the service started in anticipation of the weekend holiday crowds. Residents and visitors alike, we are told, were 'delighted' with the trolley vehicles, which now included five double-deck Garretts (Nos 105-9) fitted with 60hp Bull motors, BTH contactor control gear, and Garrett 60-seat bodies. On the seafront section, the span wires were galvanised to resist corrosion in the salt air, an experiment which seems to have been successful, for galvanised wires were also later used on other parts of the system.

The Tramways Manager was already recommending extending the service from Priory Park along Fairfax Drive to the borough boundary, a route which it was believed 'would be a most profitable one, and would be welcomed by the residents in the locality'. One of nine routes authorised under the Corporation's 1930 Act, this 1½-mile line was brought into use on 21 January 1932. It was followed on 31 July of the same year by another new route, again about 1½ miles in length, from Victoria Circus eastwards via Guildford Road and North Avenue to Hamstel Road. Again neither of these replaced tramways, and under the co-ordination scheme agreed in 1932 between the Corporation and the local bus company, both were protected from motorbus competition.

By this time the system possessed a route length of about 5 miles, and to serve the increased needs the fleet had been augmented. At the end of 1929 the Transport Committee had adopted the Manager's recommendation that, before new routes were put into operation, the Corporation should obtain experience with new types of vehicle to determine a suitable replacement for the single-deckers, and tenders were accepted from English Electric for two double-deckers which appeared in 1930 as Nos 110 and 111. Stylish three-axle vehicles, they had a rear entrance and a forward exit to speed the unloading of holiday crowds.

A change of ideas was evident in Nos 112-115 which came into service in 1932. These were two-axle double-deckers of low-height type, decided on by the Manager not only to provide greater stability but also with a view to the possible use of such vehicles on new routes where low bridges would have to be negotiated. Moreover, four-wheelers were considered to be more suitable for routes which included several tight corners, and to be more amenable to rapid fare collection on the busier short-distance in-town sections. Based on AEC 661T chassis, Nos 112-115 had lowbridge bodies seating 24 on each deck and a distinctive appearance with full

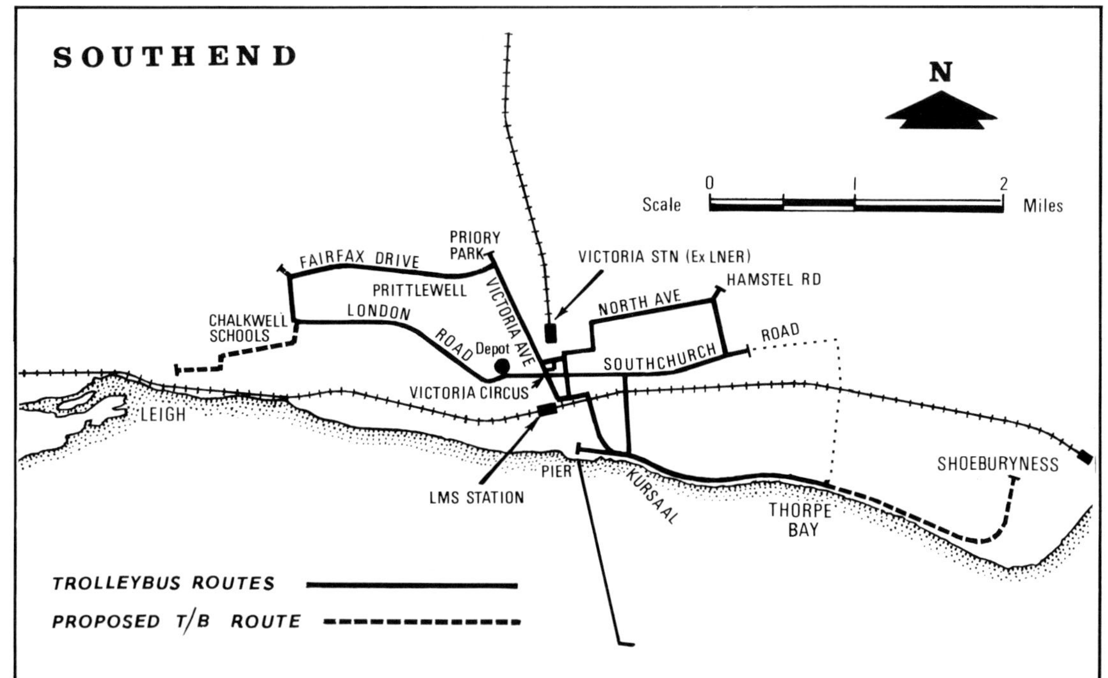

Left:

Southend-on-Sea: No 126 was a Strachans-bodied AEC 661T of 1939. *C. Carter*

Below left:

Southend-on-Sea: One of five 1936 single-deck Leylands purchased from the Teesside Railless Traction Board, No 143 mingles with the holiday crowds at the Kursaal in 1949.

V. C. Jones/Ian Allan Library

front complemented by a bus-style 'radiator'. Five similar vehicles, Nos 117-121, followed in 1933. Their success is witnessed by their long life, for several remained in evidence almost to the last days of the system, albeit with modernised front ends without the 'radiator'.

A unique vehicle in the fleet also made its debut around this time. No 116 (though not yet bearing this number in the Southend stock) was on view at the 1931 Commercial Motor Transport Exhibition following demonstration runs in Bradford and London. It was not until May 1932 that it was acquired by Southend Corporation to become No 116. Based on the AEC 663T three-axle chassis, it was fitted with English Electric equipment and body. This featured a half cab and bonnet with AEC radiator, and a forward exit fitted with a twin-hinged door, together with both rear and front stairways. Shortly after the war it was rebuilt to full-front pattern, and in 1951 it suffered the indignity of being converted to a mobile convenience! Two

further unusual vehicles came to add more diversity. Central-entrance four-wheel double-decker No 122 of 1934, a demonstrator on loan to Southend before being taken into stock, was to be the only trolleybus ever built by the Gloucester Railway Carriage & Wagon Co, while in 1935 appeared No 123, a front-entrance 56-seater and one of the only five AEC Q-type trolleybuses ever built.

In 1933 the Corporation was about to embark on the extension of the system from the Kursaal along Thorpe Bay Esplanade into Shoebury-ness, a district which in that year was incorporated into the borough. What looked like the prelude to this coastal route seemed to be taking shape in 1934, when on 21 June a short extension was opened along the Marine Parade to the Pier Head, and a Provisional Order was obtained for the 3-mile route eastwards from the Kursaal through Thorpe Bay to Shoeburyness. On 24 July 1935 the Eastchurch and Fairfax Drive trolleybuses were extended along Nelson Road to Chalkwell Schools, where they met the Leigh tramway at the London Road. By 1936 the fleet of 21 double-deckers was carrying over 8.5 million passengers a year.

The deferred question of tramway abandonment was determined in 1938, when the Transport Committee recommended that the remaining services should be replaced. This move was approved by the Town Council, and accordingly under the Southend-on-Sea Trolley

Vehicles Order of 1939 the Corporation was authorised to run trolleybuses on existing tramway routes. It was envisaged that the changeover would be completed by the spring of 1941. As a step towards this end, six Strachan-bodied AEC 661Ts (Nos 124-129) were acquired in 1939, and shortly after the outbreak of war orders were placed for 36 vehicles for delivery when conditions permitted, for the complete conversion as well as the proposed extension to Shoeburyness.

Fate ruled that the new vehicles should never be delivered and the full plan never reach fruition. It was not until 1939 that trolleybuses had taken over from tramcars between the Kursaal and Thorpe Bay, the last trams on this section running on 27 May. However, this new route was to have a curtailed life. The service was intended to be worked in summer only, since Corporation motorbuses had been running along the coast road to Shoebury Common since 1937, and the trolleybuses were withdrawn following the outbreak of war, while the wiring to the Pier Head was also to stand disused during the war years.

Wartime circumstances bought a reprieve for the surviving tramcars, since it seemed impracticable to undertake further conversions. However, the reprieve was short-lived. The final decision that the tramcars must be displaced as soon as possible was taken by the Town Council in 1941, following the sanction of the Ministry of War Transport to the move. Southend's Transport Committee had reported that, since abandonment had been contemplated for some time and therefore only essential repairs and renewals had been carried out in recent years, considerable expenditure would now be needed to put the track in good order if the tramcars were to be retained for any lengthy period. It was desirable to avoid incurring such expenditure, and therefore the trams should be withdrawn as soon as practicable. Since it would have been impossible to obtain the additional trolleybuses required for the full scheme, a modified plan had been prepared by Manager Henry Muscroft, making use of motorbuses as well as trolleybuses. It was proposed that trolleybuses should take over part of the tramway along London Road and Southchurch Road, but that motorbuses should operate in place of trams on the service to Leigh.

The last of the trams were accordingly withdrawn on 8 April 1942. Although trolleybus wires were extended during 1941-42 along the London Road tramway to join the existing wires of the Fairfax Drive route to Chalkwell Schools and thus complete a circle, this new section was not brought into use until some time after the trams had gone. In 1943 trolleybuses were extended eastwards over the former tramway to Southchurch (although they did not continue in replacement of the former sleeper-track boulevard lines which had completed a circle through Thorpe Bay, and which had succumbed to motorbuses in 1938) and in the same year along Hamstel Road to make another circle with existing North Avenue route. This addition brought the system to its maximum extent of just over 11 route miles, basically comprising three circles, but already with parts of the network out of action.

With reduced seaside traffic, Southend was able to send some of its vehicles to help more hard-pressed undertakings. The two English Electrics Nos 110 and 111 were sold in 1940 to Nottingham, where they were among the oldest in that city's fleet, in which they took fleet numbers 302 and 303. Between 1940 and 1942, by contrast, four of Southend's most modern trolleybuses were loaned to Bradford; these were 1939 AECs Nos 124-127.

Instead of welcoming the AECs envisaged before the war, fleet renewal brought nine Sunbeams in 1945 with utility bodies by Brush and Park Royal (Nos 130-138). The last new arrivals were obtained secondhand: in 1946 five single-deck Leylands (Nos 139-143) from the Teesside Railless Traction Board, dating from 1936, and in 1950 nine Park Royal-bodied

double-deck Sunbeams of 1938 vintage (Nos 144-152) from Wolverhampton.

The days of the system were numbered following a new co-ordination agreement reached between Southend Corporation and the Eastern National and Westcliff companies. This led to a revision of both corporation and company services, and the trolleybus system, by now in need of renewal and already partly moribund, found no place in the new scheme of things. Closure took place during 1954. Service on the eastern circular (via Hamstel Road and Southchurch Road) ceased on 10 February of that year, the Victoria Circus-Kursaal-Marine Parade circle on 14 July, and finally the western circular (via London Road and Fairfax Drive) on 27 October, although in latter days many of the trolley duties had already succumbed to the motorbus prior to the formal end. The final runs and the ceremonial closure, with decorated No 128, took place on the morning of 28 October 1954, so ending a system which had never developed to its full potential.

References
'Municipal Transport in Southend' *Modern Transport*, 4 September 1954.
'The Southend-on-Sea Corporation Light Railways' by R. C. Anderson — *Tramway Review* Nos 39 and 40, 1964.
'Southend Corporation Transport' — *Transport World*, 17 May 1934.
'Southend's Wartime Progress' — *Transport World*, 9 October 1941.

South Shields

Under an Act of 1935, South Shields Corporation obtained powers to abandon its tramways and to instal trolleybuses on about a dozen routes. The first route concerned, however, was not a tram replacement although it followed the tracks for part of its length. In ran from the Market Place, via Laygate, Chichester, Mortimer Road and King George Road, to a terminus in Prince Edward Road at Fremantle Road where it served a growing new housing estate. For the first in-town mile, both trams and trolleybuses used the same positive wires.

Four double-deck Weymann-bodied Karriers (Nos 200-3) were purchased and the Ministry of Transport inspection of the new installation took place on 1 October 1936. Service started on 12 October, after the Mayor had driven the first vehicle. 'The comfort and silence of the new vehicle', *Transport World* reported, 'contrasted pleasantly with the replaced form of transport and drew high praise from those present.' An extension of the service along Prince Edward Road to the coast at Marsden Bay, planned primarily for summer traffic, was brought into use on 2 May 1937. The following day (3 May) saw trolleybuses take over from tramcars on the route between the Market Place and Stanhope Road.

To replace tramcars on all but one of the remaining services (it was not intended to convert the sleeper-track Ridgeway route which had only been constructed in the 1920s) an order was placed for 26 trolleybuses. Conversion of the tramway between Pier Head and Tyne Dock via the Market Place and Laygate took place on 11 April 1938, followed closely on 14 April by the route along Fowler Street to Westoe and Chichester.

Next came the installation of what was to be the most spectacular part of the new system, the exposed Coast Road route. The first section was opened on 9 July 1938 from Pier Head along Sea Road to the New Crown at Mortimer Road. This was followed on 23 July by the further and most open section along the coast to Marsden Bay, where it joined the Prince Edward Avenue wires. A further ½-mile to Marsden Grotto was brought into use on 22 July 1939 to provide a dramatic turning loop on the cliff top. Further extension southward beyond the borough boundary was envisaged, but this never took place.

Below:
South Shields: Photographed at a quiet moment at the Market, No 265, a 1950 Karrier F4 (though carrying a Sunbeam nameplate) with body by Northern Coachbuilders, was among the last new additions to the fleet. *R. Brook*

South Shields

Fleet Nos	Registration Nos	Chassis	Electrical equipment	Body	In service	Withdrawn	Notes
200-3	CU 3589-92	Karrier E4	Metrovick	Weymann H30/26R	1936	1955/8	a, b
204-7	CU 3593-6	Karrier E4	Metrovick	Weymann H29/26R	1937	1957/63	a
208-33	CU 3850-73	Karrier E4	Metrovick	Weymann H29/26R	1937/8	1950-63	b
234	CWK 67	Daimler CTM4	Metrovick	Willowbrook H30/26R	1938	1958	b
235	KY 6210	AEC 761T	E/Electric	E/Electric H33/30F	1942	1951	c
236	LJ 7704	Thornycroft BD		Brush B32C	1942	1950	d
237-9	KW6658/9459, KY 1360	E/Electric E11	E/Electric	E/Electric H30/26R	1945	1946/7	e
240-5	CU 4601-6	Karrier W4	Metrovick	Roe H30/26R	1945/6	1962-4	
246-8	CU 4716-8	Karrier W4	Metrovick	NCB H30/26R	1947	1962/3	
249/50	CU 4719/20	Karrier W4	Metrovick	Roe H30/26R	1947	1963	
251-60	CU 4873-7, 4943-7	Karrier W4	Metrovick	NCB H30/26R	1947/8	1964	
261-70	CU 5100-5, 5279-82	Karrier F4	Metrovick	NCB H30/26R	1950	1963/6	
236-9	GNY 301/2, FTG 234/5	Karrier W4	BTH	P/Royal UH30/26R	1957	1963	f
201-3/5-9	BDJ 74-81	Sunbeam F4	BTH	E/Lancs H30/26R	1958/9	1963	g

Notes:

a In 1952, the body of No 205 was scrapped and the body of No 200 was put on No 205, which became No 200 (CU 3589)

b No 203 was rebodied by Weymann in 1942 and No 231 in 1943; No 234 was rebodied by Roe in 1942

c Ex-Bradford No 633

d Ex-Bournemouth No 71

e Ex-Bradford Nos 582, 590 and 596

f Ex-Pontypridd Nos 8, 9, 12 and 13

g Ex-St Helens Nos 374-81

Preserved vehicle: No 204

During the war, service along the Coast Road was suspended between 1941 and 1944. Meanwhile, in order to serve the town's shipyards and the new housing at Horsley Hill, wires were installed to High Shields, along Commercial Road and Templetown on one side of the town, while on the other side they were put up along Centenary Avenue to Horsley Hill, thus enabling a useful cross-town service to be started on 28 September 1942.

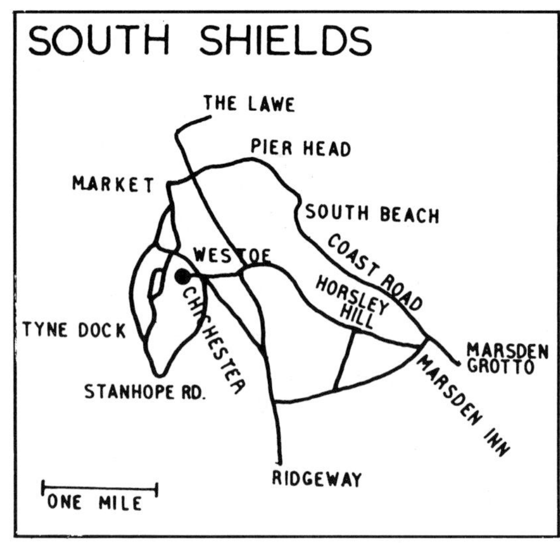

Postwar plans foresaw considerable expansion of the system and powers were obtained under the Corporation's 1945 Act for new routes, some of them to replace motorbus services as well as the remaining tramway to the Ridgeway. Several of the proposed routes never materialised, but those which did included:

31 March 1946: Along King George Road to the Ridgeway in replacement of trams.

24 July 1947: Along Commercial Road between High Shields and Market Place, and along Mile End Road to the Lawe (where a triangular reverser, the only one on the system, was installed).

5 January 1948: Along Horsley Hill Road and Highfield Road to Horsley Hill (extended to Marsden by 28 March 1948).

Wartime vehicle demands had been helped by the influx of several 'strangers' including Bradford's Q-type AEC, which became No 235 in its new home, and Bournemouth's unique single-deck Thornycroft, which took the number 236, as well as three Bournemouth Sunbeams, which had been on loan to Newcastle and then made a brief appearance in South Shields in 1943. In 1945, three Bradford English Electric six-wheelers were added to the fleet as Nos 277-9. At the end of 1945 the first postwar Karrier Ws were delivered; these were fitted with carbon-insert trolley heads instead of the wheels which had been standard up to now, and soon the whole of the fleet was so converted. More Karriers arrived in 1947 and 1948, and in 1950 came what were to prove to be the last new vehicles to be taken into the fleet, 10 Karrier F4s (though in fact with Sunbeam nameplates). Service numbers made their appearance on the trolleybuses in 1950.

The only later additions to the ranks were secondhand purchases in 1957 and 1958 from Pontypridd and St Helens, the latter being the only 8ft-wide members of the fleet. These newcomers were intended for the replacement of older vehicles, for by this time the era of expansion was over and the future of the system was in doubt. Indeed, 1958 saw the first contraction, when on 10 February buses took over the Coast Road section. In this case special factors prevailed, for traffic was generally light and corrosion of the overhead in the sea air was a severe and costly item.

A report by the General Manager in 1959 proposed total replacement of the trolleybuses by motorbuses over a period of years. It was not a question of profit or loss, he explained, since either vehicle could earn a profit when there was a sufficient density of passengers. It was a case of 'providing an elastic transport service capable of expansion to meet new needs, and in this respect the trolleybuses are at an obvious disadvantage'. Not all members of the Transport Committee were anxious to see them go; some pointed out the longer life of the trolleybus against the bus, as well as the fact that it used home-produced fuel and was not dependent on imports. A nice calculation demonstrated that

the coal needed to generate the electricity consumed by the town's trolleybuses was sufficient to keep 10½ miners in employment.

In the outcome, the changeover was deferred for two years, and it was not until 1961 that the process got under way. From 2 October 1961, trolleybuses were withdrawn from the route between the Lawe and Ridgeway. In 1963 buses gradually took over the Marsden and Horsley Hill routes, the last trolleybus to Marsden running on 1 May 1963. By the early months of 1964 the number of trolleybuses in action was steadily decreasing as buses took over their duties, until by the final day of operation — 29 April 1964 — only three trolleybuses were to be seen in service. The last run was made by No 260 without ceremony.

References
The Trolleybuses of South Shields by G. Burrows (Trolleybooks, 1976).
'South Shields Trolleybuses': *Transport World*, 12 November 1936.
The Tramways of Jarrow & South Shields by George S. Hearse (Author, 1971).

Stockport

Interest in trackless cars was shown in Stockport as early as 1911, when the tramways manager was asked to visit the new systems at Bradford and Leeds. He later also went to Bremen to look at the experimental Lloyd-Kohler system in use there. As a result of his

Below:
Stockport: Cars Nos 1 and 2 exchange trolleys on the Offerton route.

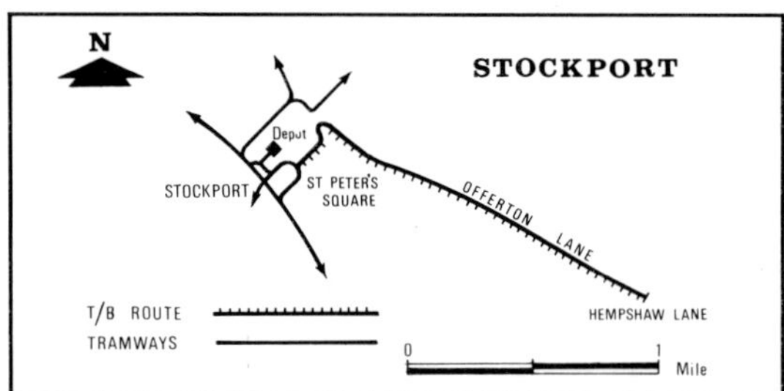

findings, the Corporation applied for Parliamentary powers to operate trolleybuses from the town centre to Offerton Lane. An extension to Marple was also under consideration, but since this would have gone outside the borough boundary, agreement with the Urban District Councils of Marple and Hazel Grove was necessary. Despite much discussion on questions of road costs, profit-sharing and the responsibility for any losses that might be incurred, agreement was not forthcoming.

Consequently Stockport went ahead and constructed its route from St Peter's Square to the borough boundary at Offerton Lane, a distance of about 1¾ miles. Service started on 10 March 1913, with the first car conveying the Deputy Mayor and members of the tramways committee.

Three vehicles (Nos 1-3) were supplied by Brush with 22-seat single-deck rear-entrance bodies. As the technical press reported, these vehicles had 'some element of novelty' in that 'the change speed control system is operated entirely by pedal action, leaving both hands of the driver free for steering purposes'. Each car had a single 35hp motor.

The new installation also claimed the distinction of being (in the words of the contemporary press) 'the first in this country equipped with a flexible trolley connection'. This was the Lloyd-Kohler or 'Bremen' system developed in Germany, with 'the two wires being erected in perpendicular parallel', the advantage of this arrangement being that 'one pair of wires is sufficient for vehicles travelling in either direction, the current collector gear being unhooked and exchanged by drivers coming in opposite directions, at any convenient meeting place'. The Stockport route thus had only one pair of wires, and the collector (known locally as the 'monkey') was transferred when two cars met. It was not unknown for the 'monkey' to drop off the wires into the roadway, with consequent disruption to service, not to mention hazard to pedestrians. Stockport was to remain the only user in Britain of the Bremen system.

Problems of maintenance and spares arose

during the war; back axle failure seemed to have been a particular problem, and on occasions the service was suspended entirely. In 1916 one car was sold to Mexborough & Swinton to become No 24, and in 1919 both remaining cars were out of action awaiting new gears and motorbuses were substituted. Thereafter the trolley vehicles ran only occasionally, and the end finally came on 11 September 1920.

References
'Stockport Trolley Omnibus Service': *Tramway & Railway World*, 10 April 1913.
Stockport Corporation Tramways by Maurice Marshall; (Manchester Transport Museum Society, 1975).

Teesside

Located in an industrial area east of Middlesbrough, the Teesside system was not one of the largest or the best known, but it possessed several claims to distinction. Apart from the limited and short-lived Ramsbottom installation, it was the only system in Britain to have developed completely unconnected with a tramway undertaking; it was the only one to have been operated by an example of that peculiarly English local government institution, the Joint Board; it was the last of the systems to open a route extension; and it was the last-but-one to cease operation, being outlived only by Bradford.

After abortive attempts to establish a tramway system, the genesis of the Teesside trackless was the 1912 Act of the comprehensively-named North Ormesby, South Bank, Normanby & Grangetown Railless Traction Co, which proposed a railless system serving the localities delineated in its title, primarily to convey workers to and from the steel works on Teesside. World War 1 delayed fulfilment of the project and, although the depot had been built by 1915, four of the 10 cars on order were reported to be almost complete by 1916 and the overhead was in position, it was not until 8 November 1919 that services were inaugurated. By this time, however, the undertaking had come into municipal ownership, following the formation of the Teesside Railless Traction Board.

Middlesbrough Corporation had been negotiating for the municipalisation of the tramways operated in its area by the Imperial Tramways Co, a process which at last became effective in 1921, and in this spirit of municipal enterprise it had looked also to the takeover of the company-promoted railless project. Follow-

Teesside

Fleet Nos	Registration Nos	Chassis	Electrical equipment	Body	In service	Withdrawn	Notes
1-10	AJ 5857-65	Cleveland	D/Kerr	E/Electric B32R	1919	By 1932	a
11-16	AJ 5866-71	Daimler	Brush	Brush B28R	1920	By 1932	b
17	AJ 7513	C/Smith/S/Squire	Straker-Clough	Straker-Clough B36F	1920	By 1936	
18-21	AJ 8607-10	S/Clough	BTH	Straker-Clough B36F	1921/2	1936	
22	PY 1845	T/Stevens TS3A	T/Stevens	Roe B32F	1924	1926	c
1-8	VN 3751-8	RS&J	RS&J/BTH	RS&J B32R	1932	1944/5	
9-13	VN 9434-8	Leyland TB3	GEC	Massey B32R	1936	1945	d
14	BVN 694	Sunbeam MF2A	BTH	E/Lancs B32R	1942	By 1969	
10-13	CPY 308-11	Sunbeam W	BTH	Roe UH30/26R	1944/5	1970-2	e
15-18	CPY 286-9	Sunbeam W	BTH	Weymann UH30/26R	1944/5	1970-2	f
1-7	GAJ 11-17	Sunbeam F4	BTH	E/Lancs H30/26R	1950	1970-2	g
8-12	VRD 183-6/192	Sunbeam F4A	BTH	Burlingham H38/30F	1969	1970-2	h

Notes:

a No 4 withdrawn before registration

b Ex-Rhondda Nos 55-60

c Petrol-electric trolleybus

d Sold to Southend-on-Sea where Nos 139-43

e Rebodied Roe H35/26R 1960-2. No 11 scrapped 1961. Nos 10 and 12 renumbered 19 and 14 respectively in 1969. No 13 renumbered T293 in 1970

f Rebodied Roe H35/26R 1960-2. Nos 16 and 17 renumbered T294 and T295 respectively in 1970

g Rebodied Roe H35/26R 1962-5. Renumbered T281-7 in 1970

h Ex-Reading Nos 183-6 and 192. Renumbered T288-292 in 1970

Preserved vehicles: Nos T285 and T291

ing negotiations started in 1918, the Railless Traction Co agreed to sell its undertaking for the sum of £40,000, excluding cars. Meanwhile, Eston Urban District Council (whose territory much of the railless routes traversed) expressed its willingness to co-operate in the purchase and operation of the system, which would then be placed under the control of a Joint Board representing the two local authorities.

Consequently, the Middlesbrough Corporation Act of 1919 gave powers for the establishment of the Teesside Railless Traction Board, 'for the purpose of acquiring by purchase and carrying on the undertaking' of the Railless Traction Co. The Board, which held its first meeting on 22 September 1919 (a few weeks before services started), consisted of three representatives each of Middlesbrough Corporation and Eston Urban District Council. Eston was to be responsible for two-thirds of the undertaking, and Middlesbrough for one-third.

The new system amounted to just over 5 route-miles. From a terminus at North Ormesby (not far from the terminus of the main Middlesbrough-Stockton tramway) the railless cars ran along South Bank Road to South Bank, where the two routes diverged; one turned into Normanby Road to reach High Street, Normanby, while the other continued along Middlesbrough Road and Eston Road to the Market Square at Grangetown.

The 10 cars which inaugurated the service (Nos 1-10) were single-deckers (the Board of Trade had refused to sanction the use of double-deckers) supplied by Railless. The chassis, built by the Cleveland Car Co of Darlington, were fitted with English Electric bodies with seats for 28 'as well as liberal space for standing room', according to a contemporary description (a reflection of the heavy workmen's traffic expected). Each car was powered by two 23hp motors, and was 'capable of maintaining a speed of 16mph even when overloaded'. The 'car shed

Left:
Teesside: No 5, a Sunbeam F4 with East Lancashire body, seen new in 1950, was later rebuilt with new Roe body. *Ian Allan Library*

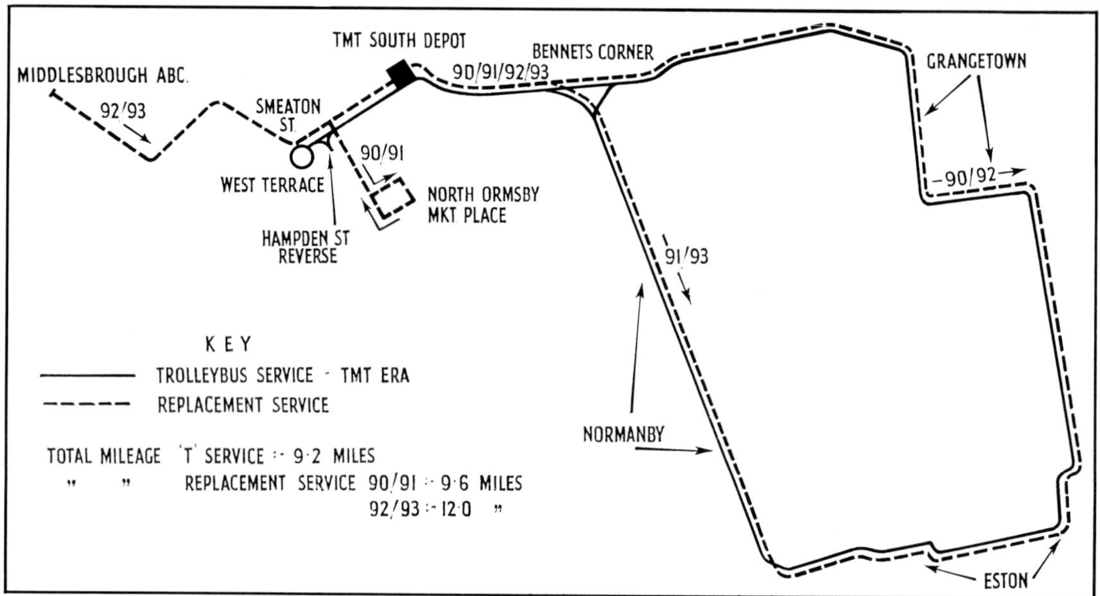

with ample room for 20 cars' was erected at South Bank. Electric power for the system was supplied by Bolckow Vaughan & Co (later Dorman Long) from its Cleveland Iron & Steel Works at South Bank, an unusual arrangement which continued until 1955, after which time the supply was taken from the grid. In order to avoid a railway level crossing at South Bank, a new bridge had been built over the line to carry the road and the trackless route, as required by the 1912 Act; in 1966 a temporary diversion was made over the level crossing while the bridge was undergoing repairs.

Traffic soon flourished to such an extent as to call for additions to stock, and these were met by the acquisition of six vehicles (Nos 11-16) from the ill-fated Rhondda system, which had ceased operation in 1915. At busy times, as many as 15 vehicles were required to maintain the service. In 1921 the first of the new Straker-Cloughs went into commission, following experience gained over the previous year or so with two contrasting vehicles developed by Clough Smith and Straker-Squire with the object of producing a modern-style trolley vehicle which would meet the requirements of the growing number of transport operators who were showing interest in this mode of transport. Of the two models, one was fitted with two motors and a hand-operated controller, while the other pointed the way ahead in having only one motor and a foot-operated controller, and it was this latter arrangement which was adopted for the new design of Straker-Clough trolleybus. A 36-seat forward-entrance body was fitted.

With a view to extending the Board's sphere of influence beyond the wires, a novel addition in 1924 was No 22, a vehicle designed to operate either as a trolleybus or as an independently-powered petrol-electric bus. Built by Tilling-Stevens, to the designs of the Teesside Manager, J. B. Parker, it was based on that company's TS 3A type of petrol-electric bus chassis, duly modified and fitted with trolley poles to enable it to take current from overhead wires. For this purpose the generator was arranged to supply a voltage equal to that of the overhead, while the control system incorporated suitable change-over switches and interlocking devices. The 32-seat, forward-entrance body was built by Roe.

This hybrid vehicle was reported to have given 'highly gratifying results under test and in actual use under normal working conditions'. It was hoped that this type of vehicle would enable the Board's operations to include an extension of service from the Normanby Road trolleybus terminus to Eston Square, as well as to facilitate through running to Redcar and into Middlesbrough. Although the vehicle worked for a time beyond the Normanby wires to Eston, great expectations were to remain largely unfulfilled and No 22 was to remain unique.

By the late 1920s, competition from independent buses, combined with the high capital expenditure that would have been needed to construct new routes, prompted serious consideration of the possibility of abandoning the trolleybus system entirely. Eight new double-deck buses, it was argued, could quite adequately do the work of 16 single-deck trolley vehicles. Nevertheless, the crisis was weathered, and during the early 1930s, when Middlesbrough was abandoning the last of its trams, there were thoughts that trolleybuses might take their place and so result in a considerably extended system. Even to their last days, the Board's trolleybuses optimistically carried the destination 'Middlesbrough' on their indicator blinds.

The fleet remained exclusively single-deck until World War 2, with deliveries during the 1930s including vehicles from both Ransomes and Leyland. The Ransomes batch of 1932, described as 'specially adapted for use in the crowded areas in which they are to operate', were rear-entrance, 32-seaters 'with a low-loading platform giving ample room for standing passengers'. Similar-style Leylands of later vintage were sold for further service at Southend-on-Sea. The last new single-decker was a solitary Sunbeam in 1942, and then in 1944 Teesside's first double-deckers made their debut in the shape of utility-bodied Sunbeams, and these were followed by further Sunbeams in 1950.

Between 1960 and 1965 the fleet was transformed when both the 1944 and the 1950 batches of Sunbeams were given new 61-seat bodies by Roe. The last to be dealt with — No 5 in 1965 — earned the doubtful distinction of acquiring the last new trolleybus body to be built for operation on any of the British systems. The still profitable trolley vehicles were carrying some 7 million passengers a year, compared with about 3½ million carried on the Board's motorbuses. Meanwhile, the Grangetown route, already extended to Kingsley Road in 1951, gained a further ½-mile extension on 23 June 1964, to bring the service to a new terminus at Fabian Road, in anticipation of the long-proposed linking of the Grangetown and Normanby routes via Eston: 'we have had this in mind for a great number of years', the general manager stated. In fact, the idea had been mooted as early as 1922.

This new route was not only the last extension to the system but also the last extension made to any of the British trolleybus systems. It was opened on 31 March 1968. Running through Eston and traversing a newly constructed road through a housing estate, just over a mile of new wiring connected the hitherto separate termini at Grangetown and Normanby, thus enabling 'circular' services to be operated. At the same time the Market Square terminus at Grangetown was taken out of use.

The date was also significant in being the last day of the Board's separate existence. From 1 April 1968 the Teesside Railless Traction Board was merged with the municipal transport undertakings of Middlesbrough and Stockton to form Teesside Municipal Transport, following the creation of the new County Borough of Teesside. Trolley vehicles soon began to appear in the new body's turquoise livery. More ominously, the small squadron of some 15 trolleybuses constituted only a small element in the combined municipal fleet, thus inducing further doubt as to its future. Indeed, not only was the new route extension seen as the last, but the life of the system itself was already regarded as limited.

Notwithstanding, in 1969 the purchase of five forward-entrance Burlingham-bodied Sunbeam F4As of 1961 vintage from Reading helped rejuvenate the ranks. At North Ormesby, road reconstruction caused the terminal loop to be replaced by a reverser at Hampden Street from 2 March 1970; the reverser itself was the one removed from South Bank the previous year. In 1970 also a renumbering of the fleet saw the trolleybuses taking the numbers T281-T295. But in that same year the admitted difficulties of maintaining the trolley vehicle services foreshadowed an early cessation. And so it turned out. The last public trolleybus service ran on 4 April 1971, to be followed after a rather protracted interval by a ceremonial final journey by decorated No T291 on 18 April, so closing one of the longest-lived and most distinctive of systems.

References
'The Tees-side Railless Traction System', *Tramway & Railway World*, 18 December 1919.
50 Years of Teesside Trolleybuses, National Trolleybus Association, 1969.

Below:
Teesside: Posing for the photographer when new in 1932, No 3 was a Ransomes, Sims & Jefferies vehicle with 32-seat rear-entrance body. *Ian Allan Library*

Walsall

The Walsall system was remarkable for its late expansion; route mileage more than doubled between 1955 and 1963. However, by this time the scales were already heavily weighted against the trolley vehicle, and only seven years later the entire network had been abandoned.

Although Walsall showed interest in the trolleybus as early as 1911 and obtained its first powers in 1914, primarily for the use of such vehicles as tramway feeders, it was not until the mid-1920s that developments actually took place. The Walsall Corporation Act of 1925 gave powers to operate trolleybuses on any of the town's tramways, on certain other roads within the borough, and on routes outside the boundary to Willenhall and from the Walsall Wood tram terminus to Shireoaks and along Chester Road to Brownhills.

A joint service to Wolverhampton was also envisaged, and it was on part of this route that Walsall's trolleybuses were to make their debut. Wolverhampton Corporation had replaced its trams on its route to Willenhall by buses in 1926, and then on 15 May 1927 had introduced trolleybuses. Walsall withdrew its trams to Willenhall in 1928, and a joint motorbus service was put on between Walsall and Wolverhampton. Walsall then decided to instal overhead from the town centre to Willenhall to link with Wolverhampton's wires so that the through service could be worked by trolleybuses. Walsall's first trolleybus service started on 22 July 1931 to Willenhall. However, it was not until the following 16 November that the through Walsall-Wolverhampton service could be introduced, since a low bridge at Horseley Fields in Wolverhampton had to be rebuilt to permit double-deckers (Wolverhampton had used single-deckers on the route). For its part Walsall purchased four six-wheel double-deckers, two AEC 663Ts with English Electric bodies (Nos 151/2) and two Guy BTXs with Brush bodies (Nos 153/4).

In 1927 consideration had been given to the conversion of the Walsall Wood tram route to trolleybus operation, but this was rejected in view of the exposed character of part of the route and because a section of the road was subject to mining subsidence which had been causing problems with the tramway track and overhead. The service was therefore taken over by motorbuses in 1928.

However, the successful operation of the Willenhall service prompted the decision in 1932 to convert the Bloxwich tramway (half of which was already wired for trolleybuses to enable vehicles to travel to and from the depot at

Above:

Walsall: An AEC 663T with English Electric body, No 152 was one of Walsall's first trolleybuses of 1931, introduced for the through service to Wolverhampton. The central headlamp on the 'radiator' is noticeable. *Ian Allan Library*

Below:

Walsall: Among the first trolleybuses put into service in Walsall in 1931 was this Guy BTX with Brush body. *Ian Allan Library*

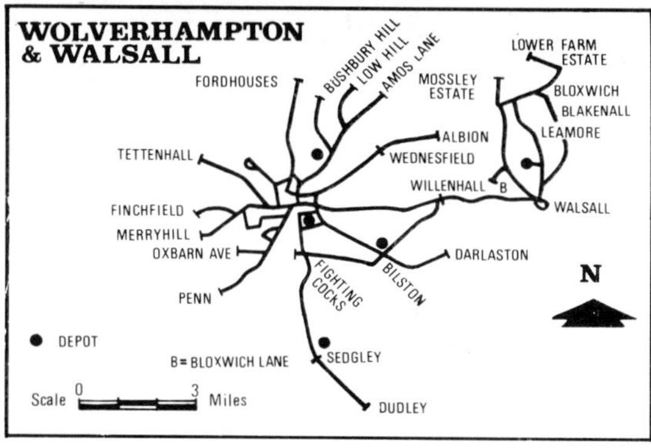

Birchills). The new route was officially inaugurated on 29 September 1933, the last trams ran on 30 September, and full public service started on 1 October, worked by a batch of 15 Sunbeams (Nos 155-169). Although there were proposals also to establish a circular route through Wednesbury and Darlaston, this was rejected because sharp corners and narrow streets were considered unsuitable, and in the event no further extensions were to be made to the system for more than 20 years.

Wartime traffic demands were eased by the addition of utility-bodied Sunbeams (the first four-wheelers in the fleet) and the loan of two Bournemouth vehicles between 1943 and 1945, while the first postwar additions were 10 Sunbeam F4s (Nos 334-343) put into service in 1950/51 to replace prewar veterans. Meanwhile, trolley wheels were replaced by carbon-insert trolley heads in 1947.

The 1950s proved to be the era of expansion with new routes and new-type vehicles following the appointment of R. Edgley Cox as General Manager in 1952. In anticipation of fleet renewal and expansion, an unusual prototype appeared in 1953. Six-wheel Sunbeam S7 No 850 had a Willowbrook-built body designed for pay-as-you-enter operation, with rear entrance and central exit and a single straight stairway opposite the exit. The doors were electrically operated under the control of the conductor at his cashdesk. No 850 did not prove popular, and it was subsequently rebuilt to more conventional layout and renumbered as No 350.

More successful and hardly less striking were the 15 Sunbeam F4As (Nos 851-65) put into service in 1954 and 1955. With 70-seat Willowbrook bodies they were of specially lightweight build, with a tare weight of only

Walsall

Fleet Nos	Registration Nos	Chassis	Electrical equipment	Body	In service	Withdrawn	Notes
151/2	DH 8311/2	AEC 663T	E/Electric	E/Electric H33/27R	1931	1946	
153/4	DH 8313/4	Guy BTX	Rees-Stevens	Brush H32/28R	1931	1945	
155-9	ADH 1-5	Sunbeam MS2	BTH	Beadle H32/28R	1933	1951	
160-4	ADH 6-10	Sunbeam MS2	BTH	Short H32/28R	1933	1951	
165-9	ADH 11-15	Sunbeam MS2	BTH	Weymann H32/28R	1933	1955/6	
187/8	EDH 863/4	Sunbeam MS2	BTH	P/Royal H32/28R	1938	1956	
216-9	HDH 211-4	Sunbeam MS2	BTH	P/Royal H32/28R	1940	1956	
225/6	JDH 29/30	Sunbeam W	BTH	P/Royal UH30/26R	1943	1959/61	
228-30	JDH 331-3	Sunbeam W	BTH	Brush UH30/26R	1945	1959	
231/2	JDH 339/40	Sunbeam W	BTH	P/Royal UH30/26R	1945	1965/1	
233	JDH 334	Sunbeam W	BTH	Brush UH30/26R	1945	1965	
234-7 *	JDH 430-4	Sunbeam W	BTH	Roe UH30/26R	1946	1965	
334-43	NDH 951-60	Sunbeam F4	BTH	Brush H30/26R	1950/1	1964-70	a
850	RDH 990	Sunbeam S7	BTH	Willowbrook H38/24D	1953	1967	b
851-72	TDH 901-15, XDH 66-72	Sunbeam F4A	BTH	Willowbrook H36/34R	1954-6	1970	c
301/2	FTG 697/8	Karrier W	BTH	Roe UH30/26R	1956	1962/3	d
303-10	BDY 806/8/11-14/ 16/19	Sunbeam W	BTH	Weymann H30/26R	1959	1970	e
850	HBE 541	Crossley TDD42/3	Metrovick	Roe H29/25R	1961	1970	f
873	HBE 542	Crossley TDD42/3	Metrovick	Roe H29/25R	1961	1967	g
874	GFU 692	BUT 9611T	Metrovick	NCB H26/26R	1962	1970	h
875/6	GFU 693/4	BUT 9611T	Metrovick	NCB H39/30F	1962/3	1970	i
877	GFU 695	BUT 9611T	Metrovick	NCB H37/30F	1962	1970	j
344-7, 351-4	ADX 193-6, 189-92	Sunbeam F4	Metrovick	P/Royal H30/26R	1962	1966/70	k

* Under 1950 renumbering, Nos 155 to 237 were renumbered 301-33 respectively.

Notes:

a No 342 rebuilt to H34/31R

b Rebuilt to H36/27R and renumbered 350 in 1961

c No 866 rebuilt to H37/34F

d Ex-Pontypridd Nos 14 and 15

e Ex-Hastings Nos 31, 33, 36-9, 41 and 44

f Ex-Cleethorpes No 63

g Ex-Cleethorpes No 64

h Ex-Cleethorpes No 59

i Ex-Cleethorpes Nos 60/1, rebuilt

j Ex-Cleethorpes No 62, rebuilt

k Ex-Ipswich Nos 123-6, 119-22

Preserved vehicles: Nos 862, 864 and 872

7¼ tons, and were the first in Britain to be constructed to 30ft length on two axles. No 851 entered service before the regulation had been amended to permit such a length on two axles and it had to receive a special dispensation from the Ministry of Transport. A further batch of seven (Nos 866-72) came in 1956 and these were to prove to be the last new vehicles to be acquired. In 1954 a new depot was opened at Birchills to replace the former tram shed which the trolleybuses had used until this time.

The expansion of the system under the Corporation's 1954 Act was planned to meet the needs of new housing development to the north of the town. The first of the extensions, opened on 6 June 1955, was the route to Blakenall on which traffic was already demanding a peak 2½min motorbus service and on which the larger-capacity trolleybus had obvious merit. In the same year another new route was opened on 12 September to Gypsy Lane Estate (later to be called Beechdale) and then on 10 October the wires were extended from Blakenall to meet the original Bloxwich route and enable circular services to be run.

North of Bloxwich, trolleybuses reached Mossley Estate on 3 June 1957, with a continuation from Abbey Square to the Eagle Hotel on 20 September 1959. The Beechdale route was extended on 13 November 1961 to Bloxwich, to complete another circle, followed by another northward extension to Lower Farm Estate on 31 December 1962. This marked the completion of this phase of development, and the only later extension was a ½-mile spur off the Beechdale route at Stevenson Avenue, along Bloxwich Lane to Cavendish Road. Installation was delayed by uncertainty about the course of the M6 motorway, but with housing development making a service necessary, construction was completed and the new line was opened on 2 September 1963. The intention was that it should eventually form part of a link back to the town centre by way of Bentley and the

Above:
Walsall: New in 1933 was No 166, a Weymann-bodied Sunbeam MS2. *Ian Allan Library*

Above right:
Walsall: No 860 was one of the 22 two-axle 70-seat Willowbrook-bodied Sunbeam F4As delivered between 1954 and 1956. At 8ft wide and 30ft long, they at first operated under special dispensation from the Ministry of Transport. *V. C. Jones/Ian Allan Library*

Right:
Walsall: Joint working: Walsall Corporation No 354, a Park Royal-bodied Sunbeam purchased from Ipswich, stands at the terminus of the Walsall-Wolverhampton route in 1965. A Wolverhampton Corporation vehicle is turning the corner in the background. Note how the destination 'Wolverhampton' is fitted into the restricted space on the indicator. *V. C. Jones/Ian Allan Library*

Wolverhampton road, but this plan was thwarted by the building of the motorway in its line of advance.

What could have been the prototype of a new generation of trolleybuses was on the drawing board around this time, when Manager Edgley Cox prepared a design for a 35ft-long two-axle 100-passenger pay-as-you-enter vehicle with three doorways and two stairways. This was never to see the light of day, and instead the expanding network was served by secondhand purchases from Pontypridd, Hastings, Grimsby Cleethorpes and Ipswich. By the mid-1960s the fleet was at its zenith with a strength of some 60 members.

Agreement had been reached with Wolverhampton that, notwithstanding Wolverhampton's abandonment programme, the through service between the two towns should continue until 1967. However, the building of the motorway across the line of the route caused the changeover to be brought forward. Hence the first Walsall closure came on 31 October 1965 with the withdrawal of the service to Wolverhampton. By this time, the rising cost of electricity (which had increased by some 50% over the previous 12 years) and the problems of obtaining spares and new equipment were telling against the trolleybuses, the popularity of which was not enhanced when a new one-way street system introduced in the town centre in 1967 included a section where they were obliged to run against the traffic flow.

Nevertheless, as late as 1969 a Parliamentary Bill was seeking provision for five additional lengths of route, primarily as connecting links between existing routes, and there was hope that a bevy of Sunbeams might be purchased from Bournemouth. Meanwhile Sunbeam No 866 was reconstructed to a forward-entrance layout which could have foreshadowed the introduction of one-man operation at a time when this was under consideration for double-deck buses. But after the Walsall municipal transport undertaking passed in 1969 to the newly-formed West Midlands Passenger Transport Executive in which the trolleybuses constituted only a minor part of the new combined organisation, the outcome appeared inevitable. From 16 February 1970 partial replacement by buses took effect, and 2 October saw the last day of normal operation, with a special 'farewell' service running on the following day to mark the final closure of the system.

References
Walsall's Trolleybuses 1931-1970: West Midlands Passenger Transport Executive, 1970.

'Transport in the Walsall District'; *Modern Transport*, 18 December 1954.
'Tramways of Walsall' by R. Hetherington; *Tramway Review* Nos 34 and 35, 1963.
The Walsall Trolleybus System by T. J. Brown (West Riding Transport Society).

Wolverhampton

(See map on page 148)
Developed under the managership of that doyen of the trolley vehicle, Charles Owen Silvers, the Wolverhampton system established a reputation as a model undertaking, visited and emulated by many operators from both home and abroad who were considering adopting the trolleybus. One of the first towns to complete a changeover from tramways to trolleybuses, Wolverhampton for a time enjoyed the distinction of owning the largest system, not only in Britain but in the world. As well as serving the town itself, the network extended well beyond the municipal boundaries to the adjacent Black Country towns of Willenhall, Darlaston, Bilston, Sedgley and Dudley. It is therefore something of a surprise to recall that the system had virtually attained its maximum extent by the mid-1930s. No new vehicles were added after 1950, and in the 1960s the network was rapidly dismantled at a time when neighbouring Walsall — which had been prompted to embrace the trolleybus to enable a through service to be operated with Wolverhampton — was still extending its wires.

Below:
Wolverhampton: On parade outside the depot in 1932 stands No 95, the first Sunbeam trolleybus produced, with its three companions Nos 92-94.
Ian Allan Library

Wolverhampton's Tramways Committee had for some time been considering the question of reconstructing the single-track Wednesfield tramway, and early in 1923 it recommended that, rather than rebuild or double the tramway, trolley vehicles should be introduced instead, since they would be 'the most suitable form of transport for this route'. The scheme was approved by the Town Council in April 1923. The tram route, from Princes Square to the Rookery Bridge at Wednesfield, was just over 1¾ miles in length, but the bridge was widened and the wires were extended into the village of Wednesfield to Pinfold Bridge, to give a route 2¼ miles long. Although Wolverhampton did not yet have powers to run trolleybuses, the Ministry of Transport made no objection to their operation on this route, provided that the Corporation included in its next Parliamentary Bill clauses authorising the running of trolley vehicles.

Because of a low railway bridge, single-deckers had to be employed, and the first fleet comprised six Tilling-Stevens TS6s with central-entrance Dodson bodies. They were fitted with tandem-type motors and contactor control. Tramcars on the route were withdrawn and motorbuses ran for several months while the new overhead was being installed, and the service was formally opened on 29 October 1923.

Such was the immediate success of the venture that in May 1924 the Town Council authorised the Tramways Committee 'to obtain and accept tenders for the supply of the necessary vehicles and equipment for installing a trolley omnibus service on the existing tramway route from Waterloo Road to Bushbury and an extension of just over a mile along Stafford Road'. The tramway in question was also of single track and was in need of renewal, and again it was considered that replacement by trolleybuses would be 'a more favourable proposition'. The proposed extension was regarded as fully justified in that it would serve a developing area. Since some 300yd of the tramway together with the proposed extension were within the area of Staffordshire County Council, it was necessary for the Corporation to reach agreement with the County Council for the new service.

Tramcars on the Bushbury route accordingly ceased running in August 1924 and again motorbuses were used temporarily until on 9 March 1925 the new 3-mile trolleybus route to Fordhouses was opened. The type of vehicle now introduced, *Electric Railway & Tramway Journal* reported, 'is practically the same as used on the Wednesfield route, the difference being less

seating capacity but more standing accommodation for rush hour traffic, a wider doorway and slightly higher roof'. Again a low railway bridge constituted a hindrance: although double-deck tramcars could negotiate the arch since the track was in the centre of the roadway, double-deck trolleybuses would have fouled the arch if they had deviated from the centre. At the inauguration of the new service, the chairman of the Tramways Committee was happily able to state that the result of the 'experiment' made on the Wednesfield route 18 months previously 'had been to make a non-paying route into a paying route', an auspicious augury for the future of the trackless trolley in his town.

With further conversions envisaged, the Corporation proceeded to rectify its lack of the requisite powers by obtaining the Wolverhampton Corporation Act of 1925 to provide general powers to instal and operate trolleybuses within the borough and on scheduled routes outside. The Act also provided for the Corporation to take over tram routes operated by the Wolverhampton District Electric Tramways Co to Dudley, Bilston and Willenhall, and it was intended that these in turn should be replaced by trolleybuses. The Dudley changeover took place in stages. The new service started from Snow Hill, Wolverhampton, to Fighting Cocks on 26 October 1925, and was extended to Sedgley Bull Ring on 10 November, with trolleybuses reaching Sedgley depot on 11 May 1927. Finally the through service to Dudley started on 8 July 1927, when a six-wheel double-decker inaugurated the service, carrying representatives of the Councils of Wolverhampton, Dudley, Sedgley, Coseley and Willenhall. The new terminus at Dudley Market, off Priory Road, was located a short distance beyond the former tram terminus.

Above left:
Wolverhampton: No 92, one of the 1932 trio of Sunbeam MS2s with MCW bodies. *Ian Allan Library*

Top:
Wolverhampton: New in 1934 was No 202, one of five Guy BTXs with bodies by Metropolitan-Cammell-Weymann. *Ian Allan Library*

Above:
Wolverhampton: Among the last new single-deckers in the fleet, No 206 entered service in 1934. A Sunbeam MF1, it had a 32-seat Park Royal body.
Ian Allan Library

Other conversions were also carried out during 1927: to Willenhall (Neachells Lane) on 15 May, extended to Willenhall Market Place, in anticipation of the through service to Walsall, on 16 September; to Penn Fields on 11 July; and the Tettenhall route on 29 October. Trolleybus service to Bilston started on 19 November 1928, and was extended to Darlaston on 28 May 1929. With these extensions, the Corporation's system now earned the claim to be the largest in the world. More than 36 million passengers a year were being carried on 25 miles of route.

Powers also existed for trolleybuses to supersede tramcars to Bradley, but in fact these powers were never exercised and buses were used on this route. On the Whitmore Reans route, trolleybuses started on 27 January 1930 after two years of motorbus operation, while later in the same year (on 27 October) the 'cross-country' service between Willenhall and Fighting Cocks via Bilston was started, again after two years of bus working.

'A new six-wheel trolley omnibus constructed by Guy Motors for Wolverhampton Corporation had a trial run last week on the Wolverhampton-Sedgley route, carrying the members of the Transport Committee and officials, together with an inspector of the Ministry of Transport', *Electric Railway & Tramway Journal* reported in November 1926, 'and great satisfaction was expressed with the vehicle's performance.' The first trolleybus to be produced by Guy Motors, No 33 was also the first six-wheel double-deck trolleybus with articulated twin rear axles, running on pneumatic tyres. Powered by a single 60hp compound-wound motor and fitted with regenerative control, it had a covered-top Dodson body with open staircase and a total of 61 seats. It was put into service on the Snow Hill-Sedgley route on 2 December 1926, and orders were soon placed for 10 more. By the time No 33 was eventually retired from Corporation duty in 1937 it had run more than half a million miles. Further batches followed, incorporating gradual improvements including enclosed-stair bodies, and by 1931 the Corporation's fleet included 50 Guy BTX six-wheel double-deckers. That same year saw the debut of the first Sunbeam trolleybus, No 95, with a 61-seat Weymann body. Between them, locally-produced Guy and Sunbeam vehicles were to continue to dominate the fleet.

The long-awaited through service between Wolverhampton and Walsall via Willenhall was inaugurated on 16 November 1931, with a through joint service of double-deckers, following the completion of road reconstruction. Hitherto a low bridge had limited Wolverhampton's Willenhall service to single-deckers.

Closely following, on 30 November 1931, Wolverhampton trolleybuses started running to Bushbury Hill, a route which had never been served by tramcars. Now the new mode of transport was spreading farther beyond the confines of the former tramway network, with more new routes to serve developing residential areas: to Amos Lane and Low Hill (Pear Tree) on 21 March 1932, followed on 10 April 1933 by routes to Bradmore and along Brickkiln Street and Jeffcock Road. Meanwhile, the Penn Fields route was extended to Penn on 10 October 1932, and later (on 8 April 1935) another route to Penn was opened by way of Penn Road. In 1934 the Wednesfield route was extended to Lichfield Road on 10 February, while on the following day trolleybuses replaced buses to Oxbarn Avenue to round out the Penn group of services.

By the mid-1930s the network was virtually complete. The 1936 fleet total showed a stock of 90 double-deckers and 18 single-deckers. Double-deckers replaced single-deckers on the Fordhouses route in 1938, but the Wednesfield route continued to be restricted to single-deckers until 1943 when the roadway under the railway bridge was lowered to allow the passage of double-deckers, and the single-deck vehicles were then sold out of service.

On 6 September 1936 a new terminus at Fighting Cocks was brought into use at Ward Road, replacing Dudding Road. After this there were only two fairly short postwar route extensions. On 10 January 1955 the Wednesfield route was extended along Lichfield Road to the junction with Linthouse Lane at the Albion in order to cater for new housing. Finally on 24 June 1956 the Amos Lane route was extended about 600yd along Lower Prestwood Road to the Pheasant Inn.

A new depot primarily built for trolleybuses was opened at Park Lane on 6 October 1938, with accommodation for 56 vehicles. The other depots were inherited from tramway days. Cleveland Road depot enjoyed a centrally-situated location, but formed one of the most unusual in operation, since it possessed no yard but opened out directly on to a main road, into which trolleybuses made a practice of emerging backwards, to the consternation of unsuspecting motorists. Other depots at Sedgley and Bilston were both outside the borough boundaries and were former Wolverhampton District Electric Tramways premises.

Wartime traffic needs were met by a total of 38 additional vehicles, while postwar fleet replacement saw the arrival of 50 Guy BTs between 1948 and 1950. No new trolleybuses appeared after this, but more than 50 earlier vehicles were given new bodies by Roe and Park Royal between 1952 and 1962.

The first signs of contraction seemed to come almost by default. From 22 January 1961 the Penn Road services were temporarily replaced by buses because of road works at the in-town end. The Penn, Penn Fields and Jeffcock Road services were reinstated on 21 May, but the Oxbarn Avenue route was not reopened to trolleybuses; instead it was covered by augmenting the paralleling bus service, of which it had been virtually a short working.

By now, however, fate was closing in on the trolleybuses. In 1961, at which time the fleet stood at a total of some 150 vehicles, the Transport Committee recommended that all trolleybuses should be withdrawn. Factors weighing against them included their route-bound nature, their higher failure rate (hardly surprising in an ageing fleet), and the fact that most of the vehicles were nearing the end of their useful life (in spite of the rebodying programme which had not yet been completed). It recommended that no new trolleybuses should be obtained, and that the policy of rebodying should be ended. In 1962 a replacement programme was announced, envisaging the reduction of the fleet by about one-third within 12 months.

As the first stage in the programme, on

Below left:
Wolverhampton: Two-axle double-deckers joined the fleet in 1936, among them No 241, a Sunbeam MF2 with Park Royal body. *Ian Allan Library*

Below:
Wolverhampton: No 284 was one of two Roe-bodied Sunbeam MF2s delivered in 1940. *Ian Allan Library*

Wolverhampton

Fleet Nos	Registration Nos	Chassis	Electrical equipment	Body	In service	Withdrawn	Notes
1-6	DA 7741-6	T/Stevens TS6	BTH	Dodson B36C	1923	1934	
7	DA 8814	T/Stevens TS6	BTH	Dodson B36C	1924	1934	
8-14	DA 9008-14	T/Stevens TS6	BTH	Dodson B36C	1925	1937	
15-32	UK 615-32	T/Stevens TS6	BTH	Dodson B36C	1925	1937	
33	UK 633	Guy BTX	Rees-Stevens	Dodson H33/28ROS	1926	1936	a
34-40	UK 634-40	Guy BTX	Rees-Stevens	Dodson H33/28R	1927	1938	
41/2	UK 3941/2	Guy BTX	Rees-Stevens	Dodson H33/28R	1927	1938	
43-50	UK 4243-50	Guy BTX	Rees-Stevens	Dodson H33/28R	1927	1938	
51-6	UK 5951-6	Guy BTX	Rees-Stevens	Dodson H33/28R	1928	1938	
57-61	UK 6357-61	Guy BTX	Rees-Stevens	Dodson H33/28R	1929	1940	
62-6	UK 7962-6	Guy BTX	Rees-Stevens	Dodson H30/31R	1930	1944	
67-70	UK 8767-70	Guy BTX	Rees-Stevens	Dodson H30/31R	1930	1944	
71-8	UK 9971-8	Guy BTX	Rees-Stevens	Guy H33/26R	1931	1945	
79-82	JW 579-82	Guy BTX	Rees-Stevens	Guy H33/26R	1931	1946	
83-91	JW 983-91	Guy BTX	Rees-Stevens	Dodson H33/26R	1932	1948	
92-4	JW 992-4	Sunbeam MS2	BTH	Weymann H31/28R	1932	1948	
95	JW 526	Sunbeam MS2	BTH	Weymann H33/28R	1931	1948	b
96-8	JW 3396-8	Sunbeam MS3	BTH	MCW H33/25R	1934	1948	
99, 200-3	JW 3399-3403	Guy BTX	Rees-Stevens	MCW H33/25R	1934	1948	
204-5	JW 4104/5	Sunbeam MS3	BTH	MCW H33/25R	1934	1947	
206-9	JW 4106-9	Sunbeam MF1	BTH	P/Royal B32R	1934	1949	
210-3	JW 4310-3	Guy BT	Rees-Stevens	P/Royal B32R	1934	1945	
214-7	JW 4314-7	Sunbeam MS2	BTH	Beadle H33/25R	1934	1948	
218-21	JW 4318-21	Guy BTX	Rees-Stevens	Beadle H33/25R	1934	1949	
222	OC 6567	Sunbeam MS2	BTH	MCW H31/28R	1934	1949	c
223-6	JW 7323-6	Sunbeam MS2	BTH	P/Royal H33/25R	1935	1949	
227-30	JW 7327-30	Guy BTX	Elec Con Co	Brush H33/25R	1935	1949	
231-3	JW 8131-3	Sunbeam MF1	BTH	P/Royal B32R	1936	1949	
234-8	JW 8134-8	Guy BT	Elec Con Co	P/Royal H28/26R	1936	1949	d
239-44	JW 8139-44	Sunbeam MF2	BTH	P/Royal H29/26R	1936	1949	
245	JW 8145	Sunbeam MS2	BTH	P/Royal H33/25R	1936	1949	
246-51	AJW 46-51	Sunbeam MF2	BTH	Beadle H28/26R	1937	1949	
252-8	AJW 52-7, BDA 358	Guy BT	Elec Con Co	Beadle H28/26R	1937	1949	
259-63	BDA 359-63	Guy BT	Elec Con Co	Roe H29/25R	1938	1950	
264-75	BDA 364-9, BJW 170-5	Sunbeam MF2	BTH	P/Royal H28/26R	1938	1950	e
276-81	BJW 176-81	Guy BT	Elec Con Co	Roe H29/25R	1938	1950/3	
282/3	DDA 182/3	Sunbeam MF2	BTH	P/Royal H28/26R	1940	1952	f
284/5	DDA 184/5	Sunbeam MF2	BTH	Roe H29/25R	1940	1950	
286-90	DDA 986-90	Sunbeam MF2	BTH	P/Royal H28/26R	1942	1952	f
291-5	DDA 991-5	Sunbeam MF2	BTH	Roe H29/25R	1942	1952	f
296-9, 400/1	DJW 596-601	Sunbeam W	BTH	Weymann UH30/26R	1943	1953	
402-7	DJW 902-7	Sunbeam W	BTH	P/Royal UH30/26R	1944	1965	g
408	DJW 938	Sunbeam W	BTH	Weymann UH30/26R	1945	1965	g
409-18	DJW 939-43, DUK 14-8	Sunbeam W	BTH	P/Royal UH30/26R	1945	1965	g, h
419-33	DUK 419, 820-33	Sunbeam W	BTH	P/Royal UH30/26R	1946	1967	h
434-55	EJW 434-55	Sunbeam W	BTH	P/Royal H28/26R	1947	1967	j
456-81	FJW 456-81	Sunbeam F4	BTH	P/Royal H28/26R	1948	1965	
482-99, 600-7	FJW 482-99, 600-7	Guy BT	BTH	P/Royal H28/26R	1949	1965	
608-30	FJW 608-30	Sunbeam F4	BTH	P/Royal H28/26R	1949	1965	
631-54	FJW 631-54	Guy BT	BTH	P/Royal H28/26R	1949	1965	

Notes:

a The first Guy trolleybus.

b The first Sunbeam trolleybus.

c Ex-Birmingham No 67. Built 1934, acquired by Wolverhampton 1934.

d The first two-axle double-deck trolleybuses in the fleet.

e Nos 264-9, 271/3/5 sold to Southend-on-Sea, where Nos 144-52.

f Nos 282, 286-95 sold to Belfast, where Nos 235-45.

g Nos 402-17 rebodied Park Royal H28/26R 1952.

h Nos 418-33 rebodied Roe H32/28R 1958/9.

j Rebodied Roe H32/28R 1960/2.

Preserved vehicles: Nos 433, 616, 654.

Above:
Wolverhampton: Representative of the postwar Wolverhampton fleet is No 623, a Park Royal-bodied Sunbeam F4 of the 1949 series.
V. C. Jones/Ian Allan Library

9 June 1963 the routes to Penn (11) and Penn Fields (4) ceased, and 15 trolleybuses were withdrawn. Closely following, on 30 June the Tettenhall route (1) came to an end. With the next stage, on 3 November 1963, 25 trolleybuses were withdrawn on the closures of the services between Finchfield and Low Hill (12), Merry Hill and Low Hill (13), Amos Lane and Jeffcock Road (9), and to Wednesfield (6 and 59). On 26 January 1964 the Fordhouses- Bushbury Hill service (3) was withdrawn. This was followed later in the year, on 26 October, by the Willenhall-Bilston-Fighting Cocks route (25), the closure of which was precipitated by the rebuilding of a railway bridge at Willenhall (ironically for the purposes of electrification).

Closures in 1965 involved the Whitmore Reans-Bilston-Darlaston services (2, 7 and 47) on 8 August, and the joint interurban route to Walsall on 31 October with the withdrawal of the Willenhall service (5) and the jointly-worked Wolverhampton-Walsall service (29). There had been hopes that this latter operation might have enjoyed a longer life, since Walsall by contrast had considerably expanded its trolleybus system in the previous few years. The last Wolverhampton route (to Dudley) continued in operation until 1967, when on 5 March No 446 had the distinction of being the last Wolverhampton trolleybus to run in public service at the final closure. This took place without official ceremony, a sad reflection of the decline in the esteem in which the trolleybus was held since the days when the Wolverhampton system had occupied a prominent position among the foremost networks in the country.

References
'Wolverhampton Trolleybus System' — National Trolleybus Association Newsletter No 13, March 1965.
'A Farewell at Wolverhampton' by F. W. York; *Buses*, January 1967.
'Trolley Omnibus System in Wolverhampton'; *Tramway & Railway World*, 20 December 1923.
'Municipal Transport Undertakings: 4 — Wolverhampton; *Transport World*, 12 January 1939.
Black Country Tramways Volume II, by J. S. Webb (Author, 1976).

Wigan

Wigan's tramways laboured under the disadvantage of having been laid to two different gauges, and the Corporation had spent considerable sums of money in reconstruction, until by 1924 only one of the narrow-gauge routes remained. This was the 1½-mile route to Martland Mill; should this too be rebuilt to standard gauge? The Tramways Committee estimated that instead conversion to trolleybus operation could be made for £10,000, only about one-third of the cost of regauging the tramway. After some doubts had been expressed by the Council, who were not entirely convinced that trolleybuses would provide adequate capacity, it was agreed to go ahead with the change.

Four vehicles were ordered from Clough Smith. Numbered 1-4 (EK 3967-70) they had Straker Squire chassis with BTH electrical equipment, and Brush 37-seat central-entrance bodies. Originally running on solid tyres, they were fitted with pneumatics in 1929.

In the town centre, a turning circle was provided at the corner of Market Street and

Below:
Wigan: Three of Wigan's fleet of four trolleybuses seen in 1925.

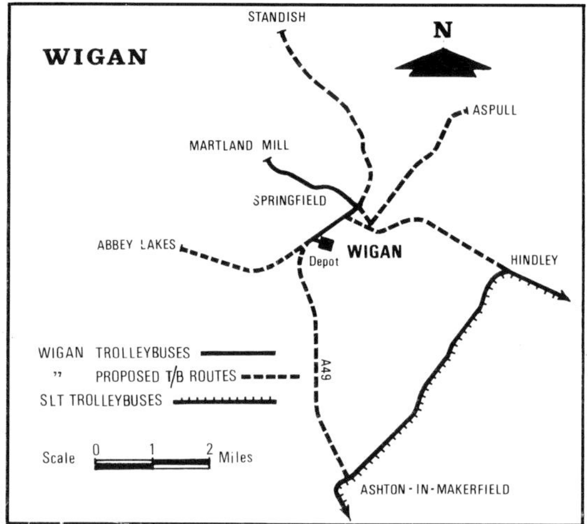

Woodcock Street, since the Watch Committee would not consent to the new vehicles turning in the Market Place, while at Martland Mill a triangular reverser was installed in Horton Street. A turning circle was also erected at Springfield for short workings. The trolleybuses were housed in the central depot at Melverley Street, about a mile from their town terminus; on their depot workings they used the tramway overhead and a skate in the track. The opening ceremony, with the tramways committee chairman driving the first trolleybus, took place on 7 May 1925, and the new vehicles replaced the tramcars during the afternoon of that day.

In 1930 there were proposals for the conversion of the Standish, Hindley, Ashton and Orrell tramways to trolleybus operation, but these were rejected and by the early months of 1931 the last tramcars had been replaced by motorbuses. This left the Martland Mill route on its own, and moreover in the anomalous position of still requiring tram tracks to be maintained for its depot working. Now considered outdated, and already being supplemented by motorbuses, the four trolleybuses were not judged worth retaining. Accordingly, the final journeys were made on 30 September 1931.

A curious feature was that throughout their lives the trolleybuses operated without legal authority. Wigan Corporation did not have powers to run trolleybuses, and while it was proposed that such powers should be obtained by means of a private Act, in fact this was never done.

References

The Tramways of Wigan by E. K. Stretch (Manchester Transport Museum Society, 1978).

'Trolleybus to Wigan Pier' by E. K. Stretch — *Trolleybus Magazine*, May 1969.

York

The City of York's trolleybus 'system' boasted only one short route, but it effectively enjoyed two lives, albeit that both were brief. Something of a network could have developed, for the Corporation obtained powers in 1914 to operate trolleybuses on four routes, basically as supplemental to the existing tramways. These were the railway station to Clifton Green South, together with a branch along Burton Stone Lane to Ratcliffe Street and Haughton Road; from Nessgate, via East Parade, to Heworth; and from Nessgate to Haley's Terrace, where it would have served the Rowntree chocolate factory.

Because of the war, actual construction was delayed until 1920, when a 1¼-mile route was equipped from Pavement, via St Saviour Gate, Peasholme Green and East Parade, to Heworth, and service started on 22 December 1920. The four vehicles (Nos 6-9) obtained from Railless were two-motor single-deckers with 24-seat bodies designed for one-man operation in which (in the words of the contemporary press) fares were 'dropped into a pay-as-you-enter device'. Since the route abounded in narrow streets and sharp corners, the vehicles were only 6ft 3in wide overall. Only two buses were needed at first, with a 15min service from noon to early evening and a half-hourly service at other times, but it was anticipated that traffic would increase when a municipal housing estate near the suburban terminus was completed.

The other proposed routes did not come into being, and although in the mid-1920s an extension off the Heworth route from East Parade to Tang Hall and Hull Road to serve

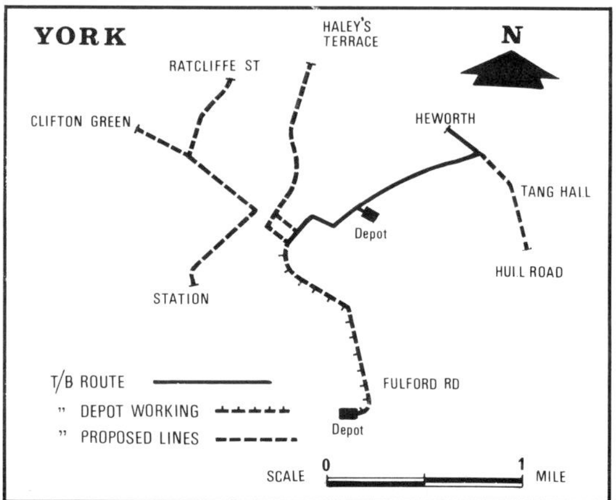

York

Fleet Nos	Registration Nos	Chassis	Electrical equipment	Body	In service	Withdrawn	Note
6-9	DN 2986-8/5	Railless	Railless	Railless B24F	1920	1929	
30-32	VY 2991-3	Karrier-Clough E4	BTH	Roe B32R	1931	1935	a

Note:

a Sold to Chesterfield.

Above left:
York: No 30, one of the three 1931 Karrier-Cloughs, photographed in Whip-Ma-Whop-Ma Gate.

Above:
York: No 7, one of the original Railless fleet of 1920, photographed in East Parade, Heworth.
Courtesy R. Brook

further housing development was considered, this did not materialise. The cars were fitted with pneumatic tyres in 1925, but as early as 1927 abandonment was being planned. The move was deferred at the time, but eventually the service was withdrawn on 31 December 1929 and replaced by motorbuses.

This was not to be the end of the story, for in the light of the rapid advance in trolleybus design over the previous few years, the Corporation decided to modernise the install-ation, and during 1930 and 1931 the overhead was remodelled and realigned to permit higher-speed operation, and new vehicles were ordered. After an official reopening ceremony, service restarted on 7 October 1931 with the three newcomers, Nos 30-32. Again these were single-deckers, but this time with rear-entrance Roe bodies on Karrier-Clough E4 chassis, the first E4s to be produced. Trials had been made with a 60-seat, six-wheel double-decker (Don-caster's Karrier E6 No 22) but this had been found unsuitable for the narrow and sinuous streets and the light traffic that was to be handled.

To allow access to the new Fulford Road depot, which was situated on the Fulford tram route and was opened in 1931 with provision for the accommodation of trolley vehicles, a single set of wires ran from the Pavement turning loop, where the trolleys were manually trans-ferred to and from the main wires. Depot working involved a journey almost equal to the route itself! The vehicles were also fitted with a skate to permit operation along the tram tracks.

The new era proved to be short-lived. In 1934 an agreement between York Corporation and the West Yorkshire Road Car Co resulted in the disappearance of York Corporation Transport as a separate entity and the withdrawal of both tramcars and trolleybuses as the newly consti-tuted York/West Yorkshire organisation's buses took over. The last of the tramcars ceased running late in 1935, while the trolleybuses continued only until 5 January 1935. The three trolley vehicles found a new home in Chester-field (where they became that undertaking's Nos 18-20) but they served for only another three years there before that system also ended.

References
'The York Trolleybuses' by D. K. Kain — *Trolleybus Magazine*, March 1972.
'Railless Traction at York' — *Tramway & Railway World*, 17 March 1921.
'Reconstruction of York Trolleybus Route' — *Tramway & Railway World*, 14 January 1932.

First and Last

System	Opened	Closed
Aberdare	15 January 1914	July 1925
Ashton-under-Lyne	26 August 1925	30 December 1966
Belfast	28 March 1938	12 May 1968
Birmingham	27 November 1922	30 June 1951
Bournemouth	13 May 1933	20 April 1969
Bradford	20 June 1911 (a)	26 March 1972 (b)
Brighton Corporation	1 May 1939	30 June 1961
Brighton, Hove & District	3 March 1946	24 March 1959
Cardiff	1 March 1942	11 January 1970
Chesterfield	23 May 1927	24 March 1938
Cleethorpes	18 July 1937	4 June 1960
Darlington	17 January 1926	31 July 1957
Derby	9 January 1932	9 September 1967
Doncaster	22 August 1928	14 December 1963
Dundee	5 September 1912	13 May 1914
Glasgow	3 April 1949	27 May 1967
Grimsby	3 October 1926	4 June 1960
Halifax	20 July 1921	24 October 1926
Hastings	1 April 1928	31 May 1959 (c)
Huddersfield	4 December 1933	13 July 1968
Ipswich	2 September 1923	23 August 1963
Keighley	3 May 1913	31 August 1932
Kingston-upon-Hull	23 July 1937 (d)	31 October 1964
Leeds	20 June 1911	26 July 1928
Llanelli	26 December 1932	8 November 1952
London	16 May 1931	8 May 1962
Maidstone	1 May 1928	15 April 1967
Manchester	1 March 1938	30 December 1966
Mexborough & Swinton	31 August 1915	26 March 1961 (e)
Newcastle upon Tyne	1 October 1935	1 October 1966
Nottingham	10 April 1927	30 June 1966 (f)
Notts & Derby	7 January 1932	25 April 1953
Oldham	26 August 1925	5 September 1926
Pontypridd	18 September 1930	31 January 1957
Portsmouth	4 August 1934	27 July 1963
Ramsbottom	14 August 1913	31 March 1931
Reading	18 July 1936	3 November 1968
Rhondda	22 December 1914	March 1915
Rotherham	3 October 1912	2 October 1965
St Helens	11 July 1927	1 July 1958
Southend-on-Sea	16 October 1925	28 October 1954
South Lancashire	3 August 1930	31 August 1958 (g)
South Shields	12 October 1936	29 April 1964
Stockport	10 March 1913	11 September 1920
Teesside	8 November 1919	4 April 1971 (h)
Walsall	22 July 1931	3 October 1970
West Hartlepool	28 February 1924	2 April 1953
Wigan	7 May 1925	30 September 1931
Wolverhampton	29 October 1923	5 March 1967
York	22 December 1920	5 January 1935

Notes

(a) Public service started on 24 June 1911.
(b) Public service ended on 24 March 1972.
(c) Ceremonial final journey on 1 June 1959.
(d) Public service started on 25 July 1937.
(e) Ceremonial closure procession on 27 March 1961.
(f) Ceremonial closure on 1 July 1966.
(g) Ceremonial closure on 1 September 1958.
(h) Ceremonial closure on 18 April 1971.

Bibliography

The following publications deal with the subject in general; references to individual systems are given at the end of each respective section.

R. A. Bishop; *The Electric Trolley Bus*; Pitman, 1931.

British Electrical & Allied Manufacturers Association; *Why Trolleybuses?*; BEAMA, 1950.

British Electrical Development Association; *The Case for Electric Road Passenger Transport*; BEDA, 1952.

British Insulated Callendar's Cables; *Trolley-Bus and Tramway Overhead Equipment*; BICC, 1954.

Harold Brearley; *The Development of the Trolley Bus*; Oakwood Press, 1957.

Ian L. Cormack & David Kaye; *Trams and Trolleybuses*; Spur Books, 1980.

A. S. Crosley, *Early Development of the Railless Electric Trolleybus*; Newcomen Society, 1961.

J. Joyce; *Trolleybus Trails*; Ian Allan, 1963.

David Kaye; *Buses and Trolleybuses before 1919*; Blandford Press, 1972.

David Kaye; *Buses and Trolleybuses 1919 to 1945*; Blandford Press, 1970.

David Kaye; *Buses and Trolleybuses since 1945*; Blandford Press, 1968.

David Kaye; *Discovering Old Buses and Trolleybuses*; Shire Publications, 1972.

Nicholas Owen; *History of the British Trolleybus*; David & Charles, 1974.

R. D. H. Symons & P. R. Cresswell; *British Trolleybuses*; Ian Allan, 1967.

Buses (originally *Buses Illustrated*); *Modern Transport*; *Omnibus Magazine*; *Passenger Transport* (originally *Electric Railway & Tramway Journal*); *Tramway Review*; *Transport World* (originally *Tramway & Railway World*); *Trolleybus Magazine*.

Below:

Birmingham: No 15 was one of five AEC 663Ts of 1932 with bodies by Brush.   *Ian Allan Library*